THE SOCIOLOGY OF DEBT

Edited by Mark Featherstone

First published in Great Britain in 2019 by

Policy Press
University of Bristol
1-9 Old Park Hill
Bristol
BS2 8BB
UK
t: +44 (0)117 954 5940
pp-info@bristol.ac.uk
www.policypress.co.uk

North America office:
Policy Press
c/o The University of Chicago Press
1427 East 60th Street
Chicago, IL 60637, USA
t: +1 773 702 7700
f: +1 773-702-9756
sales@press.uchicago.edu
www.press.uchicago.edu

British Library Cataloguing in Publication Data
A catalogue record for this book is available from the British Library

Library of Congress Cataloging-in-Publication Data
A catalog record for this book has been requested

ISBN 978-1-4473-3952-6 hardcover
ISBN 978-1-4473-3955-7 ePub
ISBN 978-1-4473-3956-4 Mobi
ISBN 978-1-4473-3953-3 ePdf

Cover design by Robin Hawes
Front cover image: Alamy
Printed and bound in Great Britain by CPI Group (UK) Ltd, Croydon, CR0 4YY
Policy Press uses environmentally responsible print partners

FSC
www.fsc.org
MIX
Paper from responsible sources
FSC® C013604

Contents

Notes on contributors		iv
Acknowledgements		vii
Introduction: towards a sociology of debt *Mark Featherstone*		1
1	Debt, complexity and the sociological imagination *Lisa Adkins*	27
2	Debt drive and the imperative of growth *Ole Bjerg*	49
3	Memory, counter-memory and resistance: notes on the 'Greek Debt Truth Commission' *Joshua Bowsher*	69
4	'Deferred lives': money, debt and the financialised futures of young temporary workers *Mark Davis and Laura Cartwright*	91
5	'Choose your moments': discipline and speculation in the indebted everyday *Samuel Kirwan, Leila Dawney and Rosie Walker*	119
6	Digital subprime: tracking the credit trackers *Joe Deville*	145
7	Debt, usury and the ongoing crises of capitalism *Nicholas Gane*	175
8	The art of unpayable debts *Max Haiven*	195
9	Ecologies of indebtedness *Mark Featherstone*	231
Index		251

Notes on contributors

Lisa Adkins is Head of the School of Social and Political Sciences at the University of Sydney, Australia, and Academy of Finland Distinguished Professor (2015-19). Her contributions to the discipline of sociology lie in the areas of economic sociology, social theory and feminist theory. Recent publications include *The Time of Money* (2018), *The Post-Fordist Sexual Contract: Working and Living in Contingency (*with Maryanne Dever, 2016) and *Measure and Value* (with Celia Lury, 2012). She is joint Editor-in-Chief of *Australian Feminist Studies* (Routledge/ Taylor and Francis).

Ole Bjerg is Associate Professor in Business Philosophy at the Copenhagen Business School, Denmark, where he also lectures on the Masters Programme in Philosophy and Business Administration. He is the author of several books on the topic of money in English, Danish and Russian, including *Parallax of Growth: The Philosophy of Ecology and Economy* (Polity, 2016), *Making Money: The Philosophy of Crisis Capitalism* (Verso, 2014), *Poker: The Parody of Capitalism* (Umich Press 2011), *Как делаются деньги? Философия посткредитного капитализма* (AdMarginem 2018), *Vores penge i vores bank* (Informations Forlag, 2017) and *Gode Penge* (Informations Forlag 2013). His current research is focused on emerging forms of money such as cryptocurrencies and central bank digital currency. Ole Bjerg is also co-founder of the Danish monetary reform movement *Gode Penge.*

Joshua Bowsher received his PhD in Critical Theory at the University of Nottingham in 2016, and has worked in the Sociology Department at Keele University. He is now a Leverhulme Early Career Research Fellow at Brunel University, UK. His research critically explores transitional justice and collective memory and their relationship to broader social processes, particularly the interrelated dynamics of financialisation and neoliberal globalisation. His work also investigates the way in which contemporary forms of social relations and subjectivity have been transformed by neoliberalism and financialisation.

Laura Cartwright is a Research Fellow in the Bauman Institute at the University of Leeds, UK, working on the 'Financing for Society – Crowdfunding Public Infrastructure' project. Her research interests are primarily centred around young people and how macro-level changes in political economy, policy and culture are affecting youth biographies and trajectories.

Mark Davis is Associate Professor of Sociology at the University of Leeds, UK. His work blends Zygmunt Bauman's analysis of modernity with insights from economic sociology in order to assess how money organises social life, and thereby how to enhance democratic control over finance. His first monograph *Freedom and Consumerism: A Critique of Zygmunt Bauman's Sociology* was published in 2008 (Routledge) and he is the editor of *Liquid Sociology: Metaphor in Zygmunt Bauman's Analysis of Modernity* (2013, Routledge) and *Bauman's Challenge: Sociological Issues for the Twenty-First Century* (2010 with Keith Tester, Palgrave). His current research is evaluating the democratising claims of financial innovations such as crowdfunding and cryptocurrencies.

Leila Dawney is a Senior Lecturer in Human Geography at the University of Brighton, UK. As a theorist of power, affect and embodiment, her research concerns the forms of experience and subjectivity that are produced in and through spaces of late capitalism, and the development of conceptual and methodological tools for thinking about the politics of experience. She is a member of the Authority Research Network.

Joe Deville is a Lecturer at Lancaster University, UK, based jointly in the Department of Sociology and the Department of Organisation, Work and Technology. His research interests include the everyday life of debt, questions of informational mobility and methods of algorithmic prediction, disaster preparedness and the production of risk, and Open Access and the politics of scholarly knowledge production. His first book *Lived Economies of Default* was published by Routledge in 2015 and he has published widely in journals including *British Journal of Sociology, Consumption Markets and Culture, Journal of Cultural Economy*, and *Cultural Studies*. He is also a co-founder and co-editor of Mattering Press, an Open Access book publisher and UK-registered charity focusing on work within the field of Science and Technology Studies.

Mark Featherstone is Senior Lecturer in Sociology at Keele University, UK. His main fields of interest are critical theory, cultural theory, and psychoanalysis. He is author of two monographs on utopia and contemporary social and political thought, *Tocqueville's Virus* (2007) and *Planet Utopia* (2017) (both Routledge). He is co-editor of the Duke University Press cultural studies journal, *Cultural Politics*.

Nicholas Gane is Professor of Sociology at the University of Warwick, UK. His current research addresses questions of crisis, debt and money. His previous publications include *Max Weber and Contemporary Capitalism* (Palgrave, 2012).

Max Haiven is Canada Research Chair in Culture, Media and Social Justice at Lakehead University where he is co-director of the ReImagining Value Action Lab (RiVAL). He writes articles for both academic and general audiences and is the author of the books *Crises of Imagination, Crises of Power: Capitalism, Creativity and the Commons* (Zed Books, 2013), *The Radical Imagination: Social Movement Research in the Age of Austerity* (2014 with Alex Khasnabish, Zed Books) and *Cultures of Financialization: Fictitious Capital in Popular Culture and Everyday Life* (Palgrave Macmillan, 2014). His latest book is *Art after Money, Money after Art: Creative Strategies Against Financialization* (Pluto Press, 2018).

Samuel Kirwan is a Leverhulme Early Career Research Fellow and Lecturer in Criminology and Social Policy at the University of Bristol, UK. His research focuses upon experiences of debt and debt advice in the context of welfare reform measures and precarious labour conditions in the United Kingdom. He recently edited the text *Advising in Austerity: Reflections on Challenging Times for Advice Agencies* (2017), published by Policy Press, and is writing a book for Agenda Publishing on Financial Inclusion.

Rosie Walker is an independent researcher and writer interested in housing, inequality, employment rights and debt. As a researcher she has worked for the London School of Economics, University of Bristol and University of Brighton. As a journalist she has written for *The Guardian, The Observer, Inside Housing* and *Third Sector*. Her co-authored book, *The Rent Trap*, about private renting and the inequality it produces, was published by Pluto Press in 2016.

Acknowledgements

The idea for this collection emerged from two workshops focused upon the sociology of debt which took place at Warwick University in February 2016 and Keele University in May of the same year. A number of the speakers from these events have contributed to this collection and I would like to thank them for their hard work which has brought this book to completion. I would also like to thank the contributors who came to the project later when I was looking to expand the coverage of the collection in particular areas. I could not have hoped to work with a better group of people. They made my role as editor of the book extremely easy. As editor of the collection I must also thank the anonymous reviewer who read the draft copy of the collection and provided such encouraging feedback, and the editors at Policy Press who have been extremely efficient and endlessly patient when I needed extensions early in the project. I'm extremely grateful for their understanding. In particular I would like to thank Shannon Kneis, Victoria Pittman and Rebecca Tomlinson from Policy Press for their hard work on the book. Finally, on a personal note, I would like to thank Siobhan, Paddy, John and Susan. When I started this project I was interested in thinking through the relationship between different kinds of debts and each of the contributors to the collection has broadened my understanding in this regard. I am now more aware than ever before of the debt I owe to Siobhan, Paddy, John and Susan. In particular, I would like to recognise my unpayable debt to John, who taught me what it means to think.

Introduction: towards a sociology of debt

Mark Featherstone

A brief history of the politics of debt

There can be little doubt that thinking through the problem of debt and the related experience of indebtedness has become central for understanding social, economic, political, and cultural conditions in the early 21st century. Following the 2007-08 financial crash, consequent credit crunch, and subsequent turn to austerity in many of the world's major economic powers, the apparent need to 'balance the books' and 'live within our means' in a world characterised by low economic growth has pushed the problem of unsustainable public and private debt centre stage. Against this backdrop, indebtedness and financial and economic insecurity have become a kind of 'new normal' for many people. In the UK, where economic growth has been largely based upon consumption, borrowing, and financial innovation since the 1980s, government plans to cut public debts have pushed private, household debts in the opposite direction, with the result that the ratio of personal debt to GDP is heading back towards levels seen in the boom years before the financial crash, when there seemed to be no end to what one could borrow (Inman and Barr, 2017). Given economic uncertainty and insecurity, however, current rises in household debt cannot easily be explained away in terms of a reckless desire to consume based on a belief in endless growth and wage increases, but rather reflect the problem of 'making ends meet' in an economic situation defined by sluggish productivity and increasing prices. This is, of course, not simply a British problem, though my own experience of living in an society defined by indebtedness has undoubtedly shaped my understanding of what being in debt means and how it impacts upon social life. The US has similarly grown its economy on the back of consumption and consumer debt in recent years in a way that now seems largely unsustainable. The situation is similarly problematic in Canada, where household debt has rapidly increased on the basis of a property boom which has pushed house prices to record levels in urban areas (Inman and Barr, 2017). The situation is worse in the

Eurozone PIIGS (Portugal, Ireland, Italy, Greece, Spain), which are still deep in debt and struggling with the legacy of the financial crash (Inman, 2018). The highest levels of household debt in the world are now found in Australia, currently running at 120% of GDP (Heath, Cadman and Dormido, 2018). Of course, it would be shortsighted to trace the root of the problem of indebtedness back to 2007-08 and stop there: it was clear in the boom years of the 1990s that debt was likely to become a global, rather than simply regional, problem in the near future. In his book *Specters of Marx* (1994), the French philosopher Jacques Derrida explored the problem of the end of the Cold War, the collapse of communism, and triumphant capitalism through a discussion of the end of dialectics, the lack of serious opposition, and the problem of unrestrained exploitation and profit making.

Against the backdrop of Francis Fukuyama's (1992) famous declaration of the end of history, which suggested that the collapse of communism left liberal, democratic, global capitalism the only game in town and that the only real threats to this hegemony would come from disenchantment, boredom, and primitive religious resistance movements, Derrida (1994) explained that 'time is out of joint'. He meant that the new global capitalist hegemony had lost perspective and become intoxicated with a utopian vision of the free market that was, in his view, totally unrealistic and irresponsible in its extremism. Derrida quoted Shakespeare's Hamlet, who complains about the disjointedness of the kingdom of Denmark and his own situation in having to try to put things right after encountering his father's ghost. Derrida's view was that post-communist, global capitalism would never be able to escape the spectres of its others, the spectres of Marx, that insist upon its responsibility, or debt, to those who have no place in the system and are forced to live on the very edge of existence. Fast forward to the present when it seems that Fukuyama's end of history capitalism is in a state of terminal decline, simply because of its over-leveraging of value in the virtual, utopian space of finance, and it is possible to argue that Derrida's spectres have truly returned to haunt a world characterised by debt, indebtedness, and responsibility for a refusal of limits. Of course, the political coordinates of this situation are clear, and revolve around whether the spectres speak of the responsibility of the reckless debtors, who now find themselves weighed down by repayments they can no longer afford to meet, or on the contrary haunt the champions of finance capitalism itself, the bankers who have created mountains of debt and sought to profit from the desire of the other by making money from money, and now must face up to the very real consequences of their utopian fantasies.

In many respects, these two positions can be seen to frame the contemporary politics of debt, which centre upon the struggle between two different visions of 'economy' defined on the one hand by market forces and the objective neutrality of exchange and on the other hand by morality and wider human concerns relating to health, well-being, freedom, respect and generosity. In this way, these two positions support contradictory visions of economic obligation, where debtors must take responsibility for their debts, and moral responsibility, where creditors must be held to account for their reckless exploitation of the needs and desires of debtors. Since the focus of this collection is the *sociology* of debt, each contribution in some way revolves around a consideration of the interface between economic and social, political, and cultural concerns and the political debates and struggles that emerge from these relationships. This is, essentially, the terrain of the sociology of debt: understood in the narrowest sense this concerns the ways in which finance and debt are grounded in social life. More broadly, it relates to the way these understandings of financial debt relate, contrast and conflict with other visions of what it means to be responsible, to be accountable, and to be indebted; these, in turn, define what it means to be social in some way or other. Although Derrida (1994) seeks to open up this space (where economic and financial responsibility is always situated in broader social and political concerns about what it means to care for others and the world that sustains life) through reference to Hamlet's commentary on the rotten, disjointed state of Denmark, he might equally have based his discussion of the politics of debt and responsibility upon an exploration of one of the great English commentators on Victorian capitalism and the effects of debt, Charles Dickens. In much the same way that Hamlet learns about responsibility from the ghost of his father, Dickens' own understandings of debt and the experience of indebtedness were clearly influenced by the memory of his own father's incarceration in the infamous debtors' prison the Marshalsea, which became central to his later novel, *Little Dorrit* (White, 2016). Indeed, Dickens wrote perhaps his most famous work, *A Christmas Carol* (2003), in order to escape his own debts, and in doing so, I would suggest, produced the clearest expression of the politics of debt in Western culture.

Published five years before Marx and Engels evoked the spectres of communism haunting Europe in *The Communist Manifesto* (1998), Dickens' *A Christmas Carol* reflected the condition of modern industrial capitalism and the experience of indebtedness in the relationships between Ebenezer Scrooge, Bob Cratchit, Tiny Tim, and the visitations of the ghosts of Marley and Christmas past, present, and yet to come.

While the spectre of communism that appears in *The Communist Manifesto* imagines a social form of responsibility, where the individual is rooted in inescapable relations with those that came before, those that make the world in the present, and those who will create in the future, Dickens' story contrasts Scrooge's economic starting point (the miser who sees the solution to poverty and indebtedness in the prison and workhouse) with the moral place he ends up occupying (an alternative model of indebtedness and responsibility symbolised by Christmas) in order to suggest the superiority of the economy of the gift and the social ethic of generosity. Here, indebtedness is no longer measured by the cold logic of the market which speaks through Scrooge – 'the cold within him froze his old features, nipped his pointed nose, shrivelled his cheek, stiffened his gait; made his eyes red, his thin lips blue; and spoke out shrewdly in his grating voice' (XXV: 2003) – but rather understood through the sociological, theological morality of Christmas, where the inescapable debt to others is expressed in the transformations of surpluses or profits into presents or gifts that recognise the necessity of human interdependence. Returning to the present, it is precisely this interdependence, this sociological morality, that the neoliberal politics of the contemporary period marked by processes of financialisation have sought to deny in favour of a kind of speculative, voracious individualism that has no sense of 'the other' beyond their ability to deliver profit. In this respect, the culture of financialisation Max Haiven (2014) explores in his book of the same name seems to be founded upon a kind of 'Scroogean ethic', where the other is a source of profit, rather than the moral position the miser ends up occupying in the final pages of Dickens' book.

Writing on the origins of financialisation, Haiven explains that it is important to understand the link between the rise of finance and postmodern culture which recognised the separation of signifier and signified and the constructedness of meaning systems. Connected to the rise of the postmodern, capitalism after World War II started to shift from an industrial system based upon mass production, towards a post-industrial system defined by knowledge, information, and short-run flexible production in the name of innovation, development, and centrally freeing up demand in the new expanding consumer society. Under these conditions – where production, but more importantly consumption, was organised around the infinite demands of desire – a new flexible model of investment was necessary to drive innovation. Although the complete postmodernisation of money was only finally realised when Nixon suspended the link between the dollar and gold in 1971, the need for ever-increasing liquidity was clearly present in the economic developments that had taken place since the end of World War II. As the post-war period wore on, and particularly from the late 1970s onwards, liquidity was necessary to enable constant investment and centrally consumption to drive production and ensure continued growth. In seeking to capture the novelty of this period, Zygmunt Bauman (2000) wrote of liquid modernity, and transformed the concept of liquidity into a metaphor for the breakdown of structure and the fragmentation of a more stable, solid version of modern society. But it may also be possible to connect his metaphor to the rise of finance, and particularly the way finance crosses boundaries in search of investment opportunities, in order to ground his exploration of the wider sociological processes that have seen the bonds of solid modernity weaken towards their new highly mobile, liquid form. Under these conditions, Bauman's concept of liquidity shows how place becomes far less important (place is ironically nowhere in this new world) and one is always caught somewhere in-between here and there. Of course, in the universe of finance this is precisely where it is possible to make easy money by exploiting price differentials between here and there, now and then through the practice of arbitrage, which requires the trader to take advantage of or move faster than the slowness of information. Reflecting on this concern with speed in the world of finance, Haiven refers to Karen Ho's ethnography of Wall Street, *Liquidated* (2009), in order to argue that financial markets are possessed by delimited horizons, 'the strategy of no strategy', concerned with making fast money which means that it is highly unlikely that they will reflect on the social consequences of financial risk or the political morality of indebtedness.

Indeed, in much the same way that the trader suffers from a myopic focus upon short-term profit and the creation of money, the contemporary debtor is equally constrained in their ability to imagine the future, simply because there is no end to debt in the fully financialised system. Despite the hypermobility of the former engaged in the circulation of weightless money around the world markets and the total immobility of the latter crushed and unable to move under the weight of their debts, the complete enclosure of the temporal horizons of those who make money from money, seemingly conjuring it out of thin air, and those who labour under what feels like the unbearable weight of financial debts, is very similar: it precludes thinking beyond financialisation and the creation of virtual bank money on the one hand and, on the other hand, indebtedness and the dead weight of a lack of liquidity and – most importantly – cold, hard cash. Beyond a fully worked-out phenomenology of finance and debt that is beyond the scope of this introduction (but which would probably revolve around an exploration of the (im)mobility and weight of money and the way this impacts upon lived experience), the key to understanding contemporary political economy thus resides in a recognition of the frozen dialectic of financialisation and indebtedness; this has narrowed the horizons of social and political change at both a collective and individual level and meant that banks have continued to speculate and borrowers remain buried in debt. Understood in terms of the emergence of finance itself, Randy Martin's (2002, 2007) work shows how the narrowed horizons of the fully financialised world have emerged as a result of the temporal expansion of the imperial logic of capitalism. While David Harvey (2005) has shown how capitalism sought to export capital in search of new markets, cheap labour, and available raw materials, and in this way provide a spatial fix for the falling rate of profit, Martin's work illustrates how the speed of finance involves a new temporal fix for the globalised world. When there is nowhere else to exploit, time becomes the final horizon of profitability, and the route to making money becomes about moving faster, exploiting price differentials, and, importantly for Martin, managing risk in the name of taking advantage of potential gains, while heading off possible losses. This is why, in Martijn Konings' (2018) view, the hegemonic understanding of capital or, perhaps we should say, financial time is ultimately ironic, since it is simultaneously founded upon a vision of the possibility of making money from speculation, but also closing off the very uncertainty that might enable the creation of speculative value through pre-emptive risk management strategies designed to mitigate against damaging losses.

In the boom years of the 1990s and early 2000s, a period later named 'the great moderation', financial risk management was essentially organised around first, an idea of endless growth, which meant that all debt would be repayable in the long run stretching way off into the future, and second, processes of securitisation, which enabled the construction of complex derivatives or futures that were then sold to hedge against losses on the market. The result of these two processes was that losses on the volatile financial markets could, so the theory went, be managed away by spreading risk and basically creating a new paradoxical condition, 'riskless risk'. Unfortunately, what this thesis failed to take into account was the relationship between the financial sector and the real economy and the enormous gap that had opened up between the levels of debt created on the markets and the money generated to meet repayments in the real, productive economy where debtors earn a wage. This problem was particularly acute in the subprime sector of the US mortgage market, where debtors found themselves unable to meet repayments and started to default, leaving creditors holding bad debts. Under these conditions, it soon became clear that the logic of securitisation designed to spread risk out of existence had created a situation of system exposure and that insurers with high levels of liability would be unable to meet the costs of investors' bad debts, resulting in the potential insolvency of the entire financial system. At this point, the globalisation of the major financial institutions and their complete entanglement with the real economy meant the threat of a global lack of liquidity, credit, and potential bankruptcy that would have very real immediate impacts upon everyday life. As a result, the lender of last resort, the state, was forced to step in to underwrite the balance sheets of the financial institutions based in its territories and provide liquidity in order to free up finance for the real economy. However, in order to cover costs the knock-on effect of the bailout and injection of liquidity into the market was a politically motivated cut to public spending and attempt to balance the books through austerity measures meant to produce leaner, meaner societies ready for even more financialisation.

Of course, the problem with austerity adopted across the UK and Europe in order to shrink the social state and expand the reach of the neoliberal idea of individual responsibility was that it completely missed the root cause of the crisis in the first place: the behaviour of creditors seeking to make money from money by making risky loans. The problem was never the public sector, which represents an investment in society that pays dividends down the line in the form of healthy, educated workers who generate value and pay taxes, but rather a financial sector that had become about making profits from transactions, instead of investment in infrastructure that would be productive in the long term. This view of the role of lending in making profit was evident in the wake of the bailout when the banks preferred to use the liquidity produced by QE (quantitative easing) to speculate in order to generate profits, rather than undertake longer-term investments in projects that might produce value in the real economy. The effect of this return to 'business as usual' in the financial sector was, therefore, that finance escaped the worst of the crash, which more seriously impacted the real, productive economy that absorbed the effects of the slow down and the wider problems brought about by the new regime of austerity. Moreover, it was precisely this lack of investment in the real economy that has led to the general decline in productivity and the rise of private debt that is fast returning to unsustainable levels in the UK because of wider economic sluggishness (Inman and Barr, 2017). Supporting this view, economist Ann Pettifor (2018) notes that the problem of contemporary finance is easy but expensive credit, based on the desire to make profits from interest repayments. The objective here is never to invest in society itself in order to develop sustainable production, but rather to generate surpluses by lending to borrowers who want to consume or more recently simply survive the economic slowdown. Given this situation, which suggests that fully financialised capitalism is unsustainable because of its inability to effectively reproduce itself, the German sociologist Wolfgang Streeck (2017) writes of the impending collapse of capitalism itself.

The cultural impact of credit and debt

While modern economists from Mandeville through Smith to Hayek thought that the strength of capitalism was based in its ability to translate individual action into some kind of social coherence, Streeck's (2017) view is that finance capitalism has lost the ability to transform private vice into public virtue, meaning that it has to fall back on the most basic form of social regulation – Weberian *Zweckrationalität* or legalism – in order to generate some level of collective integration. In this way, Streeck provides economic support for the French philosopher Bernard Stiegler's (2011, 2012, 2014) exploration of disbelief and discredit in the contemporary capitalist system, which he puts down to the failure of the Weberian spirit of capitalism based in an idea of the Protestant work ethic and sense of the credibility of the capitalist symbolic order. Writing from a psychoanalytic perspective (informed by the work of his teacher Derrida, who theorised the origin and function of writing in Western history), Stiegler argues that the problem of late capitalism resides in the way it has pushed the psychic economy of desire, where we want and wait for gratification, towards the short circuit of drive, where there is no waiting, but only instant gratification that never really satisfies. The result of this short circuit in Stiegler's view is that the symbolic system that creates the link between wanting and having – in the Protestant model, this is hard work, discipline, application and so on – breaks down towards a much more basic form of reactive, unthinking behaviourism where there is nothing between wanting and having but instinctive reflex or reaction. Under these conditions we are more like animals than civilised beings who understand the need to delay gratification in the name of production that benefits everybody, rather than the individual. Effectively, then, Stiegler's theory supports Streeck's vision of the end of capitalism that manifests itself in (a) the stagnation of the productive sector of the economy, simply because there is no long-term investment, (b) the rise of a global super-rich who make their money in the universe of finance without ever touching the productive economy, (c) the plunder of the social sector, which is seen to be a waste of resource and a poor investment on the basis that it is entirely unproductive in the short term, and (d) the kind of cynical corruption made possible in a system where the rules are meant to be broken and the type of innovation and manipulation of norms Robert Merton (1938) wrote about in his study of anomie in the US is considered shrewd and entirely normal.

Under these conditions, the sociological concept of debt – where we are indebted to others through the necessity of our social interdependence – breaks down, and indebtedness becomes a purely individual phenomenon concerned with taking up credit for the purposes of consumption and then managing the burden of repayment. As Streeck notes in his recent book, *How Will Capitalism End?* (2017), in the post-social situation (which he writes of in terms of the post-capitalist interregnum, because clearly the mistake of the financiers is to imagine that capitalism and profit are possible outside of durable social relations supported by some kind of belief system) there are no lasting institutions, but only free-floating individuals who must live by their wits. In the past, individuals might have lived through social symbolic systems that taught them how to think and behave in such a way as to make society possible, but Streeck points out this is no longer the case. On the contrary, the contemporary late capitalist symbolic system is heavily based upon individual responsibility and, in his view, concepts of disruption and resilience. While disruption explains that individuals need to be flexible and able to respond to redundancy and so on, resilience is about how we cope, hope, dope and shop our way through this turbulence in order to survive. Of course, one of the key ways people manage the collapse of durable social institutions in a period of low economic growth is by taking on private debt; this only contributes to their problems, but conversely creates massive profits for the financial sector.

However, Streeck sees no future in this set up (based upon the Matthew principle where the rich become richer and the poor become poorer) and regards it as entirely unsustainable. In his view this system, which seems to engineer a lack of investment, productivity and demand in the name of the exploitation of the poor, represents the final expression of the suicidal tendency of capitalism first observed by Marx and Engels (1998) in the 19th century. In this way, Streeck sees capitalism collapsing under mountains of debt, because it has no sustainable plan for investing in production, and writes the conclusion to the story of the period after World War II which includes a moment of upturn from the mid-1940s through to the early-1970s and then a long period of decline or downturn stretching from the 1970s through to the present. In Streeck's view, this history starts with a period of recovery and reconstruction from the devastation of World War II, which eventually resulted in a moment of over-production and exhausted demand, before lapsing into a long struggle to find ways to create demand and capacity. It is precisely this period of systemic stagnation that has been masked by processes of financialisation, which really took off with the suspension of the connection of the dollar to the gold standard and the declaration of the semiotic freedom of money: this meant that there was practically and theoretically no limit to the amount of bank money that could be created and injected into the system in the form of debt. While there is a sustainable strategy for growth in the possibility of the free creation of money for investment, because investment will drive production and the creation of demand, the problem with the creation of money for consumption and the extraction of profit in the form of interest is that it does not necessarily increase productivity or contribute to a sustainable social and economic system.

Now it is the bursting of this consumer bubble, and the potential end of the consumer society in unsustainable levels of debt, that Streeck suggests has led to the rise of what he calls the consolidation or austerity state, which regards both public and private debt as economically and morally problematic. However, since bankers have not changed their ways since the crash and are unwilling to risk investment in long-term projects, it is difficult to see how consolidation will overcome the problem of debt. This is precisely why Pettifor (2018) argues from a Keynesian point of view that finance needs to be reformed in order to create tighter, cheaper credit for investments in production. In this respect, the problem of debt requires a new political morality based in the need to invest in society and the real economy, rather than short-term profits and the pursuit of consumer goods. Of course, this is unlikely to be very popular with electorates attached to ideas of consumption and self-realisation through commodities; it would represent a move away from consumerism as, on the one hand, the central objective of the individual and, on the other, the main route to economic growth and reproduction. As Mark Horsley (2015) explains in his excellent psycho-political analysis of the indebtedness of contemporary society, falling into debt in the name consumption is not only about physical survival in late capitalist society, but also represents a way to fend off the bottomless anxiety brought about by the lack of social and institutional support engineered by neoliberal economic policy. Given the lack of a social world, we make private worlds out of commodities, and take out ever more debt in order to engage in consumption in the hope that we will be able to buy our way out of our asocial condition. Unfortunately, this 'cruel optimism', to refer to Lauren Berlant's (2011) term, founded upon the new spirit of individual consumer capitalism only plunges people further into the asocial nightmare they want to escape. It locks them into the cold power relation of the creditor and debtor that Maurizio Lazzarato writes about in his book, *The Making of the Indebted Man* (2012), where this relation comes with the demand to keep turning a profit in order to ensure repayment is possible.

The irony of Lazzarato's indebted human, or *homo debitor*, is that their forced transformation into human capital, the entrepreneurial self that estranges and disciplines their own body and emotions in search of profitability, is presented positively in neoliberal culture that mistakes this self-mutilation for the height of individual freedom and self-realisation. That this transformation takes place under the shadow of indebtedness, in a precarious society that provides little sense of the stability necessary to ensure sustainable repayment and should therefore by understood in terms of the exercise of force, forms the basis of Di Muzio and Robbins' (2016) idea of debt as power. According to Di Muzio and Robbins' thesis, the basic creditor-debtor relation enables the exercise of debt power which essentially takes the form of a desperate need to seek out endless growth and somehow overcome the paradox of seeking infinite value in a finite world. Polanyi (2002) wrote about this in terms of the stark utopia where the ideal world of signs, symbols and perfect systems runs into its limit in the hard materiality of the real world of bodies living within an ecosystem that knows no other. Although he never uses the words utopia or dystopia to talk about debt in his book *The Bonds of Debt* (2011), Richard Dienst understands the space of indebtedness in perfectly utopian/dystopian terms by suggesting that what characterises living in these spaces – because one is, of course, always *in* debt, contained, trapped, imprisoned by it the way one is, to some extent, by any space – is that it is simultaneously everywhere and nowhere. This is precisely how the key writers of utopia and dystopia have always imagined their spaces, which are reflections of reality and 'everywhere' by virtue of the way that they somehow capture the essence of what it means to live in the present, but also clearly fictional, virtual, and found 'nowhere' in the real world. Of course, the financial world is essentially a kind of 'real utopia' of banking, accounting and balance sheets, where mathematical fictions produce massive profits for the financial elites and a very real dystopia for debtors, who occupy an economy characterised by a lack of investment, stagnation, deflation, depressed wages, redundancy, and ever increasing mountains of debt.

Living in this dystopia entails trying to survive the very real effect of financialisation: the dead weight of debt which hangs in the atmosphere and pollutes the life world of the debtor. Following the work of Lazzarato (2012), it is possible to understand the way power functions in this situation through reference to work of Gilles Deleuze (1997), who updates Foucault's theory of institutional power in his short essay on the emergence of the control society. Where Foucault (1977, 2006) shows how modern power works in contained spaces – the prison, the school, the workhouse, the hospital, the asylum – and shapes the bodies held inside these institutions, Deleuze's point is that postmodern power operates through networks and a process of dispersal or control. In this regard, Deleuze contrasts the logic of indebtedness, where power works upon the body of the debtor everywhere and nowhere, to Foucault's logic of enclosure, which operates in closed spaces or places. Although there is a sense in which this thesis concerned with the dispersed nature of power was already contained in Foucault's theory, which emphasised the way domination focused upon the body and soul of the individual and thus would be clearly operative beyond the institution, there is equally a sense in which Deleuze makes this point explicit by contrasting the postmodern idea of control he takes from the work of William Burroughs with Foucault's modern concept of discipline. In Deleuze's theory the specular power of the panopticon is, thus, operative beyond the walls of the prison. It is no longer reliant upon Bentham's architecture, but rather operates through the balance sheet, which translates into a kind of scopic drive that follows the debtor, gazing upon them, transforming them into an object, and producing the kind of emotional responses – including, centrally, shame and anger – that Sartre (2003) explores in his phenomenology.

It is precisely this movement from the virtual utopian world of finance, where money is made through the practice of writing numbers on a balance sheet, to the harsh reality of the dystopia of debt, where money is absolutely scarce and seems impossible to obtain, that Joe Deville (2015) explains in his book, *Lived Economies of Default*. In his work, Deville explains that debt is not simply a quantitative phenomenon, but rather a qualitative experience that is lived and felt by real people. The power of his book is to show how finance becomes debt through a range of technologies or devices, including the credit card, which *lures* people into debt, and the letter and phone call, which enable debt collectors to create the emotional attachment of debtor to debt by insisting upon the debtor's responsibility for their borrowing. In this way Deville shows how the abstract universe of finance, which seems to be characterised by the absolute freedom to make money, becomes the very real world of debt, defined by weight, heaviness, immobility and a sense of complete unfreedom. Referring to Deleuze and Guattari's (1987) example of the orchid and the wasp machine, which they had based upon Von Uexkull's (2010) theory of the animal environment or ecosystem, Deville shows how finance enters the world in the phenomenological sense of the word and becomes debt through the credit card and then the collection letter and phone call. But centrally the creation of the life world of debt does not stop there because the effect of the realisation of finance in debt through particular devices is that it then becomes manifest in the emotions Sartre (2003) attributes to the person who is subject of the objectifying gaze of the other – worry, anxiety, shame, anger and so on. This is the life world of the debtor, a world defined by the experience of negative emotions – worry, anxiety, shame, anger, despair – and made through a range of objects that come together to make manifest the wider networks of the Deleuze's control society. Although this is not strictly Foucauldian discipline, in respect of the way that it operates outside of an institutional place, it is clear that the ways in which this debt power works upon the individual debtor very closely resembles what Foucault (1977) calls 'biopower', by virtue of the manner in which it invades every aspect of the person's embodied and emotional life.

Indeed, reading Annie McClanahan's (2018) recent work on the cultural effects of mortgage debt in the US, we might conclude that what the Deleuzean control society has really achieved through its manipulation of media and so on is to take power out of the institution, which has become a kind of relic in the post-social individualised society, and to project it into the home, which in turn becomes a distinctly uncomfortable, unhomely, or uncanny place. Drawing upon Freudian psychoanalysis, and in particular theories of repression and the uncanny (Freud, 2003), McClanahan shows how the real cultural impact of housing debt has been to transform the home from a space of comfort and security into a precarious place haunted by anxiety and insecurity. Under these conditions, the home is no longer a place of stability, but rather a haunted house defined by the looming, ever present threat of repossession and eviction. By explaining the cultural effects of this situation, ranging from strange uncanny photographs of abandoned property, through the rise of ruin porn, up to the popularity of horror films expressing anxiety about the unhomely nature of the contemporary home, McClanahan shows that excessive leveraging and extreme debt have made the home a uniquely unsuitable place for raising kids into balanced adults who feel secure in themselves. Despite her use of Freud and psychoanalysis, what McClanahan does not illustrate is how it might be possible to resolve this situation by drawing out the other side of this uncanny, unhomely situation. What might that look like? Following Freud, my view would be that what financial and mortgage debt – and by extension the abandoned home – really reveals is the inescapable Oedipal debt to the father, the history of the family, and beyond this the social inheritance that makes people who they are. This is precisely what is denied by neoliberal finance that relies on an ideology of individual responsibility that is completely unsustainable simply because 'we' (where 'we' refers to humans) inhabit and live through collective units.

What is truly uncanny about the indebted or abandoned home in contemporary financialised capitalism is not, therefore, what was uncanny about the home for Freud (2003), which is that it was haunted by repressed conflicts and tensions issuing from the history of the family. In the case of the contemporary abandoned spaces McClanahan describes, what is really uncanny is the history of the family, the space of security, safety, and socialisation from childhood into adulthood, which has been repressed by a neoliberal capitalism that takes everybody for an individual and the experience of indebtedness that transforms the home into a space of anxiety, uncertainty, and insecurity. Of course, there is little doubt that this situation, which revolves around increased insecurity in the wake of the financial crash, the subsequent turn to austerity, and then the prolonged period of economic stagnation, has led to the rise of political extremism, nationalism, and the election of populists, including Donald Trump, who say that they will somehow cure the economic ills of globalised society by throwing up walls against poor migrants. But the irony of this turn to an authoritarian version of capitalism is that the strong man, clearly attractive to voters because he symbolises and captures the spirit of the authoritative Oedipal father, is highly unlikely to ever challenge the hegemony of finance that makes money out of money through the creation of debt that suppresses demand, productivity, wages, and increases inequality, anxiety, and insecurity. Instead of seeking to address the real problem of financialised capitalism revealed by McClanahan's uncanny homes (that the unsustainable burden of financial debt hides the truth of a deeper, sociological indebtedness relating to the family and wider social bonds that connect past, present, and future in a symbolic system that creates a secure space where people can live), the strong man of authoritarian capitalism ignores the work of finance and the burden of debt preferring to translate public anxiety into fear of the foreign other who, he explains, wants what we have. Rather than taking responsibility for the other, and recognising our inescapable interdependence in a shared world, the strong man looks to scapegoat the poor and vulnerable in order to evade the need to consider the ways in which the fear, anxiety, and insecurity of the people is produced by an economic system that benefits the financial elites through the creation of a society of debtors.

It is because of this general political problem relating to the violent scapegoating of the other rather than taking responsibility for and responding to their plight, and the related financial concern around the creation of money from money through the expansion of unsustainable levels of individualised debt, that it is important to consider Pettifor's (2018) suggestion for a new ethics of debt. This would regulate finance and the creation of credit on the basis of religious morality and centrally a return to the theological critique of usury, or excessive interest. This had been a cornerstone of the majority of religious thinking about finance, including Christian thought, until Calvin suggested there was virtue in charging interest for the use of money for the production of value. Although Calvin made an ethical defence of charging interest (because the lender is unable to use their money when it is in the hands of the borrower), he made a clear distinction between fair and unfair levels of interest. Pettifor supports this need to regulate finance, noting that loans must be made repayable. Where debts become unsustainable she calls for redemption and a clean slate to enable the debtor to escape from their bondage to the creditor. Generally, Pettifor calls for a model of finance based upon tight but cheap money for investment in production and socially worthwhile projects that will break the current debt deflation cycle by creating value for society, rather than for a small group of financiers. But, in her view, this could only be achieved through regulation or the creation of publicly owned banks, because private banks always have a vested interest in making their own profits. In this way, Pettifor raises perhaps the key problem of the contemporary politics of financialised capitalism and the indebted society: it is extremely difficult to imagine change in a situation where the true nature of finance and the production of money is poorly understood by the people who would need to challenge the hegemony of the financial elites.

In his now classic work, *The Nature of Money* (2004), Geoffrey Ingham explains that the basic understanding of the nature of money – that money is simply a mediator to enable the exchange of goods between individuals – is mistaken; money is really about the creation of credit and debt that presupposes future exchange. What this means is that money represents the promise to pay, that the endless circulation of money really represents the endless circulation of promises, and that this is how social relations function in capitalist society. The truth of money is, therefore, based upon the creativity of promising, the trust that promising means something, and the moral authority that ultimately stands behind and supports the legitimacy of the practice of producing and circulating promises. For Ingham, this theory of the idealism of money is more reflective of its truth than the Marxist labour theory of value, which suggests that value emerges from productive work in the world, because the latter takes money for a thing produced in relation to finite resource, whereas in reality money is simply created with a view to future payment. From this point of view, money is always already potentially 'finance' because its creation as promise points towards the possibility of investment in useful goods or in more or less speculative ventures in the name of making more money in the future. Depending whether or not this investment is socially productive and results in the circulation of money or simply causes the build-up of profits in the hands of a minority, it is important precisely because of the promissory function of money which circulates trust and reinforces sociability and exchange. When this process fails and money becomes scarce it loses its promissory function to create trust. This results in the kind of wider social breakdown and crisis of belief that Stiegler (2011, 2012, 2014) writes of in his books on disbelief and discredit, where mistrust takes over and asociality becomes the norm.

At this point money – at least in its social, promissory, form – starts to disappear, there is a crisis in liquidity, and nobody really wants to take up credit or debt because there is no confidence in the anomic, disenchanted, alienated system. Under these conditions, people only take up expensive credit and fall into debt when they feel they have no choice but to resign themselves to living life in the red, because the future orientation of money no longer functions. There is no hope in money. One might say that the utopian function of money relating to its future possibility is no longer operative, having been replaced by its dystopian other side characterised by scarcity, desperate need, and indebtedness to creditors. This is the dead weight of debt and the reason Pettifor (2018) suggests the creation of tightly regulated, cheap money in order to restore its utopian function through the production of liquidity, and open up the endless possibility inherent in the condition of indebtedness Elettra Stimilli writes of in her book, *The Debt of the Living* (2018). For Stimilli, debt is not simply about finance, but is rather an ontological condition relating to the way humans are thrown into the world, in the Heideggerian sense of the term 'thrown'. This is the original debt, the debt of the living to existence itself, and the reason we are endlessly productive. Following in the footsteps of Marx (1988), who wrote about the creative 'species being' of humanity, Mauss (2001) and Bataille (1991), who similarly wrote of the excessive economics of primitive peoples, and finally Stiegler (1998), who explains that the original default of the human animal is what leads to our productivity, Stimilli says that we are always in debt to existence, the world, and others and that because of this unpayable debt we are ultimately condemned to freedom.

According to this theory, which recalls the existentialism of Heidegger and Sartre, we cannot but live in a state of infinite indebtedness, which means that we are always giving and in excess of ourselves in our interactions with others and the world; to pretend otherwise and to somehow imagine that debts are ever really payable is the ultimate conceit of a class-based society operating through a miserable economics founded upon inequality and an idea of individual responsibility outside of social context. Although this may seem like a purely philosophical discussion about the nature of existence, reference to Ingham's (2004) discussion of the old English concept of *wergeld* (or 'worth payment') illustrates that debt is endless and provides the backdrop to our freedom in social context. In Ingham's account *wergeld* refers to the sacrificial practice of payment to make up or compensate for injury or damage in recognition of the essential nature of sociability. Recalling Derrida's (1998) work on the origins of writing, Ingham notes that keeping track of who owes what to whom required writing through keeping accounts, and that this is how money began its life in the settling of scores for past wrongs. Of course, once the mnemotechnical practice of holding to account for the past in order to ensure stability in the present was in place, the next step was to create credit and debts stretching forward in time in order to enable investment in the future. At this point it is possible to start to identify the social and economic system we call capitalism that relies on the depersonalisation of the *wergeld* system in the form of money, which is always about making promises to settle debts and pay up in the future.

Towards a sociology of debt

According to Miranda Joseph (2014), the problem of the debt society is essentially based in processes of depersonalisation. In her view money, which starts out representing real social relations, becomes problematic when it is disembedded, rendered purely abstract, and centrally depoliticised. At this point the importance of human relations and the monetary function of settling scores and righting wrongs are lost in the new supremacy of quantitative data. Now human value is subordinate to a new mathematical reality which appears entirely neutral, objective and devoid of bias or interest. This allows capitalists and financiers to take control of the new monetary universe and exert influence without appearing to have any particular political orientation. Apparently, there is no power involved. However, this process of objectification is never complete and the moral economy that originally underpinned the system of money returns in the form of spooks and spectres including those found in the works of Marx and Engels (1998), Dickens (2003), and Derrida (1994). The work of these ghosts is to remind people that money was originally about justice, rather than purely abstract legal obligation. In this respect, recognition of their spectral presence might be seen to form the basis of a sociology of debt and indebtedness, simply because they raise the possibility of understanding these conditions outside the coordinates of quantitative value where there is never much doubt about what one owes to one's creditors. When one accepts these coordinates and plays by the rules of the financial system one is immediately caught in the biopolitical regime set out earlier, where finance translates into debt, taking on unbearable weight in the process. However, it is on the basis of the possibility of resistance to this system that Joseph calls for a new model of social accounting, and in this way recalls Ingham's reference to the politics of *wergeld* in the name of opposing moral economy to the objective violence of processes of financialisation. At the time of writing, money is largely controlled by financiers who produce credit that translates into debt for the vast majority of people who struggle to repay what they owe under conditions of low economic growth. Beyond any particular focus, the general objective of a sociology of debt must be to reveal the politics of this situation and, following Joseph's (2014) lead, suggest an alternative model of accounting based upon social responsibility that breaks the domination of the economic and financial way of seeing and understanding the phenomenon of debt and the experience of indebtedness. This is so important because it is only when this ideological shift has taken place and people have truly listened to the spectres of the morality of debt that it will be possible to really change the situation and free people from the unbearable weight of their debt through political action, recalling Jesus' original attack on the money lenders who he thought had transformed the temple into a den of robbers.

Given this discussion of what a sociology of debt might look like, the general approach of the chapters included in this collection revolves around an exploration of the condition of debt and experience of indebtedness outside of the hegemonic worldview of economists and financiers. Each of the contributions examines a particular aspect of the financialised society, the phenomenon of debt, or the experience of indebtedness from the point of social relations or the social construction of reality; in this way, each moves beyond the norms of economic and financial understandings of these conditions. In order to provide thematic coherence, the chapters are divided into three parts which address (1) the macro politics of debt, (2) the social construction of indebtedness, and finally (3) the possibilities of escape from weight of financial debt. In the first chapter of the collection, Lisa Adkins highlights the need for sociology to engage with the causes, rather than the effects of indebtedness. Noting that sociologists need to avoid the temptation to knee-jerk moralism, where debt is always necessarily bad, Adkins explains that it is essential to understand the way finance works in order to understand what debt means. However, this does not mean Adkins is a cheerleader for financial capitalism: she explains that a proper understanding of finance reveals the emergence of a new class system based upon a risk class that holds the power to appropriate the money of the masses through interest repayments. Under these conditions the old Marxist proletariat is no longer defined by the ways in which its labour power creates value for capitalists, but rather by its transformation into the postmodern debtor who repays loans endlessly projected into the future in order to create liquidity for the risk class to speculate in name of making money from money. Where Adkins speculates on the class division between the risk class of financiers making money from money and the debtor class of Minskian borrowers endlessly living in the red, in Chapter 2 Ole Bjerg uses the work of Slavoj Žižek to seek to understand the debt drive of contemporary financial capitalism. Relating to Adkins' piece, which highlights the importance of understanding the concept of liquidity for getting to grips with the way the financialised society works, Bjerg employs the Freudian-Lacanian concept of 'drive' to theorise the capitalist tendency towards pure circulation.

Starting with a discussion of the way banks make use of deposits to create money and debts, Bjerg explains that there is essentially less money and more debt circulating in the global financial system, because interest paid to banks is always greater than interest paid to savers, thus leading to the emergence of a permanent debt drive necessary to service the ever-increasing mountain of debt. The knock-on effect of this situation is that economic growth becomes essential to ensure that repayment is possible, but under conditions when this is no longer possible debt ends up having to be created to service itself. At this point, where debt equals more debt ad infinitum, Bjerg notes that the problem is the separation of Wall Street from Main Street, or the radical difference between the worlds of finance and debt, which enables mountains of debt to stack up in a situation characterised by a kind of financial apartheid. Picking up on the politics of debt explored in different ways by both Adkins and Bjerg, in Chapter 3 Joshua Bowsher explores issues of debt, responsibility and shame in the context of the Greek debt crisis. Bowsher starts by explaining that debt relies on memory and the practice of remembering necessary to make and fulfil promises, before noting that remembering is never a natural phenomenon, but rather one that is constructed by narratives of responsibility. Following this work, he explains that the hegemonic narrative of Greek debt mobilised by the EU and Troika in the teeth of the debt crisis relied on a vision of the Mediterranean leisure zone, which he then contrasts with the counter-narrative or counter-memory developed by the TCPD (Truth Commission on Public Debt) that revealed the Greek debt as odious (meaning illegitimate, illegal, and unsustainable) and a violation of the human rights of the citizens of the country.

According to the forensic analysis of the TCPD, the Greek national debt was actually the creation of excessive interest charges on borrowing from 1980 onwards, huge defence spending, and low corporation tax which meant a lack of revenue flowing back to the state. The essential point of the TCPD was, therefore, that the Greek debt was in no way a social debt, but rather a construction of the neoliberal, financial system that then held Greek society responsible in order to save international creditors from taking a hit when it became clear that the Greek state could no longer meet scheduled repayments. From this point of view, Bowsher notes, the imposition of savage austerity cuts upon Greek society takes on a very different appearance. Against the hegemonic view, which relies on the idea of the lazy Greek living beyond their means, austerity is revealed to be an act of political violence in a new framework for understanding, where the creditor is irresponsible, parasitical and shameful in their lack of concern for the people of Greece. Drawing on the work of Joseph (2014), Bowsher argues that the value of this 'accounting of innocence' is that it can create a new alternative, political subject, a collective 'we', and suggests the possibility of supplementing the financial logic of keeping accounts with a different way of thinking animated by the need for accountability and 'holding to account'. Expanding upon Bowsher's work on the politics of debt, and centrally the relationship between debt and possible futures, Chapter 4 begins the second section of the collection with Mark Davis and Laura Cartwright exploring the ways in which young people manage their debt careers and how this suspends their transitions to adulthood. Based upon empirical research carried out in the UK, Davis and Cartwright argue that young people accumulate debts on the basis of a need to survive in a low wage economy, rather than because of frivolous spending. However, the result of this is that they are unable to think beyond the short term and possess what Davis and Cartwright call 'precariatised minds'.

Although the young people who speak in Davis and Cartwright's piece are aware that their situation is systemic, rather than individualised, they remain negative about the future and ever starting a family or owning their own homes. In this way, Davis and Cartwright show how the debt society is impacting upon young people and suggest the potential longer-term effects of this generational immobility and lack of future possibility. Following Davis and Cartwright's chapter on youth, debt, and cancellation of the future, in Chapter 5, Sam Kirwan, Leila Dawney and Rosie Walker explore the 'calendrics of debt repayment' through a consideration of the work of debt advice managers. According to Kirwan, Dawney and Walker the priority for debt advice managers is to try to create debt management plans for debtors that avoid extreme discipline, allow for speculative time, and centrally create a horizon of debt freedom, even though it may be clear that this is simply an ideal, rather than any kind of realistic objective. Explaining that the calendrics of debt repayment are entirely flexible, and open to renegotiation with creditors who want to recoup what they can, Kirwan, Dawney and Walker reveal that the discipline required to repay debts is often supported by speculative time or small luxuries that sustain the illusion of the possibility of escape from debt. Hope is essential. By drawing upon an advertisement for the UK's largest rent-to-own company, Brighthouse, which encourages customers to choose their moments, the authors' point is that it is only possible to survive a life of indebtedness when one can hold out hope of escape. For this reason we must understand the ways in which deficit time (or the time of repayment and indebtedness) contrast with and connects to speculative time (or the time of consumption and appropriation).

Of course, that both these temporalities are part of the process of financialisation suggests that, even in their most hopeful moments, the debtor is in actual fact in the process of sinking ever further into debt, and that this downward spiral is in actual fact supported by financialised consumer capitalism. On the basis of this view, we might conclude then that there is no easy way out of the cycle of indebtedness. For the reader who would like to imagine that the financial sector might respond positively to this situation in order to ease the burden of debt, Chapter 6 by Joe Deville should provide a reality check. Deville's focus is networked credit/debt, online payday loans, and fringe finance. An exploration of this sector enables him to show how what he calls 'the digital subprime' makes use of big data, data mining, and algorithmic power to assess the credit-worthiness of people with 'thin' credit ratings. Exploring the work of companies on, in his words, 'the fringe of the fringe', Deville explains strategies for assessing applications for credit, including the type of internet device being used to make an application and whether the applicant completes their application form in capital letters, in order to suggest that the digital subprime is evolving in ways that recall Deleuze's (1997) theory of control. Thus an online applicant's credit-worthiness is no longer assessed by reference to their credit history, simply because this may not be available, but rather on the basis of their use of social media, digital identity, and online behaviour. Against the truly nightmarish future that Deville enables his reader to imagine, where we are entirely financialised and leveraged in order to produce easy financial profit on the one hand and on the other hand mountains of personal debt through the use of our social media profiles, the final section of the book concerns potential escapes from a future of indebtedness.

In the first chapter of this section, Chapter 7, Nick Gane focuses on the key issue of excessive interest or usury which, in his view, means that debt is now entirely financialised because it is endlessly rolled over into the future. While Adkins notes that the endless nature of debt ensures endless liquidity for financial speculation, Gane's point is that this means that there is no escape from debt for debtors. Tracking the politics of usury through the history of debate in philosophy and political theory, including the discussion of usury in Aristotle, Smith, and Bentham, Gane suggests that the key device that sustains the class system highlighted by Adkins is excessive interest and that this may be an important political pressure point for those who want to reform the unsustainable debt system in the future. Beyond Gane's critique of usury, which suggests an end to the financialised debt system, in Chapter 8 Max Haiven considers the history of unpayable debts hidden beneath financial debts that form the creditor-debtor power relation which Lazzarato (2012) thinks has become central to contemporary capitalism and, beyond this, sustains a history of oppression. In this way, Haiven suggests that the violent work of financial debt is not only to extract surplus value from debtors in the form of interest repayments stretching out into the future, but also to mask deeper debts hidden in the past that may revise and even reverse our understandings of responsibility. By exploring three case studies from the world of art, Haiven suggests it is possible to reveal these deeper sociopolitical debts, and not simply unsettle the financial debts of the contemporary moment, but in fact reverse the constructions of responsibility implicit in financialised creditor-debtor power relations. Thus Haiven offers readings of UK artist Darren Cullen's 'Pocket Money Loans', Argentine artist Marta Minujín's 'Payment of Greek Debt to Germany with Olives and Art', and Anishinaabe artist Rebecca Belmore's 'Gone Indian' in order to reveal the truth of intergenerational, international and historical colonial debts that transgress the narrow understanding of indebtedness found in the financialised world.

Finally, and to close the book, my own Chapter 9 offers a philosophical debate about the nature of debt and responsibility in a finite world. The chapter starts with a discussion of Jean Baudrillard's work on the 'exorbital' debt of the US from the late 1990s and then leaps forward to the 2007-08 crash when the weightless virtuality of financialised value took on the heaviness of debt that characterises late capitalist society today. At this point, when it seems that the experience of indebtedness is absolutely inescapable, my argument is that we face a stark choice between either a dystopia of endless repayment or a utopia where we accept the reality of deeper currents of sociological indebtedness and escape the burden of our financial debts. Referring to the work of Mauss (2001), but also Bataille (1991) and Merleau-Ponty (2012), I conclude by pointing to an idea of debt that transforms universally recognised individual deficit, or perhaps it is easier to say our essential vulnerability, into a kind of sociological excess that connects self, other and world through a recognition of their essential interdependence and identification. Essentially I think that the debate between some version of this view of indebtedness, which I started to develop in my recent book on utopias, dystopias, and globalisation (Featherstone, 2017), and the economic/financial view of debt must form the theoretical core of what a sociology of debt would look like. It is my hope that the contributions which make up this collection advance this debate and come together to provide the reader with a worked-out vision of the sociology of debt able to inform future research in this area.

References

Bataille, G. (1991) *The Accursed Share: Volume I: Consumption.* New York: Zone Books.

Bauman, Z. (2000) *Liquid Modernity.* Cambridge: Polity.

Berlant, L. (2011) *Cruel Optimism.* Durham, NC: Duke University Press.

Deleuze, G. (1997) 'Postscript on Control Societies' in his *Negotiations: 1972-1990.* New York: Columbia University Press.

Deleuze, G. and Guattari, F. (1987) *A Thousand Plateaus: Capitalism and Schizophrenia: Volume II.* Minneapolis: University of Minnesota Press.

Derrida, J. (1994) *Specters of Marx: The State of Debt, the Work of Mourning, and the New International.* London: Routledge.

Derrida, J. (1998) *Of Grammatology.* Baltimore, MD: Johns Hopkins University Press.

Deville, J. (2015) *Lived Economies of Default: Consumer Credit, Debt Collection, and the Capture of Affect.* London: Routledge.

Di Muzio, T. and Robbins, R. (2016) *Debt as Power.* Manchester: Manchester University Press.

Dickens, C. (2003) *A Christmas Carol and Other Christmas Writings.* London: Penguin.

Dienst, R. (2011) *The Bonds of Debt: Borrowing Against the Common Good.* London: Verso.

Featherstone, M. (2017) *Planet Utopia: Utopia, Dystopia, and Globalisation.* London: Routledge.

Foucault, M. (1977) *Discipline and Punish: The Birth of the Prison.* London: Penguin.

Foucault, M. (2006) *History of Madness.* London: Routledge.

Freud, S. (2003) *The Uncanny.* London: Penguin.

Fukuyama, F. (1992) *The End of History and the Last Man.* New York: Free Press.

Haiven, M. (2014) *Cultures of Financialization: Fictitious Capital in Popular Culture and Everyday Life.* New York: Palgrave.

Harvey, D. (2005) *The New Imperialism.* Oxford: Oxford University Press.

Heath, M., Cadman, E., and Dormido, H. (2018) 'How Australia's Banks Became the World's Biggest Property Addicts', Bloomberg, 28 June 2018. Available at: https://www.bloomberg.com/graphics/2018-australia-consumer-debt/?terminal=true

Ho, K. (2009) *Liquidated: An Ethnography of Wall Street.* Durham, NC: Duke University Press.

Horsley, M. (2015) *The Dark Side of Prosperity: Late Capitalism's Culture of Indebtedness.* London: Routledge.

Ingham, G. (2004) *The Nature of Money: New Directions in Political Economy*. Cambridge: Polity.

Inman, P. (2018) 'Ten Years on, How Countries that Crashed are Fairing', *The Guardian*. 16 June 2018. Available at: https://www.theguardian.com/business/2018/jun/16/ireland-portugal-greece-spain-ten-years-after-crash-austerity

Inman, P. and Barr, C. 'The UK's Debt Crisis – In Figures', *The Guardian*, 18 September 2017. Available at: https://www.theguardian.com/business/2017/sep/18/uk-debt-crisis-credit-cards-car-loans

Joseph, M. (2014) *Debt to Society: Accounting for Life under Capitalism*. Minneapolis: University of Minnesota Press.

Konings, M. (2018) *Capital and Time: For a New Critique of Neoliberal Reason*. Redwood, CA: Stanford University Press.

Lazzarato, M. (2012) *The Making of the Indebted Man: Essay on the Neoliberal Condition*. New York: Semiotext(e).

Martin, R. (2002) *Financialization of Daily Life*. Philadelphia, PA: Temple University Press.

Martin, R. (2007) *An Empire of Indifference: American War and the Financial Logic of Risk Management*. Durham, NC: Duke University Press.

Marx, K. (1988) 'Estranged Labour' in his *The Economic and Philosophic Manuscripts of 1844: and the Communist Manifesto*. New York: Prometheus Books.

Marx, K. and Engels, F. (1998) *The Communist Manifesto*. London: Verso.

Mauss, M. (2001) *The Gift: The Form and Reason for Exchange in Archaic Societies*. London: Routledge.

McClanahan, A. (2018) *Debt Pledges: Debt, Crisis, and Twenty First Century Culture*. Redwood, CA: Stanford University Press.

Merleau-Ponty, M. (2012) *Phenomenology of Perception*. London: Routledge.

Merton, R. K. (1938) 'Social Structure and Anomie', *American Sociological Review*, 3(5): 672-682.

Pettifor, A. (2018) *The Production of Money: How to Break the Power of the Bankers*. London: Verso.

Polanyi, K. (2002) *The Great Transformation: The Political and Economic Origins of our Times*. Boston, MA: Beacon Press.

Sartre, J.-P. (2003) *Being and Nothingness: An Essay on Phenomenological Ontology*. London: Routledge.

Stiegler, B. (1998) *The Fault of Epimetheus: Technics and Time: Volume I*. Redwood, CA: Stanford University Press.

Stiegler, B. (2011) *Decadence of Industrial Democracies: Disbelief and Discredit: Volume I*. Cambridge: Polity Press.
Stiegler, B. (2012) *Uncontrollable Societies of Disaffected Individuals: Disbelief and Discredit: Volume II*. Cambridge: Polity Press.
Stiegler, B. (2014) *The Lost Spirit of Capitalism: Disbelief and Discredit: Volume III*. Cambridge: Polity Press.
Stimilli, E. (2018) *The Debt of the Living: Ascesis and Capitalism*. Albany, NY: SUNY Press.
Streeck, W. (2017) *How Will Capitalism End?* London: Verso.
Von Uexkull, J. (2010) *A Foray into the Worlds of Animals and Humans: With a Theory of Meaning*. Minneapolis: University of Minnesota Press.
White, J. (2016) *Mansions of Misery: A Biography of the Marshalsea Debtors' Prison*. London: Vintage.

1

Debt, complexity and the sociological imagination

Lisa Adkins

Introduction

Since the financial crisis of 2007-08 there has been a growing interest within sociology as well as within allied social science disciplines in debt and indebtedness. This has resulted in a range of analyses which, in various ways, attempt to outline the social conditions of indebtedness, that is, to define or map indebtedness in sociological terms. In so doing, such analyses have touched on a range of critical issues including austerity, the expanded powers of financial and banking institutions, and the relationship between the state and financial capital. In this chapter, I will suggest that to date much of the sociological engagement with debt and indebtedness has been limited by a number of issues. This includes a failure to engage with the dynamics of finance and finance markets and especially the long-term and embedded process of the transformation of debt into liquidity. It also includes the operation of the assumption that debt possesses particular properties or capacities in regard to the social, as well as the supposition that debt, particularly household and personal debt, amounts to illiquid and stagnant households. I will outline how such assumptions are compromising the ability of sociologists to identify and engage with the ways money, debt and finance have become deeply embedded in social life and have become central to the dynamics of social formation. This includes class formation – whose dynamics are increasingly based not on occupations but on the dynamics of financial assets and especially their distribution – and the materialisation and dynamics of what I will term here 'Minskian households', that is, households which exist in a permanent state of speculation.

This chapter therefore amounts to a call for sociologists to rethink their understandings and engagements with debt and indebtedness and offers a number of points of orientation for the development of a sociology of debt. Following Gane (2015) I will suggest one guiding principle of this development must be an engagement with the technicalities and complexities of money, finance and debt. While such an engagement is by no means straightforward, not least because of the jurisdictional hold that the discipline of economics exerts on this terrain, it is nonetheless a necessity given the centrality of money and finance to the dynamics of the social. To begin to set out these interventions I turn first to the growth of interest in debt within sociology and the social sciences more broadly stated.

Sociology faces the crisis

In the past ten years, an interest has emerged across the social sciences in debt and indebtedness. This includes household and personal indebtedness as well as sovereign debt and public deficits. Interest has therefore emerged in regard to both private and public debt (see, for example, Blyth, 2013; Deville, 2015; Graeber, 2011; Lazzarato, 2011, 2015; Montgomerie, 2009; Roberts, 2013; Streeck, 2014). Undoubtedly, the momentum for this ongoing interest is grounded in the 2007-08 global financial crisis and its aftermath. The crisis of liquidity and its immediate and long-term consequences made a number of issues explicit which were not readily apparent to many social scientists prior to the financial crisis. These issues are legion, but here I will highlight four.

First, the financial crisis and its aftermath made it overt that populations are beholden to institutions of credit and that lives are lived in and through debt. Indeed, the financial crisis and its aftermath made clear that populations are not only beholden to institutions of credit but are also exposed to movements and fluctuations of finance markets and especially to the fortunes and movements of securities (including mortgage-backed securities) traded on finance markets. The financial crisis and its aftermath made explicit, then, how populations not only live lives which are financed through debt, but also how they are thoroughly exposed to the operations of finance markets.

Second, the financial crisis and its aftermath made clear how sovereign power had become subordinate to financial capital, that is, to the key institutions and brokers of credit. This latter was evidenced in how emergency measures and monetary policies adopted in the aftermath of the crisis – including emergency bailouts of banks, the establishment of bank recapitalisation funds, the adoption of strategies of quantitative and qualitative easing, austerity budgeting and the application of austerity measures to the social state – all served the interests of financial elites and finance capital, not least by returning liquidity (and profitability) to the financial system. The subordination of sovereign power to finance capital was also evidenced in how the aftermath of the crisis saw a process of the further devolution of authority in regard to monetary policy from states to central banks, a process which has contributed to the ongoing transformation of central banks from lenders into dealers of last resort whose key role and function is to ensure the liquidity of securities markets (Mehrling, 2010).

Third, the financial crisis and its aftermath made explicit how states themselves were entangled in and reliant on debt and especially on the trading of sovereign bonds, that is, on the trading of bundles of sovereign debt in finance markets. The crisis and its aftermath, in particular, made explicit how states were beholden to finance markets and financial institutions (including the shadow banking sector and central banks) in the pricing, grading and dealing of this debt. The downgrading and collapse of the value or, more precisely, the collapse of the collateral or security function (see Gabor and Ban, 2016; 2017) of the bonds of particular states (especially the peripheral states of the European Union) following the financial crisis made this binding dramatically clear. Ultimately, and as is by now well documented, this collapse forced peripheral European states tied to the binding rules of the European Monetary Union to seek bailouts from the European Central Bank (ECB) as well as from the International Monetary Fund (IMF) to refinance their own debt. The conditions of these bailouts on the part of creditors included compulsory and severe forms of fiscal austerity (Blyth, 2013).

Fourth, it became clear that economic growth was tied to debt and in particular that demand was fuelled by debt and indebtedness especially, but by no means only, by household and personal debt and by transaction-based credit traded in fast-moving and roving finance markets. It became clear, in other words, that growth was generated by credit debt, which in turn was tied to the operations of market-based finance and banking. This entanglement of debt and growth was dramatically highlighted in the aftermath of the financial crisis, not least in how temporary credit restrictions and credit freezes contributed to drops in demand, indeed in how it became clear that the crisis of liquidity had unleashed a recession. The financial crisis and its aftermath made explicit, in other words, that capital accumulation had become finance-led.

It would surely not be an overstatement to say that, for many sociologists, the making explicit of these issues was little short of revelatory. In fact, prior to the crisis, beyond a cluster of economic sociologists, specialist sociologists of money and sociologists of science and technology interested in the operations of finance (see, for example, Dodd, 1994; Ingham, 2004; Knorr Cetina, 2003; Mackenzie, 2003; Mackenzie and Millo, 2003; Zelizer, 1994) there was little by way of engagement with finance, money and debt within the discipline. In part this was an issue of the long-lived disciplinary boundaries and especially the thoroughly embedded division of labour between sociology and economics in place since the beginning of the twentieth century, which located money and finance firmly in the jurisdiction of economics (see Ingham, 1998; Stark, 2009).[1] But the lack of interest in and awareness of the significance of money, debt and finance to the dynamics of economy, state and society in the lead up to the financial crisis on the part of sociologists should also be located in terms of more middle- and short-range trends in sociology as a discipline. In particular, it must be located as one outcome of moves across the social sciences from the late 1970s onwards towards anti-foundationalism (see, for example, Barrett, 1992). In this move, concerns with political economy, socio-economic processes and socio-economic structure were not only sidelined but also widely problematised. This was so because the modes of analysis associated with such concerns – especially materialist modes of analysis – were characterised as antithetical to anti-foundationalism, not least because of their positivistic outlook, their search for foundational value, their mechanistic determinism, and their naïve attachment to the coordinates of realism. While the terms of these critiques were both complex and contested, nonetheless one unquestionable outcome of them was a turn away within the discipline from the economic and from socio-economic phenomena.

It is in the context of this turn away from the economic – notwithstanding the emergence of a revitalised economic sociology – that the revelatory nature of the financial crisis and its aftermath for sociologists should, in part, be placed and understood. Postone (2012) has, however, argued that the crisis and its aftermath highlighted far more than a movement away from the economic within the social sciences. It also revealed, he argues, the limits of dominant modes of inquiry and especially of anti-foundationalism:

> Dominant for the last three decades, [anti-foundational] approaches now seem to have reached their limits, unable to grasp adequately our current moment of transformation. The shift away from the study of large-scale historical processes and structures has been, arguably, partially responsible for the difficulties the human sciences have had

to delineate the contours of what has become a systemic global crisis. (Postone, 2012: 228)

While I am certainly not in agreement with the sentiment expressed here that a focus on large-scale historical processes pertaining to the rise of the significance of money, debt and finance would, by necessity, be anti-foundational in orientation[2] what is of interest is Postone's contention regarding the inability of the social sciences to respond adequately to the crisis. This claim is of interest for two reasons. First, it sits somewhat uneasily with the explosion of engagement within the social sciences, including within the discipline of sociology, with the financial crisis and its aftermath. Second, this claim is of interest as it raises the question as to what extent such engagements have come to grips with the dynamics at play in the crisis and its aftermath. That is, and to use Postone's terms, it raises the question of whether or not these analyses have adequately delineated the contours of the crisis and its aftermath.

Debt as a complex and technical issue

I will return to the idea of crisis, but it is clear from my brief sketch of the issues raised by the liquidity crisis and its aftermath, that there was not one single issue which sociologists needed to grasp to unlock its dynamics. Instead, the crisis raised many broad-ranging issues, including the relationships between the state, financial markets and financial capital, the relationship between the state and central banks, the dynamics of debt and indebtedness, the governance of debt, the dynamics of debt-led growth, and the relationship between finance-led accumulation and hegemonic neoliberalism. Critically, for sociologists it also raised the issue of the relationship between the rise of finance capital and widening forms of social inequality, an issue which included within it the distribution of the costs of the crisis. If, however, there is one feature of specifically sociological engagements with the issues raised by the crisis this has been an attempt – perhaps not surprisingly – to delineate the social aspects of these issues. Sociologists in the UK, for example, have been particularly absorbed with the social aspects of austerity, the roll back of welfare state provisioning, rising household and personal debt and lived inequalities in the post-crisis era (see, for example, Atkinson et al, 2012; McKenzie, 2015)

In his recent analysis of post-crisis monetary policy, and especially of quantitative easing (QE), that is with the process of money creation by central banks ostensibly designed to stimulate economic growth, Nick Gane (2015) similarly observes that sociologists have given over far more attention to post-crisis interventions – such as austerity programmes – which are clearly social in character. In so doing, he argues, sociologists have for the most part sidestepped those interventions which are monetary, technical and financial. He reflects that the lack of attention to such interventions is 'perhaps because the monetary practices of central banks are perceived to be either too complex or too far removed from our day-to-day concerns to be of any practical or sociological relevance' (Gane, 2015: 382). Gane makes clear, however, that this lack of engagement is problematic or, as he frames it, following C. Wright Mills (1959), a sociological problem, not least because 'it is the vocation of the sociologist to tackle the public issues of our time, in spite or perhaps because of their complexity' (Gane, 2015: 382). Via his analysis of QE, Gane shows the significance of tackling such complex and technical issues. He shows how post-crisis QE interventions in the UK unambiguously boosted the value of assets of the wealthy and in particular the assets of the richest 10% of households. In this respect, Gane suggests that QE in the UK should be located as part of a post-crisis recovery package based on a principle of regressive redistribution which is indelibly linked to accentuating social inequalities. What Gane, then, opens out via his analysis of QE is a provocation to sociologists to engage with the monetary, the financial and the technical, indeed an argument that the features and contours of the social – and especially exacerbating forms of social inequality – can only be understood and properly explained by engaging with technical, monetary and financial interventions and processes. To not engage with such processes and interventions, Gane warns, is to be 'content to study the effects of social inequality rather than its root causes' (Gane, 2015: 394).

The emphasis found in Gane's analysis on the causal and on large-scale monetary and financial driven redistributive processes might be located as speaking back to Postone's claim that the social sciences are unable to grasp the contours and dynamics of the post-crisis present. This, however, would be to downplay the clear emphasis in Gane's analysis on the limits and problems with many sociological engagements with the post-crisis present, not least in their submergence in rebounding and redoubling effects and in their bracketing of the monetary, the financial and the technical in the analysis of these effects. A quick glance at sociological analyses of the post-crisis present confirms this to be the case. In sociological and allied analyses of austerity, for example, the experiential and the everyday lived realities of austerity are continuously privileged above the fiscal and the financial, including above shifts in the relationship between the fiscal and the financial and transformations to the structures of finance (see, for example, Jupp, 2017; Raynor, 2017; Stanley, 2014). Bracketing the latter is, however, to seriously downplay the significance of the financial in the making of present day austerity. As finance economists have detailed, the drive (or better said, compulsion) towards austerity can only be understood in terms of shifts to market-based banking and financial innovations which have transformed government bonds into high quality collateral (or securities) traded in and fueling shadow (specifically repo) finance markets for raising short-term funding. Sovereign bond markets have, then, been transformed into collateral (or securities) markets: they have been securitised. As Gabor and Ban (2016, 2017) have shown for the case of the Eurozone, these shifts have left the bond markets of sovereigns increasingly (and permanently) vulnerable to the movements of such markets. As they explain it 'without explicit central bank support, sudden stops [in capital flow] pressure governments to adopt fiscal consolidations' (Gabor and Ban, 2017: 135). Sudden shifts in capital flow, in other words, create austerity as a policy outcome.

The latter was dramatically illustrated during the European debt crisis where, in the context of concerns about sovereign risk and with the European Central Bank (ECB) behaving more like a market bank than a central bank,[3] demand in repo markets shifted towards safe German bonds, creating disastrous 'runs' on the bonds of southern Eurozone member states in collateral markets. The collapsed value of such bonds rendered the latter both too risky and too expensive to use as collateral, with banks systematically reducing their exposure to the degraded bonds. In this context, governments themselves had to step in to prevent the collapse of their banking systems and national economies via reductions in wages, prices and public spending, that is, via the adoption of austerity. Indeed, as Gabor and Ban (2017) make clear, the onus fell on European governments and the societies they governed to pay the price of stabilising collateral markets. As they wryly put it, 'the collateral damage of collateralization is austerity' (Gabor and Ban, 2017: 145).

There are some serious and sobering lessons here for any sociological analysis of austerity. In so many such analyses the assumption runs rife that austerity is a fiscal response on the part of governments to the financial crisis and especially to the budgetary holes created by bank bailouts and recapitalisations on the part of the state. Understanding, however, that the conditions for fiscal austerity were set long before the financial crisis and the sovereign debt crises and, in particular, were immanent to shifts to the structure of finance and to the relationship of states to finance markets, demands an entirely different orientation to (and explanation of) the austerity state. Indeed, rather than a simple fiscal response to the crisis, that is, as an outcome of the crisis, austerity should be understood as an outcome of a major reconfiguration of the relationship between states and finance markets turning on the restructuring of sovereign bonds and the growth of the shadow banking system. Consequently (and counter to the assumptions found in so many sociological analyses), the driving force of austerity cannot be laid at the door of individual governments' monetary policies, including interventions to bail out banks. Nor can the driver of austerity be positioned, as it is in so many sociological analyses of austerity in the UK, as the outcome a moral project of a particular government whose main aim in the take-up of austerity measures is to punish and shame the poor. This is certainly not to suggest that austerity measures have been taken up in the context of exacerbating inequalities, or to suggest that the burdens of austerity are not distributed unequally. Instead, it is to suggest that contemporary austerity has to be properly understood as being rooted in long-term and broad-scale shifts in the relationships between states, central banks and finance markets. It especially has to be understood in terms of how the process of securitisation of sovereign debt has created a specific fiscal environment in which state finances have become tied to movements in finance markets and especially to the movements of markets for securitised collateral. Indeed, austerity must be understood in terms of how, 'sovereigns' access to finance moves with the cyclical rhythms of shadow banking' (Gabor and Ban, 2016: 632).

What is clear is that for sociologists to understand austerity and especially to accurately understand the relationship between austerity and the traditional objects of the sociological gaze (such as social inequality), there must by necessity be engagement with the kinds of complex and technical issues highlighted by Gane (2015) in his analysis of QE. For the case of austerity, these complex and technical issues include transformations to sovereign debt, the operations of shadow banking, and the changing relationships between public funding, fiscal budgeting, and finance markets afforded by the securitisation of sovereign bonds. For sociologists not to engage with such complex and technical issues would surely be to endlessly misfire in terms of explanation and causality and especially to unceasingly mistake effects, consequences and outcomes for causes. It would be, for example, to locate the causes of austerity in the financial crisis (and especially in sovereign debt), in the party-political projects of specific national governments, and/or in post-crisis monetary interventions instead of as an always-present possible established by long-term, durable and embedded shifts to the structure of finance and the operations of finance markets. Not to engage in the complex and the technical in analyses of austerity would, then, be to produce forms of sociological analyses which are immersed in (and cannot escape) a torrent of consequences in which what are held to serve as explanations are simply redoubled and rebounded effects.

Household and personal debt: the creditor-debtor relation

It is not, however, only the cases of QE and austerity where the dangers for sociologists of ignoring the complex and the technical lurk. Household and personal debt poses another such a hazard. As I have already underscored, interest in household and personal debt has intensified across the social sciences post the financial crisis not least because the latter revealed (for many sociologists at least) that almost undetected household and personal debt had soared to record rates, indeed revealed populations to be entirely entangled in debt. This was revealed to be the case particularly – but not only – for Anglo-American households (Poppe et al, 2016). On registering this rising indebtedness, the response on the part of some sociologists can only be described as one of a rather unsociological shocked moral indignation. Fed by charts and measures of such increasing household and personal debt, including rising debt-to-income ratios, many post-crisis sociological accounts of debt were, and continue to be, fuelled by such indignation. In several such accounts, the state of indebtedness is positioned, for example, as normatively and morally suspect, not least because of specific properties or capacities which debt is assumed to possess. Foremost here is the assumption that debt disrupts, corrupts and corrodes the social order. Thus, mass debt has been located as destructive of the literal ties that bind, namely, the relations of time (see, for example, Lazzarato, 2011), as socially estranging and destructive of community ties (Graeber, 2011), and as destructive of collective mental health and well-being, in fact, to have led to collective forms of depression (see, for example, Davies, Montgomerie and Wallin, 2015).

What is clear is that many sociologists understand debt to be a threat, and in particular understand it to be a menace to meaningful and sustainable social relations. What is also clear is that a conservative and curiously unsociological agenda informs many sociological sentiments regarding the expansion of personal and household debt. Indeed, in their emphasis on the destructive capacities of debt in relation to the social order, these kinds of sociological understandings must surely be understood to reinstate the kinds of romantic and nostalgic sentiments regarding community and social bonds that the discipline of sociology – from its very inception – has struggled against. In particular, they must be understood as part of the tradition of thought which, while coterminous with it, attempted to oppose the modern via recourse to romantic sentiments regarding community and traditional modes of life. In her engagement with debt, Joseph (2014) has precisely drawn attention to these problematic sentiments fuelling contemporary analyses of debt. She quite rightly points out that such accounts of debt tend to obscure the productive capacities of debt as well as key processes that the expansion of debt has entailed, not least the amplification and extension of the creditor-debtor relation.

I will return to the issue of the productivity of debt, but first it is important that I register that the creditor-debtor relation is the focus not only of Joseph's concerns but also of a number of sociologists and allied social scientists interested in debt. This engagement is fuelled not only by the observation that populations are beholden to debt and to the provision credit, but also by an active process of extraction and dispossession necessarily entailed in this entanglement. When life is debt-fuelled and populations rely on financial institutions to provision credit, unprecedented opportunities are, for example, opened out for finance capital to extract profits directly from the indebted, not least from the payments required to service that debt. In short, it opens out unprecedented opportunities for finance capital and institutions of finance to govern populations by debt (Lazzarato, 2011). Some social scientists have argued that this governance is a matter of the extraction of profits from payments to banks and other financial institutions on the part of working populations. Lapavitsas (2009), for example, has argued that the necessity of debt has opened out a process of the expropriation of profits by finance capital from the incomes of workers on a mass scale. This expropriation, he insists, must be understood to exist alongside mechanisms of the extraction of surplus from labour power.

This expropriation, however, has a further edge: it is connected to the return to prominence of the *rentier* albeit in a revised and updated form. What distinguishes modern day *rentiers* from their historical forebears, Lapavitsas argues, is that while the latter accrued income and wealth via lending capital which they themselves owned, the former accrue income from wealth which they themselves do not necessarily possess. Comprising of finance mangers and financiers and other financial intermediaries as well as the functionaries of finance (such as lawyers, accountants, and technical analysts), the income this modern-day layer of *rentiers* command is not an issue of the profits that can be made from loaning out owned money. Instead, the income of the modern *rentier* derives from using the money of others (including the money that everyday people pay to banks and other institutions of finance to service their debts) to speculate on financial assets. Such speculative activity fuels the income of the modern-day *rentier*, not least because their income does not simply comprise of salaries but also of bonuses and dividends based on percentages of annual profits as well as payments in the form of financial assets from which income can be accrued. It is then – according to Lapavitsas – not the ownership of loanable money but position relative to the financial system which constitutes the modern-day *rentier*. As he puts it: 'modern *rentiers* ... are not plain money-holders ... [t]hey [may] own loanable capital, but their ability to command extraordinary income is mediated by position relative to the financial system.' (Lapavitsas, 2009: 142). It is in the expansion and transformation of modern finance that the return of the *rentier* should, therefore, be located and understood. In particular, it should be understood in the context of an expanded financial system whose lifeblood in part comprises the incomes of working populations who need credit in the form of mortgages and loans in order to live.

While Lapavitsas' analysis, and especially his analysis of financial expropriation, is by no means uncontroversial (see, for example, Adkins, 2015), within the discipline of economics – and especially economics with a Keynesian and/or post-Keynesian inflection – the idea that the expansion of finance and the economy of debt has marked the return of the *rentier* has been keenly debated. Indeed, within heterodox economics a debate has taken place regarding not only the sources of and increases in *rentier* income in the context of financial expansion and the economy of debt, but also the extent to which the modern *rentier* might be regarded as a new class fraction or even a distinct class, not least because of their power in relation to the class they exploit, namely renters, that is, the indebted who pay interest on the money loaned to them by *rentiers* (see, for example, Duménil and Lévy, 2002, 2005; Epstein and Jayadev, 2005; Stockhammer, Onaran, and Grafl, 2011).

The issue of class has also caught the post-crisis imagination of sociologists and they too have zoomed in on financiers and financial intermediaries in this regard. In his analysis of contemporary finance Curran (2015), for example, focuses on senior financial employees including senior bankers, pension and hedge fund managers. Curran acknowledges that such workers command substantial incomes and do so not by salaries but via bonuses and other payments such as asset options: they share in common 'the ability to gain large bonuses from financial intermediation' (Curran, 2015: 397). But, rather than understanding such workers as a newly configured *rentier* class, Curran's interest lies in the production of risk and risk distribution. He argues that such employees should be understood as a risk-class who share similar risk positions. The architectures and intense productivity of contemporary finance have placed such workers, Curran argues, in this unique position. Via complex forms of financial trading which are high risk but extremely profitable, such employees are able to appropriate value (in the form of increased salaries and bonuses) from the risk practices they themselves operationalise and sometimes also design. At the same time, however, they are able to avoid the brunt of the consequences of such risk practices because the institutional environment in which they take place distributes risk away from them.

In part, Curran suggests, this distribution concerns long-term changes to bank and financial regulations which have enabled senior employees to become shareholders in the institutions and organisations in which they work, but to assume no responsibility for ownership. These regulations have enabled such employees to occupy 'an almost proprietary or entrepreneurial position in terms of appropriating a large portion of net revenue' (Curran, 2015: 407). This position also means that in times of losses, senior employees do not bear the majority of the downside. Thus, senior bankers and those in allied positions 'benefit from the risks they create … without bearing the consequences of these risks' (Curran, 2015: 407). This mismatch between potentials for gains and losses was, Curran maintains, illustrated dramatically by the financial crisis. In the UK, for example, state and central bank interventions returned the financial system to liquidity and prompted fiscal consolidation via austerity. The latter placed 'the burden of the crisis onto the least advantaged and those who least benefited from the lead-up to the crisis' (Curran, 2015: 407). In the post-crisis period, the incomes of the financial 'risk-class' in both the US and the UK have, moreover, increased. Those working in finance therefore 'avoided the brunt of the consequences of the risks that they created and from which they richly benefited' (Curran, 2015: 408). Curran also notes that the division between those who occupy key positions in contemporary financial institutions and the rest of the population continues to grow.

While Curran's account of the financial crisis is certainly open to contestation, not least in its insistence that the value produced by finance is illusory, what is of interest in terms of this account, as well as those accounts which foreground the return of the (albeit updated) *rentier*, is how both understand these class formations to be rooted in occupational positions. Indeed, while at face value these accounts might appear to be quite distinct, not least in their different emphases on expropriation and risk, they nonetheless share in common the idea that a specific group has been able to directly benefit from the ongoing expansion and further institutionalisation of the debt economy and yield immense power because of their occupational positions. While it is undeniable that many financial workers receive excessive and outlandish forms of remuneration, and have done so (and continue to do so) during a period in which wages for the majority of workers have not only stagnated but have also been actively repressed, it is important to register that the idea that class is indelibly embedded in occupational position has been central to sociological analyses of class for decades. Notwithstanding constant skirmishes around what occupations relate to which exact class position, and recalibrations of class schemes accommodating changes to the occupational structure, the idea that class is rooted in and arises out of occupational position and employment relationships has remained central to the sociological analysis of class. Thus, and as observed countless times, in both of the predominant modes of class analysis in sociology – neo-Marxist and neo-Weberian – class is understood to arise from occupational positions and employment relationships (see, for example, Butler and Savage, 2003; Crompton, 2008). In practice, within sociology (and especially within UK and US sociology after World War II) occupational position has therefore served as a proxy for class.

Understood in this light, what is clear regarding post-crisis sociological analyses which have attempted to come to grips with the dynamics of class at stake in the expansion of finance and the economy of debt that has fuelled this expansion – including analyses of the *rentier* class and of the risk-class and their renter and at-risk doubles – is that they do not break with this tradition. Certainly, they recognise that occupational positions and the resources they involve cannot, in the context of financial expansion and the economy of debt, be reduced to wages alone. This recognition is, however, central to many established class analyses in sociology. John Scott's (1991) neo-Weberian analysis of class in Britain, for example, paid attention to executive employees (including employees working in financial institutions and finance-related occupations) who do not own but have (and directly benefit from) share interests in the corporations in which they work. Scott argued that the situation and position of these employees – which enables them to operate as entrepreneurs and financial capitalists – places them firmly in the core of the contemporary upper class. In the long history of class analyses in sociology, the post-crisis analyses of *rentier* and risk classes should therefore be positioned as not proposing anything especially new. Indeed, in stressing that these classes are rooted in occupational positions and the conditions of specific jobs, and especially in the occupational positions and employment relations found within the institutions and organisations of the modern-day finance industry, these analyses reproduce the core sociological maxim that class is indelibly connected to occupational location.

Debt as liquidity

But can or should contemporary class relations and class formations in the time of financial expansion and of the debt economy be continued to be understood in such terms? That is, should class location continue to be understood to be hardwired to occupations and employment relations? Certainly, evidence from economists interested in contemporary inequality suggests that this may be far from the case. As well as wage stagnation for the majority of workers, this evidence charts widening inequality based on distributions of wealth rather than distributions of occupationally based income and other forms of remuneration linked to jobs. This pattern has emerged from the 1970s onwards across advanced liberal societies (Atkinson, Piketty and Saez, 2011; Piketty, 2014; Piketty and Saez, 2003, 2006). Piketty (2014) understands this trend towards inequality based on distributions of wealth as well as wealth concentration to be symptomatic of the emergence of what he terms a wealth or patrimonial society in which the rate of return on capital outstrips the rate of economic growth (income and output). Piketty writes: 'the general evolution is clear: bubbles aside, what we are witnessing is a strong comeback of private capital in the rich countries since 1970, or, to put it another way, the emergence of a new patrimonial capitalism' (Piketty, 2014: 125). Some of the wealth at issue here (such as that accumulated by financiers) is certainly occupationally related, but the vast majority of it is independent of wages and other forms of occupational remuneration and instead concerns inherited wealth and capital yielding assets such as housing and superannuation.

There are two issues that are vital to grasp here. First, this body of work is plotting a shift in the dynamics of class formation away from occupation and employment relations, and especially wage distribution, towards asset distribution. This body of work is, in other words, pointing to how life chances are increasingly determined by wealth rather than jobs. Needless to say, this empirical shift raises important questions concerning the ongoing relevance and applicability of sociological forms of analyses of class as well as class schemes which are rooted in work and occupations, including post-crisis analyses –

such as analyses of the modern *rentier* class – which maintain that class formations in the era of expanded debt continue to be occupationally based. The second issue is, however, of more direct interest to the concerns of this chapter. This concerns how the trend towards inequalities based on wealth precisely coincides with the period of financial expansion and the growth in household and personal debt. As is well documented, financial expansion has at its core huge increases in the productivity (that is, the capital yielding capacities) of assets (Konings, 2010). While this intensified productivity has many sources (including monetary and fiscal policy) one critical source lies in finance markets, especially the continuous contestation of the pricing of financial assets (such as securities) traded on finance markets. What is important to underscore here is that this contestation concerns trading on the prices of securities, which sociologists continuously locate – and continue to understand – as household and personal debt. Thus, such securities include mortgage-backed securities and, more precisely, the contracted payments from households which mortgages comprise. They also include other forms of contractual payments from households such as those connected to student debt, car loans, mobile phones and household bills such as gas and electricity bills. In regard to finance markets, mortgages and other forms of household debt do not, then, function as loans through which banks and other institutions of finance simply extract or expropriate profit in the form of interest payments. Instead, they function as liquid financial assets which are in a continuous state of transformation.

What this points to are some major forms of misrecognition on the part of sociologists in regard to household and personal debt. It highlights in particular how sociologists continuously and incorrectly register household and personal debt as comprising illiquid loans operating at the heart of household and personal life. In so doing, they thoroughly bypass the fact that such household and personal debt comprises intensely productive continuous flows of contracted, securitised payments, that is, securitised flows of money, from households to finance markets. At core, this misrecognition is due to lack of attention to the specificity of debt in the contemporary present and in particular a lack of attention to the ways in which household and personal debt is securitised debt. It is the process of securitisation – that is, the process of the transformation of illiquid loans into liquidity – which is at the very heart of the expansion of the contemporary economy of debt. Securitisation has not only afforded a set of highly complex trades and trading practices on finance markets (including credit default swaps and collateralised debt obligations) which are intensely profit yielding, but also a huge expansion in the capacities of populations to bear debt. This is so not least because the structures of financial securities, and especially their slicing and pooling, have afforded a reworking of the relationship between household income and payment. Securitised loans do not demand repayment to be completed within working lives but instead seek the possibilities of payment across whole lifetimes (Adkins, 2017). This reworking is expressed in how securitised mortgages and other forms of loans are calculated not with reference to the probabilities of wages and working lives but instead with reference to the possibilities of payment, that is with reference to capacities to continuously pay rather than to repay. Indeed, just as patterns of inequality are increasingly disconnected from the distribution of wages and other occupationally based forms of remuneration and instead are connected to asset distribution, calculations of debt loading have been disarticulated from wages and waged labour and tied to the possibilities of payment. In this context, it is critical to observe that the expansion of household debt cannot be assumed to act as a measure of how an economy of debt is actively undermining and destroying the possibilities of life (as many sociologists so often assume), but instead should be understood in terms of a recalibration and recalculation of the possibilities of life in terms of the life of securities.

Because of this lack of attention to the process of securitisation, many sociologists mistake liquidity for illiquidity. To put this a little differently, what many sociologists and allied social scientists engaged with the expansion of household and personal debt fail to appreciate is that what banks and other financial institutions seek are not illiquid, indebted households from whom interest can be extracted, but liquid, securitised households whose debts function as assets and whose contractual obligations in regard to payment can be bundled, rebundled and iteratively traded on finance markets. They tend also to fail to appreciate how the process of securitisation has transformed the household itself into a source of liquidity for finance markets. While sociologists continue to mistake securitised debts and household liquidity for old-fashioned, interest-bearing, illiquid debt, political economists are well aware of the productivity and centrality of payments from households to the operations (and profitability) of finance markets. It is recognised, for example, that household payments are now central to the production of safe assets in finance markets, with household securities now producing higher yields than government bonds (Bryan et al, 2016).

There is of course another dimension to the liquid households which finance capital seeks. This is that the household, or more precisely the home, itself operates as a key financial asset for mortgage bearers. One key characteristic of the post-1970s period of financial expansion has been the massive explosion in housing prices to the extent that they bear little if any relation to incomes earned. With some specific exceptions, this growth in housing prices has taken place across advanced liberal societies and has continued, following an immediate dip, post the financial crisis. In the context of such growth in housing prices, households typically leverage their repressed and stagnant wages to access securitised housing loans to secure housing assets. In this context, it is also important to recognise that by far the majority of household debt is mortgage debt and that the majority of household wealth lies not in wages and income but in the unrealised asset potential attached to the homes in which mortgage bearers live. And while securitised mortgages on homes serve as source of liquidity for finance markets, the asset price of housing serves as a source of liquidity for households themselves. This latter is witnessed paradigmatically in the process of iterative refinancing which is now a stable characteristic of households and of mortgage finance markets (Aalbers, 2012).

Certain economists are aware that the operation of housing as an asset has shifted the dynamics of the household. Extending the ideas of Hyman Minsky (1986) concerning financial cycles and the disequilibrium states which finance both produces and thrives upon, post-Keynesian economists have suggested that a Minskian household characterises the contemporary present (see, for example, Stockhammer and Wildauer, 2016). This is not a household which has been made illiquid and inert because of debt, but instead is one which is made liquid by constant leveraging, a leveraging which itself has been made possible by changes in calculations of debt-to-income ratios and by the possibilities of refinancing. The Minskian household is therefore not one which lives in an equilibrium state in regard to income, debt loading and the asset price of the home, but rather lives in a state of disequilibrium. While many post-Keynesian economists are committed to the idea that the leveraging typical of Minskian households is driven by 'animal spirits' or by irrationality in the context of rising asset prices, it is far more significant from a sociological point of view to understand such leveraging and its very possibilities in terms of the dynamics of asset pricing itself and the securitisation of credit. That is, it is important to ground the emergence and characteristics of the Minskian household in the changing institutional dynamics of money and finance.

There are numerous issues at play here in regard to the development of a sociology of debt. One of these is that to develop relevant understandings of personal and household debt sociologists must engage with the considerable implications of the transformation of debt into liquidity. While, like the case of QE, this transformation is technical and complex, a failure to engage with its dynamics will ensure that sociologists continue to mistake debt for illiquidity and, moreover, fail to grasp the sociological issues at stake in this transformation. One of these implications is the emergence of the Minskian households whose sociological dynamics are in urgent need of investigation. Another and related implication concerns the dynamics of class and class formation in the face of the economy of assets. Indeed, the emergence of an economy of assets is suggestive of a class formation far more complex than the two-class model implied by analyses of the return of the *rentier* class. At issue is not simply a class structure in which a super-rich leverage their occupational locations for opportunities to directly benefit from financial expansion, including from payments that a renter class must, by necessity, give over to financial institutions. Thus, at issue is not simply the emergence of an elite class who – via powers available to them by virtue of their position in a specific occupational matrix – are able to actively expropriate the resources of the masses. Instead, it is clear that whole populations – by virtue of the dynamics of asset pricing, including the asset pricing of housing – are entangled in an economy of leverage and speculation. The pressing issues for sociologists in this context, I would suggest, include the emergent class dynamics of this latter economy, that is, the class dynamics of an economy of assets. This is an economy which necessarily involves exposure to financial risk and, moreover, is one which is increasingly taken for granted by governments in the rescaling of welfare and other forms of social provisions such as unemployment and pension provisions. This is an economy, in other words, through which the management of populations is being recalibrated and reimagined.

Conclusion

In this chapter, and through a focus on austerity and household and personal debt, I have set down a number of challenges to sociologists interested in the development of a sociology of debt. These challenges turn around the suggestion that sociologists must develop a far better understanding of the operations of money and finance if they are to understand how debt is implicated in the workings and dynamics of social life. Critical among the issues I have raised are not only the transformation of debt into liquidity, but also the long-term and embedded character of the processes at issue in the expansion of finance from the late 1970s onwards. Recognition of this latter serves as an important corrective to a range of claims that are repeatedly made in sociological engagements with the post-financial crisis era. Such recognition enables austerity, for example, to be understood as an always-present possible established by durable and embedded shifts to the structure of finance and the operations of finance markets rather than as a response to the financial crisis on the part of specific national governments. What I have stressed therefore in this chapter is that it is only by engaging with objects that have fallen outside the remit of the sociological gaze – such as liquidity, assets, securitisation and speculation – that a sociology of debt which is relevant to the current era can be built. Such a sociology would, moreover, not simply represent a 'return' to the issues which were abandoned in the cultural and linguistic turn, but instead comprise a revitalised sociology through which a new relationship with the discipline of economics is necessarily built.

Notes

[1] This enduring division has meant that sociologists have tended to focus on the social meanings rather than the social production of money (Ingham, 1998).

[2] This is so not least because of the non-foundational character of value in the neoliberal era (see, for example, Cooper and Konings, 2015).

[3] The ECB downgraded the credit rating of lower performing bonds and subjected those bonds to market-like penalties (Gabor and Ban, 2016).

References

Aalbers, M. (2012) 'European Mortgage Markets Before and After the Financial Crisis' in M. Aalbers (ed) *Subprime Cities: The Political Economy of Mortgage Markets*, Oxford: Wiley-Blackwell.

Adkins, L. (2015) 'What are Post-Fordist Wages? Simmel, Labour Money and the Problem of Value' *South Atlantic Quarterly* 14(2) 331-53.

Adkins, L. (2017) 'Speculative Futures in the Time of Debt' *The Sociological Review* 65(3): 448-62.

Atkinson, A. B., Piketty, T. and Saez, E. (2011) 'Top Incomes in the Long Run of History' *Journal of Economic Literature* 49(1): 3-71.

Atkinson, W. Roberts, S. and Savage, M. (2012) *Class Inequality in Austerity Britain*, Basingstoke: Palgrave Macmillan.

Barrett, M. (1992) 'Words and Things: Materialism and Method in Contemporary Feminist Theory' in M. Barrett and A. Phillips (eds) *Destabilising Theory: Contemporary Feminist Debates*, Cambridge: Polity.

Blyth, M. (2013) *Austerity: The History of a Dangerous Idea*, Oxford: Oxford University Press.

Bryan, D., Rafferty, M. and Tinel, B. (2016) 'Households at the Frontiers of Monetary Development' *Behemoth* 9(2): 46-58.

Butler, T. and Savage, M. (2003) *Social Change and the Middle Classes*, London: Routledge.

Cooper, M. and Konings, M. (2015) 'Contingency and Foundation: Rethinking Money, Debt and Finance after the Crisis' *South Atlantic Quarterly* 114(2): 239-50.

Crompton, R. (2008) *Class and Stratification*, Oxford: Wiley.

Curran, D. (2015) 'Risk Illusion and Organized Irresponsibility in Contemporary Finance: Rethinking Class and Risk Society' *Economy and Society* 44(3): 392-417.

Davies, W., Montgomerie, J. and Wallin, S. (2015) *Financial Melancholia: Mental Health and Indebtedness*, London: Political Economy Research Centre.

Deville, J. (2015) *Lived Economies of Default*, London: Routledge.

Dodd, N. (1994) *The Sociology of Money*, Cambridge: Polity.

Duménil, G. and Lévy, D. (2002) 'Neoliberalism: The Crime and the Beneficiary' *Review* 25(4): 393-400.

Duménil, G. and Lévy, D. (2005) 'Costs and Benefits of Neoliberalism: A Class Analysis' in G. A. Epstein (ed) *Financialization and the World Economy*, Cheltenham: Edward Elgar.

Dünhaupt, P. (2012) 'Financialization and the Rentier Income Share: Evidence from the USA and Germany' *International Review of Applied Economics* 26(4): 465–87.

Epstein, G. and Jayadev, A. (2005) 'The Rise of Rentier Incomes in OECD Countries: Financialization, Central Bank Policy and Labor solidarity' in G. A. Epstein (ed) *Financialization and the World Economy*, Cheltenham: Edward Elgar.

Gabor, D. and Ban, C. (2016) 'Banking in Bonds: The New Links Between States and Markets' *Journal of Common Market Studies* 54(3): 617-35.

Gabor, D. and Ban, C. (2017) 'Europe's Toxic Twins: Government Debt in Financialized Times' in I. Ertürk and D. Gabor (eds) *The Routledge Companion to Banking Regulation and Reform*, London: Routledge.

Gane, N. (2015) 'Central Banking, Technocratic Governance and the Financial Crisis: Placing Quantitative Easing into Question', *Sosiologia*, 4: 381-96.

Graeber, D. (2011) *Debt: The First 5,000 Years*, New York, NY: Melville House Publishing.

Ingham, G. (1998) 'On the Underdevelopment of the "Sociology of Money"' *Acta Sociologica* 41(1): 3-18.
Ingham, G. (2004) *The Nature of Money*, Cambridge: Polity Press.
Joseph, M. (2014) *Debt to Society*, Minneapolis, MN: University of Minnesota Press.
Jupp, E. (2017) 'Home Space, Gender and Activism: The Visible and the Invisible in Austere Times' *Critical Social Policy* 37(3): 348-66.
Knorr Cetina, K. (2003) 'From Pipes to Scopes: The Flow Architecture of Financial Markets' *Distinktion* 7: 7-23.
Konings, M. (2010) 'Rethinking Neoliberalism and the Crisis: Beyond the Re-regulation Agenda' in M. Konings (ed) *The Great Credit Crash*, London: Verso.
Lapavitsas, C. (2009) 'Financialized Capitalism: Crisis and Financial Expropriation' *Historical Materialism* 17(2): 117-48.
Lazzarato, M. (2011) *The Making of the Indebted Man*, Los Angeles, CA: Semiotext(e).
Lazzarato, M. (2015) *Governing by Debt*, South Pasadena, CA: Semiotext(e).
MacKenzie, D. (2003) 'Long-Term Capital Management and the Sociology of Arbitrage', *Economy and Society* 32(3): 349-80.
MacKenzie, D. and Millo, Y. (2003) 'Constructing a Market, Performing Theory: The Historical Sociology of a Financial Derivatives Exchange' *American Journal of Sociology* 109(1): 107-45.
McKenzie, L. (2015) *Getting By: Estates, Class and Culture in Austerity Britain*, Bristol: Policy Press.
Mehrling, P. (2005) *Fischer Black and the Revolutionary Idea of Finance*, Hoboken, NJ: John Wiley and Sons.
Mehrling, P. (2010) *The New Lombard Street*, Princeton, NJ: Princeton University Press.
Minsky, H. (1986) *Stabilizing an Unstable Economy*, New York: McGraw Hill.
Montgomerie, J. (2009) 'The Pursuit of (Past) Happiness? Middle-Class Indebtedness and American Financialisation' *New Political Economy* 14(1): 1-24.
Piketty, T. (2014) *Capital in the Twenty-First Century*, Cambridge, MA: Harvard University Press.
Piketty, T. and Saez, E. (2003) 'Income Inequality in the United States, 1913–1998' *The Quarterly Journal of Economics* 118(3): 1-39.
Piketty, T. and Saez, E. (2006) *How Progressive is the U.S. Federal Tax System? A Historical and International Perspective*, NBER Working Paper Series, Working Paper 12404, Cambridge, MA: National Bureau of Economic Research.

Poppe, C., Lavik, R. and Borgeraas, E. (2016) 'The Dangers of Borrowing in the Age of Financialization' *Acta Sociologica* 59(1)19-33.

Postone, M. (2012) 'Thinking the Global Crisis' *South Atlantic Quarterly* 111(2): 227-49

Raynor, R. (2017) 'Dramatising Austerity: Holding a Story Together (and Why It Falls Apart . . .)' *Cultural Geography* 24(2): 193-212.

Roberts, A. (2013) 'Financing Social Reproduction: The Gendered Relations of Debt and Mortgage Finance in Twenty-First-Century America' *New Political Economy*, 18(1): 21-42.

Scott, J. (1991) *Who Rules Britain?*, Cambridge: Polity.

Stanley, L. (2014) '"We're Reaping What We Sowed": Everyday Crisis Narratives and Acquiescence to the Age of Austerity' *New Political Economy* 19(6): 895-917.

Stark, D. (2009) *The Sense of Dissonance: Accounts of Worth in Economic Life*, Princeton: NJ: Princeton University Press.

Stockhammer, E. and Wildauer, R. (2016) 'Debt-driven Growth? Wealth, Distribution and Demand in OECD Countries' *Cambridge Journal of Economics* 40(6): 1609-34.

Stockhammer, E., Onaran, O. and Grafl, L. (2011) 'Financialisation, Income Distribution and Aggregate Demand in the USA' *Cambridge Journal of Economics* 35(4): 637-61.

Streeck, W. (2014) *Buying Time: The Delayed Crisis of Democratic Capitalism*, trans. Patrick Camiller, London: Verso.

Wright Mills, C. (1959) *The Sociological Imagination*, Oxford: Oxford University Press.

Zelizer, V. (1994) *The Social Meaning of Money*, New York: Basic Books.

2

Debt drive and the imperative of growth

Ole Bjerg

From macroeconomics to sociology

The holy grail of orthodox and even most of heterodox macroeconomics is to provide an answer to the following question: How can we increase growth in our economy? The idea is that growth increases the volume of wealth that is available for distribution and consumption in society. It is a means to achieve employment, stability and to increase overall well-being. Neoclassical supply-side economists argue that growth can only be achieved by fostering competition to increase efficiency and innovation, thus increasing the productive capacity of the economy and the supply of goods and services, which in turn creates its own demand for these goods and services. Post-Keynesian demand-side economists disagree with this as they argue that growth may be achieved by stimulating demand for goods and services through government spending, thus putting into motion a virtuous cycle of income, production, investment, employment, consumption, income, production, investment, and so on, which ultimately compensates for the deficit incurred by the government. While these two positions may fiercely debate the optimal means by which economic growth is achieved, they often fail to inquire into the mechanisms that compel our societies to strive for growth in the first place. Why must we grow?

The analysis in this chapter is framed by three 'moves': in terms of our mode of explanation, we shall make a move from macroeconomics to sociology. Macroeconomic explanations tend to identify causalities or at least correlations between variables, which can subsequently be manipulated to achieve particular ends. A macroeconomic analysis may for instance find a correlation between central bank interest rates, inflation, economic stability and economic growth, which might suggest a lowering of central bank interest rates to stimulate an increase in GDP (Gross Domestic Product). While this type of analysis may indeed also be found within the discipline of sociology, our kind of sociological analysis is looking for general social mechanisms rather than individual economic variables. In this sense, we are probably aiming to diagnose rather than to explain the phenomenon of growth.

The theoretical framework of our analysis is derived from Slavoj Žižek. In our conceptualisation of growth we make a second move from desire to drive. This distinction is developed within the context of psychoanalysis but in Žižek's reading the application is not restricted to the individual subject. In fact the move from desire to drive is also a move from level of the individual to the level or society of capitalism as Žižek calls it. While the compulsion for economic growth may appear as a desire for more commodities at the level of the individual consumer, this is the manifestation of a systemic drive that operates on the systemic level of capitalism.

The identification and diagnosis of this systemic drive is structured by a third and final move from money to debt. Money is a positive object. The individual consumer may use money as a medium of exchange to acquire consumer objects of desire or money may itself become an object of the desire of the individual. For the individual, money appears as separate from debt. Money is in the pocket, while the debt is in the bank. Money can even make debt disappear. But once we move to the level of society, we see how money and debt are much more intricately intertwined. Not only can there be no money without debt. Money itself is debt.

Our three moves are folded into each other in the sociological proposition that contemporary capitalism is marked by an imperative of economic growth, which is propelled by a debt drive.

From desire to drive

We shall begin with a rather condensed passage from Žižek. This passage contains much of the conceptual tools that we need for our analysis, although we also need to unpack some of the formulations:

> Therein lies the difference between desire and drive: desire is grounded in its constitutive lack, while the drive circulates around a hole, a gap in the order of being. In other words, the circular movement of the drive obeys the weird logic of the curved space in which the shortest distance between two points is not a straight line, but a curve: the drive "knows" that the quickest way to realize its aim is to circulate around its goal-object. At the immediate level

> of addressing individuals, capitalism of course interpellates them as consumers, as subjects of desire, soliciting in them ever new perverse and excessive desires (for which it offers products to satisfy them); furthermore, it obviously also manipulates the "desire to desire," celebrating the very desire to desire ever new objects and modes of pleasure. However, even if it already manipulates desire in a way which takes into account the fact that the most elementary desire is the desire to reproduce itself as desire (and not to find satisfaction), at this level, we do not yet reach the drive. The drive inheres in capitalism at a more fundamental, *systemic*, level: the drive is that which propels forward the entire capitalist machinery, it is the impersonal compulsion to engage in the endless circular movement of expanded reproduction. We enter the mode of the drive the moment the circulation of money as capital becomes an end in itself, since the expansion of value takes place only within this constantly renewed movement. (Žižek, 2012: 496–7, emphasis in original)

This passage provides, first of all, a definition of the concept of drive in relation to desire. Desire is directed at an object, which is at the same time overdetermined by a series of fantasmatic projections. This is why, as Žižek points out, 'the subject ... and the object-cause of its desire ... are strictly correlative' (Žižek, 2000: 28). The concept of desire is quite immediately applicable to consumer capitalism as also suggested in the above passage. Through ever more efficient forms of marketing, individuals are 'interpellated' as consumer subjects with their desires structured by the objects of consumption provided by capitalism. This is the standard analysis of contemporary consumer capitalism that every sociology student is able to recite in her sleep.

The move from desire to drive, however, provides an opportunity to push the analysis one step further. While the concept of desire certainly points to important dimensions of the ideology of growth, the distinctive characteristic of our current predicament perhaps lies rather in the domain of drive. In the second half of the passage, Žižek makes the proposition that the constitution of desire at the level of the individual subject is merely the manifestation of a drive inherent in capitalism at a much more 'fundamental, systemic, level'. In order to unfold this proposition, we shall look more closely into the concept of the drive. Žižek provides the following elaboration:

> Once we move beyond desire – that is to say, beyond the fantasy which sustains desire – we enter the strange domain of *drive*: the domain of the closed circular palpitation which finds satisfaction in endlessly repeating the same failed gesture. (Žižek,1997: 30, emphasis in original)

The field of tension between the desire of the subject and the object of desire is sustained by fantasy. This is where we find the imaginary promises of car commercials and perfume ads: 'Buy object X and become subject Y'. In the domain of drive, there is no such fantasmatic support. There is no belief in any form of satisfaction or relief brought about by the achievement of an object. In fact, the drive is not even oriented towards an object. While desire has a goal, which is the appropriation of the object, drive has an aim, which is the very process propelled by aim itself. The rhythm of drive is the failed repetition.

The move from desire to drive is exemplified in the development of addictions such as compulsive gambling, drug addiction and compulsive shopping (Bjerg, 2008). Let's make a small detour to illustrate the concept of drive: the subjectivity of the ordinary, non-compulsive gambler is largely structured by the desire for money. The goal of the gambler is to win. This desire is supported by various fantasies projected onto the sublime object of money or simply the event of winning, which functions as an 'answer of the real' somehow redeeming the subjectivity of the gambler (Bjerg, 2009).

But being exposed to the groundless chance of the game also carries the risk that the desire for money and the fantasies sustaining this desire are eroded. The oscillation between winning and losing with no apparent reason for one or the other challenges the belief that money carries any meaning at all. In gambling, money is desublimated. This is the point, where the gambler moves from the domain of desire into the domain of drive (Bjerg, 2011: 150–3). The goal of gambling is no longer to win money. The aim of gambling is to gamble. The gambler is submerged in the pure repetitive rhythm of the game, where no win or no loss can be big enough to provide a logical conclusion to the game. This is expressed in the words of the legendary gambler, Nick 'The Greek' Dandalos: 'The next best thing to gambling and winning is gambling and losing' (Alvarez, 1983: 114). It is when the gambler becomes completely caught up in the mode of the drive that the state of addiction evolves. In this mode, the gambler 'finds satisfaction in endlessly repeating the same failed gesture', which carries with it all the social, emotional and economic costs associated with compulsive gambling.

Transposing the distinction between desire and drive back into the analysis of economic growth we find a similar duality. Economic growth is propelled by the consumer demand for ever more and ever newer goods and services. And this consumer demand is itself the result of the way that capitalism functions to structure the desire of the subject. But according to Žižek's proposition quoted above, we should be able to identify, beyond or behind the desire constituted at the level of the individual subject, a more fundamental drive for growth. What is this drive and where should we look for it?

Unfortunately, Žižek himself provides little more than knee-jerk classic Marxism in his guidance also quoted previously, where he points to 'the moment the circulation of money as capital becomes an end in itself' (Žižek, 2012: 497). As this statement is so generic that it is almost impossible to disagree with, it still needs to be revised in order to fully capture the particular drive of contemporary growth capitalism. Rather than making the move from money to capital, we should make a move from money to debt. The proposition to be explored in the following section is thus stated in the following paraphrase:

> We enter the mode of the drive the moment the circulation of money as *debt* becomes an end in itself, since the expansion of *bank balance sheets* take place only within this constantly renewed movement.

From money to debt

Today we live in the age of post-credit capitalism (Bjerg, 2014). This phase of capitalism is not only, and perhaps not even primarily, defined by the constitution of the means of production of goods and services through the appropriation of value by capital. What matters today is the constitution of the means of production of money and debt.

The evolution of our current paradigm of money may crudely be conceived in an overlapping succession of two stages of decoupling. In the first stage, the creation of fiat money by the state is decoupled from the supply of precious metals such as gold and silver otherwise restricting the issuance of new money. Invoking Žižek's conception of the intricate relation between the real and the symbolic, we should be careful not to romanticise previous monetary regimes based on some form of gold standard. Žižek's definition of the real as 'that which resists symbolization' and 'as the rock upon which every attempt at symbolization stumbles' (Žižek, 1989: 69, 169) also applies to precious metals. The value of gold and silver is 'real' and yet this value can only be expressed through a price, which is derived in a process of symbolisation.

This means, first of all, that the pricing of money through a reference to gold is a highly precarious procedure and over time it seems impossible to sustain a stable price. Throughout history, functioning gold and silver standards are the exception rather than the rule. Secondly, we might ask ourselves if the value of money under a gold standard is derived from an inherent value of gold, or if it is the other way around, so that the value of gold is derived from the fact that it is incorporated into the money system.

But in order to understand our current paradigm of money, we need to include another stage of decoupling, which is the decoupling of commercial bank credit money from central bank fiat money. This is also a process that has been evolving over decades and even centuries but it has particularly picked up speed since the 1970s. Today, only a fraction of the total supply of money in Western and other comparable economies is constituted by fiat money in cash originating from state-controlled central banks (Bjerg, 2014: 167-183). The vast majority of money in circulation is commercial bank credit money (Ryan-Collins et al, 2011). This is the money sitting in commercial bank deposit accounts that we use whenever we make payments by credit cards, debit cards, bank transfers, cheques, or other forms of non-cash money transactions. From an individual money user perspective it is easy to think of bank credit money as merely a convenient substitute for central bank physical cash. Buying things in a shop, it seems to make little difference if you pay by cash or card. But shifting into a macro perspective on the economy, there are crucial and consequential differences between the two forms of money.

While physical cash is created as the central bank runs its printing press, commercial bank credit money is created when the bank issues new credit. When a customer takes out a loan of say £100,000 in a bank, this money is typically not paid out in cash but merely credited to the customer's deposit account in the bank. In this way, the bank essentially creates new money by simply expanding its balance sheet. On the one hand, the bank records the loan of £100,000 as a debt that the customer now owes the bank. This debt figures as an asset on the bank's balance sheet. On the other hand, the £100,000 that is paid out to the customer is recorded as a credit against the bank. The customer's deposit is money that is owed by the bank. This credit figures as a liability on the bank's balance sheet.

While the books of the bank still balance, it has nevertheless managed to create £100,000 worth of new money out of nothing. Or perhaps more correctly, it has created £100,000 worth of new money out of the customer's debt to the bank. The gist of the matter is of course that in our current economy, where most payments are made as bank credit transfers, credit against a bank *is* money. It is thus misleading to think of banks as merely 'financial intermediaries'. Rather than lending out money already in existence, banks are capable of making money by the same token as they lend them out (Werner, 2005: 161-80). This is how the majority of money circulating in our contemporary economy has come into being.

Debt and growth

We have already touched upon various dimensions of the relation between money and growth throughout the preceding analyses. We shall now explore how the relation between money and growth is reconfigured with the emergence of post-credit money. In the classical account, which we find in Adam Smith, money is a means of exchange to alleviate the inconveniences of barter (1776: 24-5). Money is a mere facilitator of growth as it improves the efficiency of the market. Money enables the exchange of diverse commodities and services thus liberating the butcher to concentrate on butchering, the baker to concentrate on baking and the brewer to concentrate on brewing. In other words, money facilitates the division of labour, which in turn creates growth through increased productivity.

Money, however, not only operates on the supply side of the economy but also on the demand side. Money not only facilitates growth by enabling productivity, although, admittedly, it does that too. Money plays a key role in the very constitution of the desires of the economic subject, thus creating new and increasing demands for new commodities and services that can only be provided through the market economy. In addition, money itself emerges as an object of desire thus furthering the expansive forces of the market economy. In other words, money does not only respond to pre-existing needs that are served through the market economy. Through the structuring of desire, money puts into motion a self-perpetuating movement towards more and more growth.

While both of these relations between money and growth still apply today, the system of post-credit money adds another dimension to the dialectic. In our contemporary system, the creation of money is intertwined with the creation of interest-bearing debt. On the one hand, credit money itself is nothing but the debt of the bank to the bank customer. On the other hand, credit money is created as the counter entry to the creation of a debt of the customer to the bank. On the balance sheet of the bank, the bank's debt to the customer figures as a liability and the customer's debt to the bank figures as an asset. From this immediate perspective, the two entries, money and debt, appear to be symmetrical. But if we add the dimension of temporality, the symmetry disappears. The customer's debt to the bank earns an interest depending on the conditions of the loan and the credibility of the customer. An asset-backed mortgage may earn as little as 2-3 per cent annually while a credit card loan may earn up to 20-30 per cent or even higher. The bank's debt to the customer, however, typically earns very little if any interest at all. This is because this debt functions at the same time as liquid money.

If we believe in the textbook theory of banking, debt and interest – where the issuance of a loan is merely the movement of money from one agent, the lender, to another agent, the borrower – the interest differential between debt and money makes a lot of sense. The interest paid by the borrower is a compensation to the lender because the lender foregoes the ability to dispose of the money otherwise. This is similar to the way that someone lending out their car might expect some form of compensation, as they cannot use the car while it is being lent out. But as we have seen, this is not how banks function in the age of post-credit money. Of course a bank requires initial investors in order to come into being. But, once the bank is up and running and minimal requirements for capital and liquidity are fulfilled, it does not have to wait for depositors to lend out money. It is capable of creating money through the expansion of its own balance sheet by the same token that it lends out this money. In fact, we can think of the borrower as being at the same time a lender, in so far as the money paid out through the loan is nothing but a deposit with the bank. Banks transform debt into money (Bjerg, 2014: 124-31). In this light, charging interest seems less justified by the argument that for every debt there is a creditor who has foregone the opportunity to dispose this money. In the case of banks, the money would not be there in the first place if it wasn't for the debtor being willing to borrow it.

The issue at hand is not so much the moral arguments for or against interest. The point is rather that in our current monetary system, debts tend to grow at a faster pace than the supply of money. This is due, primarily, to the basic differential between interests on debt and interests on deposits. From the perspective of the individual debtor, this is not necessarily a problem. If they have a steady job, a profitable business, or another source of income, they may be perfectly capable of recovering the amount of money necessary to make the required payments of interest and principal as it comes due. But, from the perspective of the total economy, the difference between the growth rate of debts and the growth rate of money amounts to a structural lack of money. There is simply not enough money to go around to meet the payments of debt and principal. This configuration of the money system has implications for the functioning of the economy as such. Money no longer just structures a desire for economic growth. The build-up of debt in the system of post-credit money propels the economy into a drive towards perpetual debt.

The parable of the eleventh round

In order to explore in more detail, the mechanics of money, debt and economic growth, we shall start by looking into a parable told by Berhard Lietaer (who is, by the way, one of the architects behind the Euro).

> Once upon a time, in a small village in the Outback, people used barter for all their transactions. On every market day, people walked around with chickens, eggs, hams, and breads, and engaged in prolonged negotiations among themselves to exchange what they needed. At key periods of the year, like harvests or whenever someone's barn needed big repairs after a storm, people recalled the tradition of helping each other out that they had brought from the old country. They knew that if they had a problem someday, others would aid them in return.
>
> One market day, a stranger with shiny black shoes and an elegant white hat came by and observed the whole process with a sardonic smile. When he saw one farmer running around to corral the six chickens he wanted to exchange for a big ham, he could not refrain from laughing. "Poor people," he said, "so primitive." The farmer's wife overheard him and challenged the stranger, "Do you think you can do a better job handling chickens?" "Chickens, no," responded the stranger, "But there is a much better way to eliminate all that hassle." "Oh yes, how so?" asked the woman. "See that tree there?" the stranger replied. "Well, I will go wait there for one of you to bring me one large cowhide. Then have every family visit me. I'll explain the better way."
>
> And so it happened. He took the cowhide, and cut perfect leather rounds in it, and put an elaborate and graceful little

> stamp on each round. Then he gave to each family 10 rounds, and explained that each represented the value of one chicken. "Now you can trade and bargain with the rounds instead of the unwieldy chickens," he explained.
>
> It made sense. Everybody was impressed with the man with the shiny shoes and inspiring hat.
>
> "Oh, by the way," he added after every family had received their 10 rounds, "in a year's time, I will come back and sit under that same tree. I want you to each bring me back 11 rounds. That 11th round is a token of appreciation for the technological improvement I just made possible in your lives." "But where will the 11th round come from?" asked the farmer with the six chickens. "You'll see," said the man with a reassuring smile.
>
> Assuming that the population and its annual production remain exactly the same during that next year, what do you think had to happen? Remember, that 11th round was never created. Therefore, bottom line, one of each 11 families will have to lose all its rounds, even if everybody managed their affairs well, in order to provide the 11th round to 10 others.
>
> So when a storm threatened the crop of one of the families, people became less generous with their time to help bring it in before disaster struck. While it was much more convenient to exchange the rounds instead of the chickens on market days, the new game also had the unintended side effect of actively discouraging the spontaneous cooperation that was traditional in the village. Instead, the new money game was generating a systemic undertow of competition among all the participants. (Lietaer, 50-3: 2002)

The parable is of course an illustration of the way that money is created on the basis of interest-bearing debt. It also shows how this creation of money out of debt introduces an imbalance into the economy. Since there is a lack of enough rounds to pay back the stranger, the families now have to compete against each other. Some individual families will probably do fine under this system. The most competitive families will have no problems earning enough rounds to pay back the stranger. But some other families will eventually not have enough rounds to pay the stranger. What the stranger has done is simply to create money on the back of interest-bearing debt. Over the course of the year, the amount of debt has outgrown the amount of money available for repayment.

The scarcity of money forces an environment of competition rather than cooperation.

Initially, Lietaer merely uses the parable to illustrate how the institution of debt tends to erode non-monetary forms of economic interaction such as sharing and gift-giving. Charles Eisenstein, however, expands on Lietaer's parable and shows how the competition for rounds to pay back the debts to the stranger ultimately forces the economy of the village to grow (Eisenstein, 2011). Unless the villagers choose to unite and kick the stranger out of the village, the economy of the village is, according to Eisenstein, likely to evolve into a situation of default and perpetual debt creation. In order to compensate for the lack of rounds to pay back both principal and interest, the stranger agrees to create new rounds and lend them out to the village families on the condition that these new rounds are also paid back with interest:

> So imagine now that the villagers gather round the man in the hat and say, "Sir, could you please give us some additional rounds so that none of us need go bankrupt?"
>
> The man says, "I will, but only to those who can assure me they will pay me back. Since each round is worth one chicken, I'll lend new rounds to people who have more chickens than the number of rounds they already owe me. That way, if they don't pay back the rounds, I can seize their chickens instead. Oh, and because I'm such a nice guy, I'll even create new rounds for people who don't have additional chickens right now, if they can persuade me that they will breed more chickens in the future. So show me your business plan! Show me that you are trustworthy (one villager can create 'credit reports' to help you do that). I'll lend at 10 percent - if you are a clever breeder, you can increase your flock by 20 percent per year, pay me back, and get rich yourself, too." (Eisenstein: 2011: 95-7)

Since the stranger only lends out to families that are able to put up chickens or other assets in collateral for the loan or to families able to present a viable business plan for how to produce more chickens in the future, the families are compelled to increase their production of chickens in order to remain creditworthy in the eyes of the stranger rather than to satisfy any actual demand for chickens. The financing of the economy of the village through the creation of money out of debt creates an imperative of perpetual growth.

Psychoanalysis provides a further elaboration of this imbalance introduced into the economy by the stranger's creation of money out of debt. This imbalance is structurally similar to the imbalance that is instituted with the inclusion of the subject into the symbolic order. Žižek theorises this inclusion as symbolic castration and he provides the following account:

> What Lacan calls 'symbolic castration' is a deprivation, a gesture of taking away (the loss of the ultimate and absolute—'incestuous'—object of desire) which is in itself giving, productive, generative, opening up and sustaining the space of desire and of meaning. The frustrating nature of our human existence, the very fact that our lives are forever out of joint, marked by a traumatic imbalance, is what propels us towards permanent creativity. (Žižek, 2012: 132)

If we transpose this definition into the field of money and debt, it is much in line with the standard account of the function of banks and credit. When banks create money on the back of interest-bearing debt, Žižek's 'traumatic imbalance' is instituted in the economy. In so far as the perpetually rising debt can never be repaid, this puts the economy 'forever out of joint'. But even if this state of perpetual indebtedness is indeed 'frustrating' it is at the same time also 'productive, generative, opening up and sustaining the space of' investment, innovation and growth.

This space of investment, innovation and growth not only operates on the supply side of the economy. Creativity is not just mobilised to find new ways of producing more chickens. Even though the stranger requires the families to produce more chicken, he himself is not directly interested in the chickens. For him the chickens are merely a means for the families to earn more rounds. But for this conversion of chickens into rounds to take place, the families have to be able to sell their excess production of chickens. This means that the village economy not only has to increase the capacity for the production of chickens, it also has to increase the capacity for the consumption of chickens.

We may complement the conventional notion of GDP (Gross Domestic Product) with a parallel notion of GDD (Gross Domestic Desire) (Bjerg, 2016: 114-121). The economy has to deploy its creative powers to produce consumer subjects with a capacity for consumption that is not restricted by immediate needs. Since there is a limit to the amount of chickens that one person is able to eat, it might be necessary for the village economy to diversify its production and invent new products such as chicken merchandise, chicken toys or chicken movies, which are more easily consumed. At the same time, the economy would have to market these products in a way that would make them objects of the desire of consumers.

The simplified logic of the parable illustrates how money itself is a debt owed by banks to money users. It also shows how money is introduced into the economy as the counter entry to a debt owed by money users to the bank. This second debt, however, is not money. It is only a debt. In so far as the debt owed by money users to banks tends to grow faster than the debt owed by banks to money users, a structural shortage of money is introduced into the system. There is never enough money to pay back the debt and the system thus requires a perpetual creation of new money to compensate for this shortage. But since this money can only be lent into the economy creating new debt, it only perpetuates the logic. As we have seen, Žižek describes how 'drive circulates around a hole, a gap in the order of being' (Žižek, 2012: 496). In similar fashion, money circulates around a hole, a gap in the order of the economy, which is debt.

The gist of our model of the eleventh parable is that when money is created out of interest-bearing debt, it is inherently impossible for the economy to grow itself out of debt. Individual agents may experience wealth and become free of debt and the economy as a whole may even experience an increase in productivity and the build-up of capital. But the money system necessarily increases the amount of debt at a faster rate than the supply of money available to repay the debt. As long as the economy is growing in terms of productive output and build-up of capital, the increasing level of debt may not be a problem. As long as the economy expands, banks are more than willing to keep lending new money into the economy, which are then available to make the current payments of interest and principals on outstanding loans. Such organisation of the economy, however, compels it to keep growing if the money system is not going to collapse.

Growth cannot be used to pay off the debt. Banks do not accept chickens in payment of debt and interests. While economic growth does indeed result in the production of even more goods and services, these products are only valorised as they are exchanged for money in the market. As long as new money can only be introduced into the economy together with the creation of interest-bearing debt, there will always be a deficit of money regardless of the amount of goods and services produced in the underlying economy. This is the gist of the parable of the eleventh round. Even if all families were able to double their output of chickens and other commodities, there would not be enough rounds to pay off their debts to the stranger. This Faustian feature of the economy is not immediately obvious, when we just look at the economy as a conglomeration of individual subjects of desire. We need to include the systemic level at which the logic of the debt drive is operative.

Wall Street and Main Street

Now of course the parable of the eleventh round is an extremely simplified model of the way that economies and banks function. The model does not take into account the difference between central banks and commercial banks. It also assumes that the village economy is a closed economy with no interaction with other economies. While it is beyond the scope of this text to discuss the implications of these simplifications for the transposition of the analysis onto our actual economy, we shall turn to a third simplification in the parable.

Readers with an ear for antisemitism may have already noted a very critical assumption in our model of the imaginary village. The parable of the eleventh round is the story of a solidarity community, where people live in harmony and mutual collaboration, until it is one day upset by the intrusion of a stranger, who wears a hat and lends out money for interest. It is difficult not to notice how the parable resembles the stereotypical narrative of the Jew as the alien element of greed obstructing the balance of an otherwise harmonious community. This resemblance should, however, not prevent us from examining the economic implications of the intrusion of the stranger. The crucial issue is, of course, not the race or beliefs of the stranger but rather his status as someone who is at the margins of the village economy.

One of the reasons why the introduction of the rounds into the village is destined to undermine its economy, or at least force it onto a path of perpetual growth, is that the stranger himself is not a participant in the production, trade and consumption of commodities within the economy. Suppose that rather than just visiting once every year, the stranger moves into the village after his second visit. And suppose that the stranger, who is now no longer effectively a stranger, consumes chickens, eggs, ham, beer and other commodities produced in the village, paying for these with the rounds he has earned by collecting interest. In this case, there would not necessarily be a shortage of rounds in circulation to service the debt incurred by the villagers. Rather than being pulled out of circulation, the ten rounds paid in interest every year would be recycled into the economy as the stranger spends them buying produce in the market. The village would indeed have to make a one-off expansion of its production capacity to provide the surplus demand for commodities brought about by inclusion of the stranger into the economy but there would be no need for the kind of perpetual growth seen in our initial model.

With this variation in mind, we might ask if our empirical contemporary economy is closer to the initial ideal type of the parable of the eleventh round, where 'the stranger' is truly a stranger separated from the productive economy of the village, or to the alternative ideal type, where the stranger is an inhabitant of the village fully integrated into the productive economy? In so far as the stranger represents the function of banking, the question boils down to the relationship between banks and the rest of the economy. The issue revolves around the infamous distinction between the financial economy and the productive economy, between Wall Street and Main Street. This is of course a complicated question with no simple and unambiguous answer.

It is of course true that banks are integrated within the rest of the economy. There are several ways by which interest and other profits are channelled back into the non-financial economy. For instance, banks pay out dividends to shareholders as well as salaries and bonuses to employees. This money is in principle available for spending in the non-financial economy, where shareholders, clerks and bank CEOs may use them to buy chickens, cars and other commodities. In addition, banks are also taxed on their profits, which is another way of redistributing money back into the non-financial economy. As money is spent back into the non-financial economy, it becomes available for the repayment of debt and interest without the creation of new debt.

At the same time, we may also identify a number of possibilities for a decoupling of the financial economy from the productive or non-financial economy. Rather than paying out money to shareholders, banks may choose to retain the money that is paid back to the bank by debtors and use this for the extension of even more loans and the creation of even more money. Banks may also choose to invest the money in financial markets, where some of it may indeed eventually 'trickle down' to the non-financial economy but substantial parts may also just perpetually circulate in a speculative economy, where they remain inaccessible to non-financial agents in the economy. It is also the case that some banks aid wealthy individuals and corporations in channelling money into offshore accounts, where they become unavailable for taxation.

While it is beyond the scope of this chapter to provide any extensive review to the trends of financialisation, we shall at least venture the hypothesis that our contemporary economy is marked by a trend towards a state of financial apartheid. The popular conception of this apartheid is the distinction between the 99 and the 1 per cent, which was put forward by the Occupy Wall Street Movement. This hypothesis suggests that there is an accumulation and perhaps even congestion of money in one end of the economy, while there is a scarcity of money to service the increasing levels of debt that building is up in the other end of the economy. If this hypothesis is true, it means that our current economy is closer to the first ideal type, where the stranger is indeed a stranger economically decoupled from the productive economy of the village, than to the latter ideal type, where the stranger is an inhabitant of the village. As an increasing decoupling of banking and financial industries from the non-financial sectors of the economy leads to the tensions illustrated in our model of the eleventh parable, the only way of sustaining the system is to continue the injection of ever more money created out of debt into the economy. And for this money creation to keep going, we need at least the prospect that our economy can keep perpetually growing into the future.

Debt drive

The aim of this chapter was to show how the imperative of growth that marks our contemporary economy is not only propelled by needs and desires but also by a pure drive for growth. The drive for growth does not operate on the level of the individual subject but rather on the level of the economy as a whole. The parable of the eleventh round allows us to observe this shift between the two levels. Let us recall the distinction between desire and drive within capitalism quoted at length at the beginning of the chapter:

> At the immediate level of addressing individuals, capitalism of course interpellates them as consumers, as subjects of desire, soliciting in them ever new perverse and excessive desires. … The drive inheres in capitalism at a more fundamental, *systemic*, level: the drive is that which propels forward the entire capitalist machinery, it is the impersonal compulsion to engage in the endless circular movement of expanded self-reproduction. (Žižek, 2012: 496-7, emphasis in original)

When we look at the parable of the eleventh round from the perspective of the individual people in the parable, we can explain economic growth as merely the aggregate function of the desire of individual subjects. First, the villagers want to make their economic interaction more efficient by using the new 'smart' payment technology offered by the stranger. Then, they want to earn more money. And finally, they just want to be able to pay their debts. The same applies as we look at the actual economy. It is generally possible to explain economic growth by reducing it to the subjective desires of the individuals in the economy.

In the parable there is, however, one exception. This is the stranger. What is the desire of the stranger? In so far as he does not appear as a consumer or even as an owner of capital in the village economy, he does not seem to gain anything from his intrusion into the village economy. It is true that ultimately he will be in a position to dominate the village by making demands on all the people that owe him money and all the people that depend on this willingness to extend credit. But even this kind of power seems meaningless as long as he is not part of the village economy himself.

Now of course we should be careful how far we extend the logic of the parable. But perhaps the stranger stands for the pursuit of money for its own sake, not the desire for the accumulation of capital, not the desire for commodities to be purchased for money, and not even the desire to become free of debt. There is something enigmatic about the pursuit of money for its own sake. Noam Yuran has provided an elaborate account of the way that conventional economic thinking fails to grasp pure greed as it insists on translating any pursuit of profit into the concept of utility. Yet money pursued for its own sake does not have any utility. Here is how Yuran summarises his argument:

> At this stage we can finally return to the strange inability of economics to conceptualize greed. The unthinkable nature of greed does not, obviously, result from the fact that greed is a non-economic topic, but rather that it reflects its location beyond or at the limit of the subject. For orthodox economics, greed is unthinkable because it transcends the horizon of utility-seeking individuals. It cannot be fully incorporated within the perspective of individuals. However, for Marx this is precisely what makes it an *objective* economic reality. In this sense the economic oversight of greed is not simply a theoretical mistake. It is an ideological error in the sense of an error that partakes in the social reality it observes. The unthinkable nature of greed is actually part of its structure. (Yuran, 2014: 31)

This adds another dimension to the character of the stranger. Not only is he at the margins of the village economy, but even the very constitution of his subjectivity is barely comprehensible from the perspective of the villagers. He is not only a stranger but also simply strange, as he incarnates the unthinkable phenomenon of pure greed.

The issue of money creation and the domination of people through the imposition of debt is a recurring theme in many so-called conspiracy theories that try to explain trends and events in the world economy as part of a master plan executed by a small elite of powerful people. The banking system is one of the means through which these elites exercise their powers. In some accounts, the conspiracy consists of Jews, in some of aliens, and in others of some combination or collaboration between Jews and aliens. Perhaps we can understand these theories as symptoms of this 'unthinkable nature of greed'. In order to explain the existence of pure greed, it is necessary to move beyond the domain of the ordinary subject. So the Jew, the extraterrestrial or the combination of the two is posed as this alien element that is beyond the horizon of the ordinary human subject. Žižek himself captures this in his discussion of antisemitism:

> We must confront ourselves with how the ideological figure of the 'Jew' is invested with our unconscious desire, with how we have constructed this figure to escape a certain deadlock of our desire. ... [T]he anti-Semitic idea of Jew has nothing to do with Jews; the ideological figure of a Jew is a way to stitch up the inconsistency of our own ideological system. (Žižek, 1989: 48)

There are, of course, plenty of reasons to be highly sceptical of such theories that resort to the existence of a conspiracy of Jews or aliens in their way of explaining the world. But we may still concur with the underlying philosophical point that, in order to understand the money and banking system, we need to include some extra-subjective element in our explanation. Fortunately, Žižek provides us with concepts that allow us to include this element in our explanation without resorting to the blaming of Jews or aliens. This brings us back to the concept of drive. The stranger in the parable functions to incarnate pure drive. As we have seen, the intrusion of the stranger into the village economy seems to put it on a path of forced perpetual growth that may lead to the ultimate destruction of the community. Žižek captures this feature of drive, as he defines it, as 'death drive':

> [D]rive as such is death drive: it stands for an unconditional impetus which disregards the proper needs of the living body and simply battens on it. It is as if some part of the body, an organ, is sublimated, torn out of its bodily context, elevated to the dignity of the Thing and thus caught in an infinitely repetitive cycle, endlessly circulating around the void of its structuring impossibility. (Žižek, 1997: 31)

A transposition of this definition of drive onto the domain of the economy, which sums up our argument, might look like this:

> The drive of contemporary capitalism is debt drive: it stands for an unconditional impetus which disregards the proper needs of the living society and simply battens on it. It is as if some part of the economy, the bank, is sublimated, torn out of its societal context, elevated to the dignity of the Thing and thus caught in an infinitely repetitive cycle, endlessly circulating around the void of the impossibility of debt redemption.

Note

This chapter is a revised version of Chapter 8 in Bjerg (2016), *Parallax of Growth – The Philosophy of Ecology and Economy.*

References

Alvarez, A. (1983) *The Biggest Game in Town*. London: Houghton.

Bjerg, O. (2008) *For Tæt På Kapitalismen: Ludomani, Narkomani Og Købemani*. København: Museum Tusculanum Press.

Bjerg, O. (2009) 'Too Close to the Money'. *Theory, Culture and Society* 26(4): 47-66.

Bjerg, O. (2011) *Poker: The Parody of Capitalism*. Ann Arbour: University of Michigan Press.

Bjerg, O. (2014) *Making Money: The Philosophy of Crisis Capitalism*. London: Verso.

Bjerg, O. (2016) *Parallax of Growth: The Philosophy of Ecology and Economy*. Cambridge: Polity Press.

Eisenstein, C. (2011) *Sacred Economics: Money, Gift, and Society in the Age of Transition*. Berkeley: Evolver Editions.

Jackson, A., and Dyson, B. (2012) *Modernising Money: Why Our Monetary System Is Broken and How It Can Be Fixed*. London: Positive Money.

Lietaer, B. (2002) *The Future Of Money: Creating New Wealth, Work and a Wiser World*. (New edition). London: Random House Business.
Ryan-Collins, J., Greenham, T., Werner, R. and Jackson, A. (2011) *Where Does Money Come From? A Guide to the UK Monetary and Banking System*. London: New Economics Foundation.
Smith, A. (1776) *The Wealth of Nations*. New York: The Modern Library.
Werner, R. (2005) *The New Paradigm in Macroeconomics: Solving the Riddle of Japanese Macroeconomic Performance*. Basingstoke: Palgrave Macmillan.
Yuran, N. (2014) *What Money Wants: An Economy of Desire*. Stanford, California: Stanford University Press.
Žižek, S. (1989) *The Sublime Object of Ideology*. London: Verso.
Žižek, S. (1997) *The Plague of Fantasies*. London: Verso.
Žižek, S. (2000) *The Fragile Absolute or, Why Is the Christian Legacy Worth Fighting For?* London: Verso.
Žižek, S. (2012) *Less than Nothing: Hegel and the Shadow of Dialectical Materialism*. London; New York: Verso.

3

Memory, counter-memory and resistance: notes on the 'Greek Debt Truth Commission'

Joshua Bowsher

Introduction

By 2015, the harsh economic austerity measures enforced upon Greece by the 'Troika' – made up of the International Monetary Fund (IMF), the European Commission and the European Central Bank (ECB) – in return for bailout loans designed to keep the country afloat had resulted in widespread impoverishment for the Greek people. Between 2009-14 severe material deprivation in Greece rose from 11% to 21.5% of the population, and the poorest 10% of the population lost 56.5% of their income (Truth Committee on the Public Debt [TCPD], 2015: 40). The disastrous social consequences of austerity fomented an all-out confrontation between Greece and its creditors.

The Greek general election in January 2015 brought the radical, anti-austerity party, Syriza, to power in the Hellenic parliament. In power, Syriza attempted to reverse the austerity measures at home, while also trying to renegotiate the terms of the debt with the Troika. What followed was a frenetic and combative period of negotiation between the Troika and the Syriza government, represented by Greek prime minister, Alex Tsipras, and his heterodox finance minister, Yanis Varoufakis. Syriza framed their arguments in terms of their own democratic legitimacy, culminating in the famous 5 July referendum, in which Greek citizens overwhelmingly voted 'όχι' (no) to the renegotiated bailout package set out by its lenders. They also attempted to use legal arguments to question the legitimacy of the debt. In short, Syriza's first eight months were defined by a political movement of Hellenic defiance that threatened to overturn the Troika's imposition of austerity. As we now know, however, the radicalism of the first Syriza government ended in failure, capitulation and a more 'moderate' approach in its second parliamentary term.

One of the initiatives of the first, more radical, Syriza government was the development of the Truth Committee on the Public Debt (TCPD), which was established in April 2015 and tasked with investigating Greece's sovereign debt. The TCPD was intended to support the Greek government in its negotiations with its creditors and pursued its investigations to formulate arguments concerning the cancellation of Greek debt. In June 2015, it published a preliminary report in English and Greek that challenged both the dominant narratives regarding the key causes of Greece's spiralling sovereign debt and the legality of specific debts according to international law.

Although the TCPD was prematurely closed as a consequence of political schisms that opened up within Syriza (Toussaint and Lemoine, 2017: 34-53), legal scholars have recently shown that the arguments it developed are well supported in international law and significantly challenge the Troika's narratives regarding the debt from an economic, legal and political perspective (Bantekas and Vivien, 2016). Despite its untimely demise, the TCPD thus has much to offer in terms of legal strategy and practice regarding the cancellation of sovereign debt beyond the immediate context of the Greek crisis.

Nevertheless, my interest in the TCPD does not centre upon the efficacy of its legal arguments, even if this remains important to the analysis I develop here. Rather, I am interested in the TCPD because it attempted to problematise and address broader and significant questions regarding the now ever-present social context of financialisation and debt, which has been of increasing concern for sociologists and social theorists in the decade since the 2008 global financial crash (see: Adkins, 2017; Federici, 2014; Joseph, 2014; Lazzarato, 2012, 2015; Mulcahy, 2017), and which is treated across this volume. In other words, I am concerned with how the TCPD contests the *sociopolitical problem* of debt engendered by financialisation, and what lessons we might take from its practices in our ongoing engagements with these issues.

Taking this perspective, this chapter develops a theoretical analysis of the TCPD as an important and strategic response to a specific modality of power which is central to post-crash neoliberalism. Setting out the terms of this governmental technology, the chapter follows Maurizio Lazzarato (2012; 2015) in insisting that financialised neoliberalism operates through a 'mnemotechnics' of debt, or, to put it another way, a project of memory that does the crucial work of legitimising and sustaining recourse to neoliberal austerity policies by making citizens 'guilty' and thus deserving of them. As such, my argument is that the TCPD is worth our critical attention because it responds precisely to this mnemotechnical modality of power. This chapter thus analyses the TCPD as a project of memory-making that responds to the mnemotechnics of the debt economy, by strategically reversing its logic.

Exploring the ways in which the TCPD draws from memory-making practices developed within the international human rights movement, I analyse the TCPD as a practice of counter-memory that shapes a narrative of the Greek debt which demonstrates the innocence of Greek citizens and thus frees them from guilt. The importance of this strategy, I suggest, should not be underestimated. If the mnemotechnics of debt constrains human action and social organisation within neoliberal rationalities by making us 'guilty' for our debts, then the TCPD attempted to reverse this logic and create space for alternative, egalitarian futures to emerge, even if they ultimately failed to materialise. Although it is critically important to acknowledge and come to terms with this failure, the TCPD's strategy of counter-memory, I conclude, remains an important precedent for thinking through and resisting the current conjuncture of financialised neoliberalism.

Guilt and responsibility: the 'power' of memory

Understanding the prescience of the TCPD as 'memory-making' first requires us to grasp the configuration of power operating across the Greek crisis that makes this form of resistance necessary. Above all, the situation in Greece should be understood within the general context of both the global process of financialisation and the monumental crisis of financialised capitalism that began in 2008. Literature on financialisation has long emphasised that the proliferation of finance (and thus indebtedness) emerged alongside the conjunctural shift towards neoliberalism which took place in the 1970s (Duménil and Lévy, 2005; Marazzi, 2011). As authors such as Marazzi (2011) have noted, the explosion of finance emerged as a way of supplementing the stagnant wages that followed the turn towards neoliberal economic policies. In this sense, the neoliberal project, which combines the demands of marketisation, privatisation, and deregulation with the production of individuals as 'entrepreneurs of the self' (Foucault, 2010: 224), has been fuelled by cheap credit that has extensively financialised social existence.

It was precisely this conjuncture of financialised neoliberalism that came into crisis with the 2008 financial crash. The crash represented a moment in which large rates of mortgage default destroyed the value of securities held by major banks, leading to a liquidity crisis that threatened to undermine the whole economic system. Consequently, the present is one in which the avatars of financial capital are calling in their debts. If finance was once *credit* which 'functioned to sustain our aristocratic fantasies of "conspicuous consumption",' as Yannis Stavrakakis (2013: 34) has put it, finance has now been rearticulated as *debt*, which initiates a new governmental logic of accountability: austerity and (above all) repayment. The Greek crisis represents an important node in the development of this new socio-economic conjuncture. Since the first bailout package of 2010, the Greek state has had to make round after round of social spending cuts, structural adjustments all made in the name of repaying debt, or, at least, making public debt 'sustainable'.

At the centre of this new governmental logic is a project of memory, a mnemotechnics which can be best understood by turning to Maurizio Lazzarato's now famous work on neoliberalism and the debt economy (2012, 2015). For Lazzarato, indebtedness constitutes a generalised condition of post-crash society, a conjuncture which he calls 'the debt economy'. For Lazzarato (2012: 29), debt is also a modality of power specific to this conjuncture; it functions as a ' "capture", "predation", and "extraction" machine on the whole of society, as an instrument for macroeconomic prescription and management [and] a mechanism for the production and "government" of collective and individual subjectivities'. In the present moment, debt is thus a *practice* through which power operates in simultaneous and mutually reinforcing ways at both the macro-level of social structure and the micro-level of subjectivity and human conduct.

Above all, for Lazzarato the governmental value of debt is in its ability to establish an asymmetrical and hierarchical power relation between creditors and debtors, one that is increasingly generalised across all social relations. Lazzarato argues that debt has produced a form of social organisation in which an increasingly small creditor class is constituted at the expense of subjugating the rest as debtors. It is this hierarchy of debt, Lazzarato (2015: 66) argues, that 'capitalist elites would like to apply to all of society'. While much of this framework is valuable for this analysis, what is especially important for our purposes is that it is precisely within the content of this relation between creditors and debtors that memory appears as a pivotal technique of power. For the hierarchical relation between creditors and their debtors is instituted and mediated by a mnemotechnics or 'art' of memory which is intrinsic to its workings.

Drawing from Nietzsche's *On the Genealogy of Morals*, Lazzarato (2012: 39-41) argues that debt is rendered both intelligible and operational through the promise of repayment. It thus necessitates producing a subject capable of promising, that is, someone who can stand 'as a guarantor for themselves'. It is precisely through this act of the promise that the debtor is temporally bound and subject to the creditor, or more accurately to the promise of future value for the creditor. But promising requires memory: for 'making a person capable of promising means constructing a memory for him ... a conscience, which provides a bulwark against forgetting'. In other words, promising is a speech act that requires a memory of the act to fulfil it. It is thus not a memory created 'for conserving the past' but a 'memory of the future' (Lazzarato, 2012: 45), one that makes the debtor answerable to the promise made to the creditor at a future date.

Memory acts as the conduit which gives stability to debt both as 'a specific morality of promise (to honour one's debt) and fault (for having entered it)' (Stavrakakis, 2013: 34). Memory constitutes and maintains the debt relation by forcibly inscribing concepts of responsibility (to repay one's debts) and guilt (for one's indebtedness) into the interiority of the subject. For Lazzarato (2012), this means that the mnemotechnics of guilt and responsibility is an operation of control that subjects the debtor to the power of the creditor. More precisely, memory is the means by which the creditor externalises responsibility for indebtedness to the debtor in such a way as to seize control of the debtor's future. For, in the act of promising, the debtor's field of possibilities is constrained by the memory of debt, which makes them responsible by committing them to undertake forms of conduct that make them more likely to meet their responsibilities to the creditor.

Crucially, Lazzarato shows that in the era of post-crash neoliberalism, the mnemotechnics of debt has entered new and specific configurations of governmental practice. Under the debt economy, Lazzarato (2012: 47) argues, debt has both been 'rediscovered' and scaled up as a generalised 'technique of government aimed at reducing the uncertainty of the behaviour of the governed', because it can control 'temporalities of action' by locking up 'possibilities within an established framework' (71). Debt, as a technology of memory, is now used as a governmental technique that functions by producing the human individual as a specific kind of subject capable of repaying its debts: neoliberal *homo œconomicus* or, as in Foucault's (2010: 226) famous formulation, 'an entrepreneur of the self'. Under the auspices of guilt and responsibility, debt locks the subject into a relation to the self that reduces all aspects of social and psychological life to human capital, that is, investments which can generate the profits from which one can reimburse their creditors.

What is particularly prescient about Lazzarato's analysis is that it doesn't simply concern private debts, such as those which individuals enter through contracts, but also encompasses sovereign debts, such as those at the centre of the Greek crisis for which citizens are made to become guilty and responsible. That said, understanding how sovereign debt is used to govern the subject is not straightforward; it requires a clarification of the linkage between the macroeconomic scale of public debt and the individual. After all, bonds and various other sovereign debt instruments are not contracts involving private individuals but are made between states and their lenders. What is the link that binds the individual, in a relation of guilt and responsibility no less, to sovereign debt?

For Lazzarato (2012: 123-5), the answer is that the transformation of social security from a social right to social debt forges this linkage by transforming 'welfare' into a credit issued by the state which must be repaid by the individual. In the debt economy, the logic of welfare as social debt becomes the terrain upon which the mnemotechnics of debt flourishes: social debt becomes reified as budget deficits and citizens become 'responsible' and thus 'guilty' for the 'overaccumulation' of sovereign debt through their laziness, profligacy, and general lack of entrepreneurial spirit. This mediates between the macroeconomic aspects of the debt economy and the subject by tying social spending (that individuals make use of) to sovereign debt. Within this paradigm, austerity policies are thus not only a way of making the state 'leaner' and thus more attractive to its lenders, but simultaneously a means of transforming individuals into responsible and entrepreneurial subjects by radically reengineering social policy (through privatisations, outsourcing or by making welfare policies more panoptic and punitive, for example).

A Greek mnemotechnics of debt

As the Greek crisis has unfolded, Lazzarato's analysis of debt as a governmental mnemotechnics has become a useful analytical framework for several authors (Kioupkiolis, 2014; Selmic, 2016; Stavrakakis, 2013). Among these, Radman Selmic's development of Lazzarato's framework to analyse the Greek crisis is particularly interesting, precisely because it draws close attention to the ways in which the gap between sovereign debt and the subject was mediated through the mnemotechnics of debt.

Selmic (2016: 46) follows Lazzarato in differentiating two discrete but interconnected registers of debt: the 'production of indebtedness through financial instruments, on the one hand, and the production of subjectivity on the other'. In the Greek case, Selmic argues, the 'machinic' production of debt refers to the macroeconomic work of organisations such as the ECB, which operates through a 'set of nonrepresentational, mostly abstract, quantitative decisions such as the extension of acceptable collateral for sovereign borrowers' (Selmic, 2016: 52). For Selmic, these macroeconomic and machinic elements are correlated to a representational register that operates in the orders of subjectivity and social relations. During the Greek crisis, the mnemotechnics of debt operated in this register, producing 'feelings of guilt and responsibility' that were designed to legitimise – and thus make it possible to impose – the 'machinic' transformations of the Greek economy.

In distinguishing between the machinic procedures of debt and its representational correlates, Selmic draws attention to the disjunction between the abstract, purely technical operations of sovereign debt and the (discursive, speaking) subject. To traverse this disjunction, a logic of social debt and a corresponding mnemotechnics are articulated in the representational register of discourse so that the macroeconomic aspects of the debt economy and the subject become intertwined. For Selmic:

> The manner in which responsibility and ethics *vis-à-vis* Greek public debt were discussed and structured in public and subsequently perceived and internalised by Greek citizens was one of the crucial elements in imposing and executing austerity measures … Greek citizens were publicly shamed … in order to experience a deep sense of responsibility. (Selmic, 2016: 53)

Here, the linkages between sovereign debt and the citizen are developed through a discourse in which the former is the result of a 'budget deficit' for which the latter is responsible. Sovereign debt thus becomes 'their' (that is, the Greek people's) public debt through a discourse in which social spending becomes social debt that is reified as a budget deficit.

An important implication here is that the relation between the economic fact of sovereign debt and the individual subject was by no means automatic (as it would be in the individualised debt relation created when entering into a private contract such as a mortgage). The mnemotechnics of debt was not intrinsic to Greece's sovereign debt but was constituted as part of a discourse of social debt that was designed to forge the necessary links between the machinic operations of debt at the macroeconomic scale and the subject. The demand for Greece to repay its debts was thus managed through a conscious (as opposed to automatic) project of memory that could draw Greek citizens into relation with the debt and make them both guilty and responsible. In other words, the Greek crisis necessitated a retroactive development of memory to transform Greek *schulden* (the German word for debt) into Greek *schuld* (the German word for guilt).

The media played a significant role in cultivating this memory project. Although it has often seemed a truism that in the Greek case 'feelings of guilt were purposely spread through biased press and expert analyse,' (Selmic, 2016: 53) there have now been several studies of domestic and international news media which tend to support this claim (Bickes, Otten and Weymann, 2014; Mylonas, 2014; Tseligka, 2016).

In a particularly compelling critical discourse analysis of the Greek domestic press, Yiannis Mylonas' (2014) shows how *Ekathimerini*, a large, mainstream Greek newspaper of both liberal and conservative orientation, was pivotal in fostering a Greek mnemotechnics of debt. Through his analysis, Mylonas finds that there are two separate but mutually reinforcing logics that were produced by media discourses at the time. First, Mylonas shows that media discourses tended to construct the Greek crisis as a cultural problem, one of the Mediterranean as a 'leisure zone' (Mylonas, 2014: 310). In this construction, Greek profligacy operates at the structural and individual level: the crisis is understood to be both the problem of a bloated and wasteful state and a moral failing regarding the 'lifestyle and habits of laypeople' (311). In other words, social spending becomes social debt for which the Greek people are responsible; the overaccumulation of debt here becomes the result of a culture of laziness and profligacy. As such, the discourse of social debt immediately ensnares Greek citizens in the mnemotechnics of debt: sovereign (now framed as public) debt becomes *their promise* for which they must now take responsibility.

This mnemotechnics is dovetailed by a second and interconnected discourse, which frames the crisis as a moment for the Greek people to face their responsibilities. But this is also a necessity with hidden opportunities. Through news reporting and commentary articles, 'prolonged austerity appears as essential for a "new Greece" to emerge, that is (economically) dynamic, entrepreneurial, and more European' (Mylonas, 2014: 313). Consequently, the media discourses surrounding the Greek crisis reflect a slightly different instantiation of the imperative to become a responsibilised, entrepreneurial subject. Not only is becoming an entrepreneurial subject (through significant reductions in public spending as well as other changes in social and economic policy) proffered as the only means by which Greece can meet its responsibilities, but it is also framed as 'an opportunity for the "true Greek" to emerge in his full creative and productive potential' (313). In this way, 'the signifying semiotics of the media,' as Lazzarato (2014: 14) contends, constructed a mnemotechnics of guilt and blame that not only could 'justify in the eyes of individuated subjects … the fact that "there is no alternative",' but presents these strictures as a strategic opportunity for growth.

Memory-making and counter-memory

If memory is central to neoliberalism's austerity project in Greece, then, as I will now argue, the TCPD must be understood as a crucial response to the specifically mnemotechnical aspects of this project. The argument I aim to develop is that the TCPD develops a counter-memory through its own project of memory-making. Developing this point first requires an outline of what is understood by the term 'memory-making'. From there, it will be possible to situate the TCPD within this framework.

Memory-making practices and institutions emerged most notably from within the human rights movement where the cultivation of collective memory has been understood as a bulwark against genocide and atrocity. This strand of memory-making has its roots in Holocaust memorialisation and has now become a form of globalised and cosmopolitan memory whose mission is ensure that a repetition of the past happens 'never again!' (Levy and Sznaider, 2004). Although the context of human rights and genocide seems far removed from the Greek case as it confronts us here, there are several interconnections between practices of memory-making developed within the human rights movement and the development of the TCPD which are worth exploring.

Since the 1980s, the human rights movement has developed several institutional memory-making practices that are now seen as essential to the process of post-conflict and/or post-regime peace-building. Of particular concern here is the growth of truth commissions, an institutional form developed in post-dictatorial Argentina and Chile, but which finds it most paradigmatic example in the South African Truth and Reconciliation Commission that marked the end of the apartheid regime. Typically, truth commissions are quasi-juridical institutions that endeavour to develop an authoritative version of the past, normally achieved by inviting both human rights victims and perpetrators to tell their stories in public hearings as well as by examining public documents. The truths gathered through these practices are then knitted together to make an overarching narrative about the past, usually in a published public report. Truth commissions thus create 'a version of history that informs, and is informed by, the memories of those involved – a shared truth … that allows sense to be made of a traumatic past and is a prerequisite for a stable future' (Brants and Klep, 2013: 38).

Institutional memory-making is thus not only tied to the past but also to the future. Indeed, Alexandra Barahona de Brito (2010: 361) has argued that institutions like truth commissions are 'membership-making apparatuses' that function by producing narratives (or truths) which forge new post-conflict communal identities capable of overcoming the past. Furthermore, such identities are not politically neutral. They are organised around the social and political circumstances of post-conflict transition and reflect the political agendas of social elites. Truth commissions, as memory-making, shape the future by (re)working the past. They create 'social memory' which defines 'the scope and nature of action, reorders reality and legitimates power holders'. They are thus instruments 'to legitimate discourse, create loyalties and justify political options … what and how societies choose to remember and forget largely determines their future options'.

In this sense, the discourses and practices that are used to identify and construct the key concerns of the past are central to the future that is being created. As Zinaida Miller (2008: 261) points out, institutional practices such as truth commissions are 'definitional projects' whose specific ways of seeing and constructing the past defines the nature of injustice and victimhood, as well as concepts of repair, reparation and remedy. Given their emergence from within the human rights movement, it can be no surprise that truth commissions are significantly shaped by human rights norms, values, legal codes, and discourses which determines the key concerns of the past (and, in doing so, the future).

The development of the interdependences between memory-making and human rights has advantages and disadvantages. On the one hand, the juridical grounding of human rights as a set of legal discourses recognised in international law, national constitutions, and so on, serves a strategic function. Catherine Turner (2013: 201) has argued that the legalism of human rights is useful 'as a means of transcending existing political conflict' through the legitimacy and 'formality of law and legal procedure'. From this perspective, legal discourses usefully open up a terrain for the process of memory-making that is always already legitimate, in order to overcome the divisive political claims and counter-claims of the past. Human rights law legitimises memory claims insofar as it furnishes them with a formal recognition that – ideally, at least – places it beyond the contentious realm of the political.

On the other hand, critics have argued that the overreliance on human rights in the process of memory-making is problematic. In short, they argue that institutional practices tend to produce 'invisibilities' within the memories that they fabricate (Miller, 2008). The disposition of human rights lends it to an almost pathological concern with the physical cruelties committed in the past: violence against individual bodies perpetrated by the former regime. Consequently, issues of socio-economic justice have often been excluded from post-conflict memory-making (Meister, 2011). Such exclusions tend to leave issues of social injustice unaddressed, making them 'powder-kegs' that have the potential to erupt within post-conflict societies, dragging them back into periods of renewed violence (Muvingi, 2009). In this sense, the 'technocratic' strength of human rights discourses is tempered somewhat by the limited scope within which it has defined and memorialised the past.

The interesting point about the TCPD in Greece is that it substantially borrows from this model in ways which utilise the strengths of human rights memory-making whilst also overcoming these shortcomings through an interesting reconfiguration of human rights discourses that ultimately serves to confront the mnemotechnics of debt in strategically useful ways. In other words, what the TCPD achieved was a memory-making practice grounded in the legitimacy of human rights law that does not ignore questions of 'the socio-economic'. Rather, it explicitly confronts financialised neoliberalism at a central node of its diagram of power: memory. To understand this project of counter-memory, I will now contextualise the TCPD within the framework of memory-making, showing how it expands upon these practices to confront the mnemotechnics of debt.

Counter-memory: The 'Greek Debt Truth Commission'

In developing this reading, one could begin by pointing to the lexical resonance between the Truth Committee on the Public Debt and the 'truth commission' that has become central to post-conflict memory-making. This linguistic affinity was transformed into equivalence through the development of an English language appeal website for the TCPD, a citizens' initiative backed by the Syriza government, which referred to the committee as the 'Greek Debt Truth Commission' (Greekdebttruthcommission.org, 2015). Certainly, any nominative resemblances reflect a shared memory-making sensibility and institutional approach.

Like a truth commission, the TCPD was an investigative body established to address the past through a construction of truth. Exploring Greek public debt between the years of 1980-2015, the committee was 'given the mandate to investigate the truth about the creation and the intolerable increase in the public debt' (TCPD, 2015: 7-8). Further, its investigations were also shaped by a desire to interrogate the legitimacy and legality of the Greek debt with reference to the doctrine of 'odious debt' in international law, so as to formulate 'arguments and [trace] the legal foundations concerning the cancellation of the debt'. Although the nature of some of these arguments will be explored in more detail later, it is worth mentioning that this legal approach also draws it into close conceptual proximity with human rights memory-making. Many of its legal arguments were grounded in international human rights law, insofar as debts were considered 'odious' if they violated the human rights of Greek citizens.

This mandate was pursued with investigative techniques not dissimilar to those of 'ordinary' truth commissions. The committee's investigation involved public testimonies taken from various witnesses and authorities, including the IMF representatives in Greece, and former Greek ministers such as Panayiotis Roumeliotis whose testimony would prove explosive and did much to raise the public profile of the commission (Toussaint and Lemoine, 2017: 48). The TCPD (2015: 8-9) also examined all documentation pertaining to Greece's public debt including official documents, contracts, treaties, official statistics, and so on. Finally, in keeping with the tradition of truth commissions, it encouraged members of the public to participate in 'truth-telling' as experts, witnesses and sources.

Importantly, this institutional framework was not designed simply to produce legal arguments regarding the Greek debt that could be used in ostensibly private negotiations between the Syriza government and its creditors. Rather, the TCPD (2015: 9) was designed to raise awareness amongst Greek citizens, and 'to define specific issues that need to be brought into public consideration'. The TCPD's Preliminary Report reflected this purpose. It was thus written in plain, non-technical language so it could 'be read by people without specialist technical knowledge, who however form the bulk of any society, and participate as they must in democratic deliberation' (TCPD, 2015: 9). As such, the TCPD encompassed not only the institutional trappings but also the spirit of memory-making, insofar as it used various institutional practices not only to investigate the public debt but also to give shape to a public and shared memory of it.

Of course, memory-making is more than just a reconstruction of the past for its own sake. It is a process of remembering that is always connected to, and thus serves, a particular vision future. In this sense, the TCPD should be understood as a 'memory-making apparatus' not simply because it was concerned with constructing a memory about the debt, but because efforts to construct a narrative about the debt could and should have given a different shape to Greece's future. This raises the critical question of what kind of future the TCPD engenders.

My argument is that the TCPD was designed to resist the authoritarian imposition of austerity by producing a counter-memory to the mnemotechnics of debt. Where the latter cast the Greek people as ostensibly guilty 'social debtors' deserving of their fate, the TCPD's counter-memory contested this logic by developing a narrative of their innocence, and, conversely, the guilt of Greece's creditors. The future orientation of this strategy can be understood when it is contextualised within and read through the committee's own concern with truth-finding and truth-making as both a democratic right of Greek citizens and of practical import for the purposes of democracy and 'democratic deliberation' (TCPD, 2015: 8-9). Such desires for democracy clearly stand in opposition to the Troika's authoritarian imposition of austerity and reflect the first Syriza government's broader concern with building a democratic future. Constructing a counter-memory of Greek innocence might therefore be read as a way tracing a path from the Troika's authoritarianism to the possibility of democracy by reversing the logic which gives the former legitimacy and makes austerity socially inevitable.

This can be recast in the theoretical terms I set out earlier in this chapter. If, as Lazzarato (2012: 71) argues, the mnemotechnics of debt locks the future up within the framework of authoritarian austerity, then memories of Greek innocence shatter this closure, creating a space in which democratic decision-making regarding Greece's future might (re)emerge. The TCPD's Preliminary Report (2015) 'remembered' the debt so as to give shape to new future options in a situation where the social imaginary had been closed within the framework of austerity. This reading of the TCPD can be demonstrated through an analysis of the Preliminary Report and the ways in which it confronts dominant narratives regarding Greek sovereign debt.

Against social debt: The arguments of the TCPD

Set out across several chapters, the Preliminary Report of the TCPD develops several significant arguments that challenge the terms upon which the excesses of the sovereign debt are understood to be the result of social debts accrued by a profligate, non-entrepreneurial citizenry draining the resources of the state. The first chapter is particularly prescient as it develops a historical analysis, beginning in 1980, that traces the accumulation of Greece's sovereign debt. Not only does it show that public expenditure was lower than other Eurozone countries, but that, 'rather than being the product of a high budget deficit, the increase of debt was clearly related to the growth in interest payments' (TCPD: 2015: 11). In other words, debt servicing rather than out of control social or welfare spending was a key reason for the large accumulation of the debt between 1980 and 2007.

Alongside this, the first chapter shows that in this first period before the financial crash, other factors such as excessive defence (and not welfare) spending, tax evasion by Greece's richest individuals and companies, illicit capital outflows, and huge reductions in corporation tax (from 40% to 25%) contributed to this growing debt (TCPD, 2015: 11-14). As such, the logic of social debt becomes quite dubious. The mnemotechnics of guilt is severed through a forensic accounting that demonstrates the innocence of the 'social' (and thus the individual) regarding the accumulation of sovereign debt.

But if the pre-crash history of Greek sovereign debt put the logic of social debt into question, the TCPD's excavation of post-crash sovereign debt (accumulated from 2010-15) made in Chapter 2 of the Preliminary Report is perhaps even more damning. This was a period in which the Greek state accumulated most of its debt. In fact, the bailouts saw the debt increase 'from €299.690 Billion, 129.7% of GDP, to €317.94, 177.1% of GDP' (TCPD, 2015: 20). But this was not the result of a profligate state or its citizens. The key preliminary finding of the report is that the bailouts of the Greek state were mechanisms by which first European and then Greek banks could reduce their exposure to private and public debt, rather than to rescue the state and its citizens (TCPD, 2015: 17-20).

Seemingly technocratic responses to debt problems (themselves a practical rendering of neoliberalism's famous maxim 'There is no alternative!') thus look increasingly like a monumental stitch-up, where what might be called 'the social' is totally abandoned to prop up the financial sector. As the TCPD (2015: 20) summarised, 'the two support programmes for Greece were a colossal bail-out of private creditors'.[1]

This point becomes clearer if one considers that the financial sector was prioritised over small bondholders (individuals who had invested in government bonds as an apparently 'zero risk' form of saving) who were left to incur significant losses. As the TCPD (2015: 20) argues, around 15,000 families lost their life savings in this way, with 17 suicides recorded amongst those who lost their savings.

In this way, the TCPD significantly challenges the mnemotechnics of debt so keenly developed not only by Greece's creditors but also by the media. Where a mnemotechnics of Greek guilt has come to dominate, the TCPD reverses this logic not only by severing the link between sovereign debt and the social but by articulating the guilt of the creditor class conglomerated around central and private banks and the broader financial sector. In the creation of counter-memory, creditor guilt comes to be opposed to Greek society's innocence.

Innocence and victimhood: human rights and blank slates?

This mnemotechnical reversal is significantly bolstered by its development through legal discourses. Above all, this served the purpose of shielding what was essentially a set of political claims regarding the debt within the seemingly technocratic legitimacy of law. On the one hand, this legalism meant its arguments could not, in theory at least, be ignored Greece's creditors. After all, central banks, international financial institutions and states alike are bound by international law. Consequently, the TCPD had a kind of *force majeure* – albeit sadly unrealised – such that its arguments might have reversed the logic of social debt in a substantial, material way (debt cancellation). On the other hand, by rendering its reversal of the mnemotechnics within the 'politically neutral' discourses of the law, the TCPD gave social legitimacy to its counter-memory of Greek innocence, substantiating the ground upon which alternative futures could be imagined and made.

The 'doctrine of odious debt' drawn upon and developed by the TCPD is strongly grounded in the norms, customs and principles of human rights law (Bantekas and Vivien, 2016: 543). This doctrine organised the TCPD's legal arguments into a fourfold distinction between different kinds of 'odious' debt: illegitimate, illegal, odious and unsustainable debt. Each reflects a different problematisation of the debt, as well as of the terms and conditions attached to it, including: technical irregularities related to the contract (illegal debt); terms or conditions of the debt which are morally unfair or unconscionable (illegitimate debt); conditions that conflict with fundamental human rights provisions and the democratic right to self-determination (odious debt); or, conditions that compromise the state's future capacity to protect fundamental human rights (unsustainable debt).

In the chapter titled 'The impact of the "bailout programme" on human rights', the TCPD drew on this fourfold framework to understand the impact of various loan agreements on both civil and political rights, and their less-used social and economic counterparts. In fact, the report devoted significant attention to the impact of the debt on several socio-economic human rights, including the rights to work, to health and to education, social security and so on. For example, the report concludes that the right to health was undermined by the conditionalities attached to the Greek bailouts insofar as they resulted in 'cuts to healthcare spending, lay-offs in the public health sector … decimation of hospital beds, and increasingly restricted public health insurance' (TCPD, 2015: 38). By 2015, the latter had meant that 2.5 million persons (25% of the population) were left without health insurance.

The report carefully outlines legal liability for these violations, and attributes them to various creditors. For example, the report argues that the 'IMF is required to refrain from steps that would undermine the possibility of a borrowing State complying with its own national and international human rights obligations' (TCPD, 2015: 47). In imposing certain conditions upon credit lent to Greece, the IMF has thus broken its obligations in international law. Consequently, the report finds that Greek debts owed to various creditors are illegal, illegitimate and odious. In light of these findings, the report concludes by setting out the legal routes Greece could pursue to repudiate and suspend its sovereign debt.

It is worth noting that while this approach clearly roots the TCPD within the tradition of human rights memory-making, it also overcomes the limitations of the latter by developing an accounting of the 'social' that centres the economic violences of financial institutions and processes. Crucially, in developing through legal accounting of the debt and its social consequences, the TCPD concretises the distinction between Greek innocence and the guilt of creditors through the legal categories of victim and perpetrator. Of course, the human rights victim has long been understood as an 'innocent' (Mutua, 2001; Meister, 2011). Accordingly, if the mnemotechnics of guilt is given legitimacy by the contract and by an accounting of debt, then human rights victimhood puts this guilt into question by forwarding an accounting of innocence that is underpinned by both the morality and force of law.

If this counter-memory, in theory at least, has both legitimacy and legality on its side, then this opens out onto the broader question of both its potential and consequences within the Greek crisis. To think through this question, I draw from Miranda Joseph's conceptualisation of resistance to financialised neoliberalism, and its proliferations of measurement, calculation, and accounting (Joseph, 2014). In this respect, I follow Max Haiven (2016) whose review of Joseph's *Debt to Society* begins to make connections between her concept of 'counter-accounting' and the Greek Committee. Nevertheless, I aim to develop these connections in a more substantial way to fully render the concept of memory-making as a mode of resistance.

For Joseph (2014: 140-2) projects of resistance must hope to constitute 'an alternative "we" '. Nevertheless, any attempt to forge new collectives is conditioned by the responsibilities and opportunities of the conjuncture it hopes to escape from. There is thus a danger that staking resistance out on the idea that human life and the social world are beyond the crude logics of cost/benefit calculation is doomed to fall on deaf ears because it is not sufficiently attentive to these constraints.

To create the conditions for an alternative 'we', Joseph argues, resistance to financialised neoliberalism must begin by 'supplementing accounting with accountability,' so that it can 'push accounting to its limits as we also stake a claim to goals, values, not currently articulated within the regime of accounting' (Joseph, 2014: 142) In other words, the possibility of forming new collectives emerges not by escaping the logic of accounting or measurement altogether, 'but rather through its appropriation and transformation'.

It is hard to imagine an experiment more representative of Joseph's thinking than the 'Greek Debt Truth Commission'. Through its own appropriation of actuarial and legal knowledges, it presented an alternative legal accounting of the public debt, one that subverted dominant narratives and sought to make the creditors accountable to a 'social' they had been quick to externalise and abandon in the name of financial necessity. Moreover, when understood as 'memory-making', the TCPD is also drawn into a clear relation with the production of an alternative 'we'. After all, as I showed earlier, social memory is nothing if it is not a 'membership-making apparatus' (Barahona de Brito, 2010). A key point, therefore, is to understand what kind of futures, what kind of alternative collective identities, are opened up by the memory of Greek victimhood and innocence.

Still, this is not as simple as it may first appear. Victimhood has no other qualities apart from its innocence. There is no shortage of critics who understand that the downside of human rights victimhood is its 'passivity,' and 'haplessness' (Badiou, 2001; Mutua, 2001). In other words, victimhood is not only defined by its innocence but also by a lack of agency which is deferred to a 'saviour' who 'bears witness' and swoops in to save the day. Victimhood is critically marked by an absence or lack, rather than by a substantive 'identity'. From this standpoint, it is difficult not to have reservations about the 'futurability' of victimhood.

Such pitfalls might be avoided, however, if we don't consider victimhood valuable because it contains the raw materials for producing identity in its own right. Instead, we might understand the construction of victimhood as a strategically useful intervention whose limits come precisely as it announces the innocence it is designed to establish. From this perspective, victimhood serves as the crucial prerequisite of a *tabula rasa* – a blank slate – which necessarily exhausts its contents through this process. After all, innocence creates no identity other than the freedom it affords; it is exhausted in the creation of possibilities it presupposes. Blank slates are spaces of new emergences and new becomings; they are an emptiness which is not desolate but a new horizon of potentialities upon which an alternative future could be built.

Consequently, if the TCPD creates a blank slate by nullifying neoliberalism's mnemotechnics, then the forging of new identities requires the production of other social apparatuses, assemblages, and forms of life that are necessarily outside and beyond the remit of this institution. From this perspective, the promise of the TCPD was only one first step – among others – in the construction of an alternative 'we'. For the Truth Committee and, more broadly, the first Syriza government, the substantive content of this 'we' was to emerge through democratic deliberation. Even if this project was never fully realised perhaps the night of the Greek referendum in July, only a few weeks after the release of the TCPD's Preliminary Report, provides a glimpse of this democracy yet to come. In voting 'όχι' to the terms of the third bailout, Greek citizens had not only refused the economic constraints placed upon them by the Troika, but in taking hold of this opportunity began to constitute an alternative 'we' based not on victimhood but political agency. As Alex Tsipras would put it: 'Today's no is a big yes to democratic Europe. A no to a vision of the eurozone as a boundless iron cage for its people. From tomorrow, Europe, whose heart tonight beats in Greece, starts healing its wounds, our wounds' (quoted in *The Guardian*, 2015).

Conclusion: failures and legacies

By September 2015, the political excitement which had gripped Greece in June and early July was extinguished. The referendum result didn't prove enough on its own to resist the formidable powers of the Troika, and by 2016 the 'Greek Debt Truth Commission' was largely forgotten. The capitulation of the Syriza government is reflected in the far less radical and far more accommodating stance it has taken since it won its second term following the agreement of a third Greek bailout. Furthermore, while cracks have appeared in the edifice of neoliberalism, such that even the IMF has now deemed public criticism of its key tenets a necessary PR exercise (see Ostry, Loungani and Furceri, 2016), the logics, practices and assumptions of neoliberal governance remain fundamentally in place. In judging both Syriza and the TCPD from this vantage point, it is easy to emphasise their failures.

Nevertheless, what I have tried to show is the valuable contribution that the TCPD has made in terms of both conceptual tools with which to critically approach the debt economy but also material practices that might resist it. Following Lazzarato (2012), I have argued that the debt economy functions by transforming memory into a mechanism of social control. Post-crash neoliberalism is thus defined by a mnemotechnics of debt that constrains both the present and the future within the logics of financial calculation, an accounting which transforms the social world into collateral damage sacrificed at the altar of the economy. This being the case, the value of the TCPD is in developing practices that function at the level of memory, a counter-mnemotechnics, which is capable of transforming guilt into innocence and, in doing so, prising open a new field of possibilities for the future of 'the social'.

Recent research affirming the legitimacy of the TCPD's arguments under international law (Bantekas and Vivien, 2016) affords a certain confidence in the central tenets of its approach, and as such raises the possibility of the model's appropriation, development and transformation in future. In this sense, perhaps the legacy of 'Greek Debt Truth Commission' is to sketch out a terrain of struggle – memory – and a set of tools that are equal to it and which may, someday, contribute to our escape from the debt economy. No doubt, future experiments will have to critically develop these tools, by asking, for example, whether its top-down, institutional approach is the best vehicle for a memory-making process designed to forge new solidarities, identities or grassroots movements. As such, my hope is that the TCPD marks a starting point for a new series of political experiments, rather than signalling an end.

Note

[1] The words used by the Committee here are taken from an open letter signed by a group of investors, economists and legal scholars and published by Bruegel, a German economic think tank (see: http://bruegel.org/2015/05/giving-greece-a-chance/). Though the letter makes this admission, it also advocates austerity policies as a necessity to resolve the 'Greek crisis'. The TCPD's use of their words is thus designed to weaponise them.

References

Adkins, L. (2017) 'Speculative Futures in the Time of Debt', *Sociological Review*, 448-62.

Badiou, A. (2001) *Ethics: An Essay on the Understanding of Evil.* London: Verso.

Bantekas, I. and Vivien, R. (2016) 'On The Odiousness of Greek Debt', *European Law Journal*, 22(4), 539–565.

Barahona de Brito, A. (2010) 'Transitional Justice and Memory: Exploring Perspectives', *South European Society and Politics*, 15(3), 359-76.

Bickes, H., Otten, T. and Weymann, L. C. (2014) 'The Financial Crisis in the German and English Press: Metaphorical Structures in the Media Coverage on Greece, Spain and Italy', *Discourse & Society*, 25(4), 424-45.

Brants, C. and Klep, K. (2013) 'Transitional Justice: History-telling, Collective Memory and the Victim-witness', *International Journal of Conflict and Violence*, 7(1), 36-49.

Duménil, G. and Lévy, D. (2005) 'Costs and Benefits of Neoliberalism: a Class Analysis', In G. Epsteing (ed), *Financialization and the World Economy* (17-45). Cheltenham: Edward Elgar.

Federici, S. (2014) 'From Commoning to Debt: Financialization, Microcredit, and the Changing Architecture of Capital Accumulation', *South Atlantic Quarterly*, 113(2), 231-44.

Foucault, M. (2010) *The Birth of Biopolitics: Lectures at the College de France 1978-1979.* New York: Palgrave Macmillan.

Greekdebttruthcommission.org (2015) Retrieved 1 October 2015, from http://greekdebttruthcommission.org/)

Haiven, M. (2016) 'Struggles for a collective counter-accounting', *Dialogues in Human Geography*, 6(3), 323–326.

Joseph, M. (2014) *Debt to Society: Accounting for Life under Capitalism.* London: University of Minnesota Press.

Kioupkiolis, A. (2014) 'Towards a Regime of Post-political Biopower? Dispatches from Greece, 2010–2012', *Theory, Culture & Society*, 31(1), 143-58.

Lazzarato, M. (2009) 'Neoliberalism in Action: Inequality, Insecurity and the Reconstitution of the Social', *Theory, Culture and Society*, 26(6), 109-33.

Lazzarato, M. (2012) *The Making of Indebted Man.* (Joshua David Jordan, trans.) Los Angeles: Semiotext(e).

Lazzarato, M. (2014) *Signs and Machines.* (Joshua David Jordan, trans.) Los Angeles: Semiotext(e).

Lazzarato, M. (2015) *Governing by Debt.* (Joshua David Jordan, trans.) Los Angeles: Semiotext(e).

Levy, D. and Sznaider, N. (2004) 'The Institutionalization of Cosmopolitan Morality: The Holocaust and Human Rights', *Journal of Human Rights*, 3(2), 143-57.

Marazzi, C. (2011) *The Violence of Financial Capital.* (K. Lebedeva and J. McGimsey, trans.) Los Angeles: Semiotext(e).

Meister, R. (2011) *After Evil: A Politics of Human Rights.* New York: Columbia University Press.

Miller, Z. (2008) 'Effects of Invisibility: In Search of the "Economic" in Transitional Justice', *The International Journal of Transitional Justice, 2*(3), 266-91.

Mulcahy, N. (2017) 'Entrepreneurial Subjectivity and the Political Economy of Daily Life in the time of Finance', *European Journal of Social Theory*, 20(2), 216-35.

Mutua, M. (2001) 'Savages, Victims and Saviours: the Metaphor of Human Rights', *Harvard International Law Journal*, 24(1), 201-45.

Muvingi, I. (2009) 'Sitting on Powder Kegs: Socioeconomic Rights in Transitional Societies', *International Journal of Transitonal Justice*, 3(2), 163-82.

Mylonas, Y. (2014) 'Crisis, Austerity and Opposition in Mainstream Media Discourses of Greece', *Critical Discourse Studies*, 11(3), 305-21.

Ostry, J., Loungani, P. and Furceri, D. (2016) *Neoliberalism: Oversold?* Washington, DC: IMF.

Selmic, R. (2016) 'The European Central Bank, Machinic Enslavement, and the Greek Public Sector', *Finance and Society*, 2(1), 45-61.

Stavrakakis, Y. (2013) 'Debt Society: Greece and the Future of Post-democracy', *Radical Philosophy*, (181), 33-8.

TCPD (2015) *Preliminary Report.* Retrieved 1 August 2015 from http://cadtm.org/Preliminary-Report-of-the-Truth

The Guardian (2015) 'Greek Referendum No Vote Signals Huge Challenge to Eurozone Leaders', Retrieved from https://www.theguardian.com/business/2015/jul/05/greek-referendum-no-vote-signals-huge-challenge-to-eurozone-leaders

Toussaint, E. and Lemoine, B. (2017) *History of the CADTM Anti-Debt Policies.* Brussels: CADTM.

Tseligka, E. D. (2016) 'Becoming the Other – Stereotyping of Greeks by the German Press', *Continuum: Journal of Media & Cultural Studies*, 30(6), 627-35.

Turner, C. (2013) 'Deconstructing Transitional Justice', *Law and Critique*, 24(2), 193-209.

4

'Deferred lives': money, debt and the financialised futures of young temporary workers

Mark Davis and Laura Cartwright

The systemic necessity to take on ever more unsecured credit simply to go about the business of everyday life in a financialised society is still positioned as a personal choice rather than an unavoidable means of survival. For young people endeavouring to make the transition to 'adulthood' – a state often associated with financial independence and self-sufficiency – the accumulation of debt has become an integral part of this transitional process, especially at a time of continued economic instability and with state support greatly atrophied in the name of 'austerity'.

In this chapter, we assess the lived experiences of indebted lives in the context of precarious temporary employment in the UK, in order to examine the extent to which young people are 'governed' by debt (Adkins, 2017; Lazzarato, 2015). Sociological studies of debt have tended to follow a 'left Nietzschean' line through Foucault, Deleuze and Lazzarato. We aim to fill a gap in current understanding by contextualising young people's own perceptions of debt and its impact upon their future through a qualitative analysis of their lived experiences.

Assessing the extent to which debt becomes a tool of discipline, conditioning behaviour around market imperatives, we analyse original interview data to demonstrate how young people label and rationalise the different types of debt they are now compelled to undertake – from apparently 'bad' consumer debt to 'good' mortgage debt – and how the nature of their insecure employment impacts upon such judgements. Rather than total discipline, we demonstrate how young people actively reject, resist and negotiate the debts that they undertake, challenging a moralisation of debt that seeks to condemn the character of struggling debtors. As well as this empirical work, our theoretical contribution here is to assess this data in terms of what we consider to be the *temporal dynamics* of indebtedness, which result in living 'deferred lives'.

Given our focus upon the UK, the pressure here for young people to 'get into debt' is particularly evident in the aspiration to attend university. The introduction and escalation of tuition fees has seen young people taking on significant amounts of debt in order to obtain higher education which, as current research demonstrates, may not be enough to secure the kind of well-paid jobs that would enable such debts ever to be fully repaid. A 2015 report found that 58 per cent of UK graduates are in non-graduate occupations, one of the highest rates in the OECD (CIPD, 2015: 14), with the annual number of graduates greatly outstripping the number of high-skill, high-pay roles available. In addition, young people make up a significant number of those in 'precarious' forms of work, employed on temporary or 'zero-hours' contracts that offer little job security and often pay the minimum wage (IPPR, 2010; Standing, 2014; UKCES, 2014).

Within this UK context, the ability of young people to transition to adulthood via those traditional benchmarks expressed by participants during our interviews – that is, a 'good' job, home ownership, a pension, marriage, having children – is severely impeded by previous debt accrual and the instability of income from precarious employment. The possibility of a future that is both financialised and yet somehow 'debt free' appears to imply one without the 'drag' of previous debts that prevent access to those traditional benchmarks, or that frustrate attempts to act 'as if' one was no longer 'dragged back to the past' of previous financial decisions. To achieve these markers, however, often requires more indebtedness and so embarking upon a 'debt accrual career' (Houle, 2014: 448).

Changing attitudes towards debt

'Getting out' of the debts that tie down households and burden everyday life is therefore a common and deeply held ambition (Stanley et al, 2015). Changing attitudes towards debt, and the increased cultural normalisation of borrowing, have led to high levels of personal and household debt (The Griffiths Report, 2005). The total unsecured debt level for UK households (which includes credit cards, payday loans, and student loans, but not mortgages as they are linked to an underlying asset) rose by £48bn between 2012 and 2015 to reach a total of £353bn (TUC, 2016: 4). At the time of writing, total UK credit card debt in February 2018 stands at £70.84bn, up from £63.82bn in January 2015 (The Money Charity, 2018). As restrictions on the availability of unsecured credit were relaxed, and consumer borrowing became an integral part of a UK economy thriving upon a growing pool of 'revolving debtors' (Froud et al, 2010; Montgomerie, 2007), the normalisation of using credit to access goods and services disguised the greater retrenchment of state-led welfare provision under regimes of austerity (Sandel, 2012).

The embeddedness of neoliberal policy making has replaced social and public service provision with market-oriented and profit-driven alternatives (Brown, 2015; Crouch, 2011; Mirowski, 2013). This has seen more areas of public goods and services, once funded through collective taxation and accessed by virtue of citizenship, become privatised and only accessible through various forms of consumer credit. As Mary Mellor explains:

> Citizens became consumers. Employee rights became zero-hours contracts. Welfare support became scrounging. Houses became investment opportunities. Debt became a way of life. The state became a dependent 'household'. (Mellor, 2016: 20)

In spite of evidence that since the 1980s there has been a global explosion of inequality (Oxfam, 2017; Stiglitz, 2012; Wilkinson and Pickett, 2009), the reach of markets and market-oriented thinking into aspects of social life traditionally governed by 'non-market' norms is a striking and significant development (Sandel, 2012). Being 'in debt' has ceased to be a temporary means of raising one's spending power and has today become an economic necessity for a large majority of people.

More and more UK households are finding it impossible to cover their living costs without supplementing their low, stagnant wages with higher levels of debt. A study in April 2012 found that more than 60 per cent of people who took out payday loans were doing so to pay household bills or to buy essentials like food, clothes and petrol (Clarke, 2012, cited in Flaherty and Banks, 2013: 224; see also Packman, 2014). Extreme over-indebtedness – understood as paying out more than 40 per cent of income to finance unsecured credit – is growing particularly quickly in households that are in employment but with low income(s). In 2015, 9 per cent of low-income households in employment were extremely over-indebted, up from 5 per cent in 2014 (TUC, 2016). Meanwhile, inequality in the UK has returned to the levels comparable to the period before World War I (Dorling, 2014; Weeks, 2014) in part because the basic capitalist task of generating secure employment through investment in productive industries has been abandoned (Sayer, 2016). Instead, wealth at the top has been extracted from various sources of 'unearned income', such as dividends, capital gains, interest, and rent (Mellor, 2016: 183).

Rather than the profligate use of credit to acquire luxury items, which is so often the popular image, problematic personal debt in the context of such inequality arises from a persistent disparity between income and expenditure, insecure labour market experiences, and the financial impact of normal life events. Increasing indebtedness has been associated with the deepening disciplinary power of global finance in everyday life (Langley, 2008; Montgomerie, 2007), requiring individuals to devise their own personal solutions to collective problems, while simultaneously shouldering the associated risks (Bauman, 2000; Beck, 1992). In this way, debt becomes a tool of discipline, conditioning behaviour around market imperatives.

The moral and social dimensions of debt

When it comes to the popular image of indebted lives, the moral and social dimensions of finance are played out in ways that adhere closely to the fate of 'flawed consumers' (Bauman, 1998). In a society that has for its 'meta-value' the exercise of free choice within a market setting, Bauman's (1998: 71) notion of 'flawed consumers' captures the moralising narrative that lays the blame for structural circumstances entirely upon the apparent 'wrong choices', 'bad decisions' and 'lack of competence' enacted by 'free choosing' individuals. If you exist at the margins or are excluded from the consumer market, then you must surely have 'chosen' to live that way (de Benedictus et al, 2017; Edmiston, 2018). As such, these people are doomed to be beyond both the public's moral obligation and political redemption via welfare institutions, seemingly undermining years of welfare and social justice initiatives as their plight is blamed on individual fecklessness, financial incompetence, or an inability to delay consumer gratification (Walker, 2012; Webley and Nyhus, 2001). This fundamental shift in social attitudes is neatly, if troublingly, captured by journalist Suzanne Moore (*The Guardian,* 2012), who observes that these days 'instead of being disgusted by poverty, we are disgusted by poor people themselves'.

This understanding of indebtedness as a consequence of problematic individual conduct, rather than as a necessary means of survival, is reflected in recent Conservative public policy, and in the otherwise progressive 'Econocracy' thesis (Earle, Moran and Ward-Perkins, 2016). Authored by key figures in the impressive student-led 'post-crash' and 'rethinking' economics networks, they also conclude that the central problem here is the public's lack of financial understanding. The possibility is seldom entertained that the central problem is, on the contrary, the need for economists and policy makers to improve their understanding of the public. As such, UK policy initiatives identify the key strategic priority as being to 'increase levels of financial capability and awareness alongside more transparent financial literature so individuals can take control of their finances' (DTI, 2005: 11). Those 'lacking essential financial skills, including the ability to budget sensibly, may over-commit themselves by taking on excessive debts' (DWP, 2007) and so the professed solutions focus upon equipping 'people with the capability to make savings decisions, promoting access to savings opportunities' (DWP, 2007: 39).

Within this policy framework, people's financial difficulties are not the product of top-down, politically mediated, economic mismanagement, but rather a failure of individuals to self-regulate. Those nefarious processes, inherent within a financial system that 'profits without producing' precisely through capitalising upon the securitisation and trade of ever more household debt (Lapavitsas, 2013; Sayer, 2016), are displaced by moralising narratives that simply blame individuals. As a result, financial vulnerabilities are seen as the consequence of dispositional flaws in character that require a range of interventions through neoliberal technologies of performance and governance (Lazzarato, 2015; Walker, 2012: 537).

Young people and debt

Access to relations of credit and debt is fundamental to providing young adults with the financial resources necessary to achieve many of the social markers of the transition to full adulthood. The volume of debt now required to access home ownership and university education, for example, is staggering for what were once considered by previous generations to be standard middle-class entitlements (Montgomerie, 2011; Winterton and Irwin, 2012). As early as their mid-twenties in the 1960s-70s, the 'baby boomers' followed a standard life-course script and had:

> … left their parents' home, completed their education, entered the full-time labour market, got married, and had a child in quick succession (and typically in that order). (Houle, 2014: 450)

Young adults in the UK today face a unique mix of risks that previous generations did not, creating significant and growing intergenerational inequalities (Barr and Malik, 2016). A variety of social, cultural and economic changes mean traditional life-course scripts are seldom available, not least as a result of escalating house prices, changes within higher education and the shift to 'mass' university participation, as well as difficulties in transitioning into a highly flexible, deregulated and competitive labour market. Young adults today are far less able to 'achieve' adult roles before their mid- to late-thirties, leading to a sense of entrapment in a perpetual present of limited economic resources and a 'deferral' of life objectives until 'one day' in the future.

Research by Barr and Malik (2016) found that the disposable income of pensioners has grown three times faster than that of young people, with inequality rising rapidly between the generations. Unaffordable housing, rising university tuition fees and insecure, low-waged work have led young adults to become overburdened with debt at a critical life stage, frustrating their ambition to become economically independent and increasing the likelihood of detrimental effects to their psychological well-being. Research has also found that living in this situation of 'suspended adulthood' has left large numbers of young people feeling 'worn down', lacking confidence and feeling worried about the future (Women's Trust, 2016).

A key factor in this process is the rise of unsecured debt among young adults. The necessity of taking on debt to invest in the future, for example via student loans to finance higher education, means young adults are burdened with regular debt repayments for decades. As Lazzarato argues:

> Student indebtedness exemplifies neoliberalism's strategy since the 1970s: the substitution of social rights (the right to education, health care, retirement, etc.) for access to credit, in other words, for the right to contract debt. (Lazzarato, 2015: 66)

Under the principle of a sensible 'rational choice', young people who wish to obtain higher education are now compelled to make crude economic decisions based upon what might provide 'value for money' and 'enhance employability', rather than by virtue of personal ambitions, academic interest or aptitude. This repositioning of students as consumers legitimates a narrative of individual choice and so also the acquisition of personal responsibility and accountability for the decisions taken. Consequently, student debt that cannot be repaid is seen as the result of bad decision-making, rather than the result of social structural factors (Edmiston, 2018; Irwin, 2018).

The fact that many young adults regard going to university as a significant but necessary financial risk reveals an anxiety that such high levels of debt so early in life can intensify financial vulnerability as over-indebtedness becomes a lifelong reality from which they cannot escape (Montgomerie, 2011). This then compounds the insecurity faced by young adults because of their relatively weak position in the labour market, as their 'new hire', 'temporary', or 'zero-hours' status leaves them particularly vulnerable to job loss.

As well as the financial burden, there is an often overlooked existential burden that comes with the unsecured debt of a student loan. The rhetoric of 'investing in the future' is explicitly linked to the potential for individuals to enjoy enhanced average incomes across a career by virtue of being qualified as a graduate. Of course, there is also an investment in one's 'self', requiring a range of personality, behaviour, lifestyle, and aesthetic micro-adjustments that can constitute exhaustive 'labour upon the self' in order to maximise one's employability potential for a 'good career', rather than just accepting a 'lousy job' (Lazzarato, 2011, 2015; Boltanski and Chiapello, 2007).

Although formally unsecured, the only asset tied to this debt is one's own 'self-as-human-capital', fostering a fully financialised relationship to society in both the present and the future (Adkins, 2017). The need to be as marketable as possible among the annual flux of employable graduates, and the requirement to identify fully with one's employer organisation in order to be a 'loyal employee' embracing corporate values, leads to a ceaseless process of self-monitoring that radically reduces the prospects for challenging the status quo. As Chomsky (2011, cited in Hartlep and Eckrich, 2013: 82) argues, 'when you trap people in a system of debt, they can't afford the time to think'. The need to work (primarily in order to manage one's debt burden) takes precedence over long-held ambitions and future plans. Moreover, it prevents the cultivation of a sense of awareness of the structures and processes contributing to one's own situation and can lead to damaging narratives of self-blame (Standing, 2014). This is how debt becomes a tool of discipline.

This is intensified by an awareness that there is no guarantee that graduates will find a job, let alone the specific career they hope for (Green and Zhu, 2010), as evermore graduates enter the market place and so 'crowd out' their peers (Walker and Zhu, 2013). While this process has been underway in various forms at least since the 1960s, the financialised form of today's 'eduflation' (Macdonald and Shaker, 2012) supports Montgomerie's (2011) suggestion that many of the assumptions held about the future financial benefits of higher education are being undermined by the requirement to assume vast debts and the steady decline in any 'graduate earnings advantage' (Purcell at al, 2012: 60). The idea that university should be viewed as a 'long-term investment', habitually cited by politicians as justification for raising tuition fees, is undermined when there is no guarantee of future employment nor any accurate way of estimating future earnings, and thus the 'return on investment'. As we will see, despite obtaining undergraduate and, in some cases, postgraduate qualifications, the participants in our study were still relying upon temporary employment and servicing large debts for degrees that had yet to deliver any non-academic returns. Aspirations become narrowed, intimately tied to the betterment of present financial frustrations, with the only motivation for keeping going an abstract goal of one day, finally being 'debt free'.

Our research was motivated to explore these tensions via the lived experience of financial precarity among a specific group, namely young adults in temporary work. We were interested in how they made sense of their own social and economic circumstances and how this impacted upon their future ambitions. With debt now such an integral part of the youth transition process, and central to imagining one's journey across a financialised life-course (Montgomerie, 2011), we investigated the *temporal dynamics* of debt and its impact upon young people's sense of the past, present and future (Adkins, 2017). How do they negotiate, justify and understand the different 'types' or 'qualities' of debt they accumulate? How does this frame their orientations towards future (often heavily-financialised) life goals? Given our research questions, we wanted to test the assumptions in existing literature by exploring the impact of these developments on the conceptualisation of money, debt and financial futures in the everyday lives of a social group at the centre of these transitions.

Methodology

Given the centrality of student debt to the financialisation of everyday life, young temporary workers have been acutely affected by changes in social and economic policy specifically relating to debt. Previous research has demonstrated that young people make up a significant proportion of temporary workers, and many do so in the absence of more secure forms of employment (IPPR, 2010; TUC, 2013). In identifying a sample, we wanted to foreground the biographical and employment narratives of this group, along with their self-understanding of their decision-making processes in relation to money, debt and finance. This helped us to develop a deeper sociological understanding of economic behaviours that do not rely on abstracted models of 'rational' consumer choice, and which enabled us to assess the extent of debt's disciplinary power on their lives.

Our data is drawn from a study conducted in 2012 with a group of 20 temporary workers, accessed via a gatekeeper at an employment agency in Yorkshire, in the North of England. Each participant worked in what the agency called 'entry level' employment, typically in sales, customer service, and administrative roles, with a mix of 'fixed-term' (that is, weekly, monthly) and unspecified 'rolling' contracts. Since participants were accessed through this agency, our sample is non-representative. All our participants identified as 'White British'. All had obtained a good number of GCSEs, with ten graduates, three postgraduates, and seven who had not attended university. This provided us with a diversity of views in relation to the reasons why higher education was or was not pursued. All participants were still 'temping' or in the process of seeking their next temporary contract. The sample also allowed us to explore the lived experience of debt with those inhabiting low-income households that are nevertheless in employment, and with comparative experiences of the UK's temporary labour market.

Employing an abductive approach, we drew upon theoretical work from the above literature to prepare a set of interview questions that would allow us to test assumptions through qualitative enquiry. We privileged semi-structured, open-ended discussions to allow participants to speak reflectively, and at length, on the issues that *they* felt were important. Each interview lasted approximately one hour; was recorded using a voice recorder with the consent of interviewees; and then independently coded by the authors. We have anonymised the participants throughout the analysis that follows.

Money and debt

> The everyday imposes its monotony. It is the invariable constant of the variations it envelops. The days follow after another and resemble one another, and yet – here lies the contradiction at the heart of everydayness – everything changes ... Some people cry out against the acceleration of time, others cry out against stagnation. They're both right. (Lefebvre, 1987: 10, cited in Deville and Seigworth, 2015: 624)

The ability of young people to conceive and to implement biographical plans is increasingly undermined by a precarious cocktail of insecure employment and low, stagnant wages. This experience is exacerbated by high levels of unsecured debt, typically from a mix of consumer credit spending, student loans, or various forms of 'pay-day' borrowing. In such circumstances, the difficulties of the present extend into a future that is always already heavily financialised.

A survey by The Money Advice Service (2014: 5) in the UK found that 72 per cent of respondents in their twenties identified as having made 'financial mistakes' that they regretted, including seeing credit as 'free money'. As we signalled above, as well as shouldering the moral consequences of debt, many experience a 'domino effect' with one financial decision seeming to have a cumulatively negative effect over time. For many of the participants we interviewed, incurring debts was not the result of reckless consumer spending but rather born of financial necessity, often due to inadequate support elsewhere (in the form of unemployment benefits, for example).

Thirteen of the twenty participants had attended university, amassing a substantial amount of debt mostly in the form of their student loan(s). While unhappy with owing so much money, curiously most of the graduates didn't consider their student loan to be 'real debt' because there was no specific time limit attached to the repayment period. Here the temporal dynamics of indebtedness are apparent since, as with their attitude towards their present circumstances, this was simply a *deferred* reality, to be settled 'one day' in the future:

> "Yeah I've got about £25,000 student loan. But again that bothers me even less, cos … until you're earning enough they won't take it off you anyway, so when I'm earning enough it just comes off like a tax. It's not like you've got to make the effort to pay it, it just comes off automatically, so it doesn't faze me." (Lisa, 23)

> "On my student loan, I probably owe about £35,000. It doesn't really bother me cos I know its debt, but … it's not, like, there's a guy banging on your door … it is there, but it's not gonna effect your life that much when you earn over a certain amount." (Katie, 23)

> "Yeah, I do have a student loan, which I pretend isn't there because I've never actually earned enough to pay it back!" (Eleanor, 25)

Earning little above the UK's minimum wage, most of our interviewees admitted that they were not currently earning enough money to reach the repayment threshold requiring them to begin paying back their student loan(s). As a result, their debt – along with the disciplinary control it has over them in the here and now – was continuing to grow as it sat accruing further interest. Escalating interest on student loan debt has significantly worsened for those students that entered university after 2012, as a direct result of the then Conservative-Liberal Democrat coalition government's decision to alter the terms of repayment. More recent changes mean some students are now paying interest on their student loan debt at a rate higher than mortgages or personal loans (Brignall and Collinson, 2016).

Some of our participants that had studied for postgraduate qualifications also owed additional money in the form of Career Development Loans (CDLs), or were still repaying money borrowed to fund their studies from family members:

> "I have a credit card, and I have a Career Development Loan, and a loan to my uncle. It [CDL] started at £7,000, and I've paid it off for a year so my guess is it's down to £6,000, but I'm not positive. I just know it goes out … it's just a direct debit of £168 that goes out every month to pay it back. I also borrowed £1,000 from my uncle." (Phoebe, 28)

In addition to student loan debt, the use of overdrafts and credit cards to fund basic living costs was common among all participants. This challenges the idea that unsecured consumer credit is indulged to fund lavish lifestyle spending. Instead, our participants spoke of the need to use unsecured credit to pay for everyday necessities that their low, stagnant wages could not afford in a context of ever-rising costs of living for essential goods and services.

Recently, Andrew Bailey (Head of the UK's Financial Conduct Authority since 2016) has acknowledged that the increasing over-indebtedness of young people is not linked to 'reckless borrowing', but rather 'directed at essential living costs (and) the affordability of basic living' (cited in Ahmed, 2017). Such forms of unsecured credit are readily available while a student, but often require sudden repayment after graduation to avoid incurring high interest rates or additional charges. This debt was a more immediately pressing worry for the participants, with many of them struggling to pay off their overdrafts and credit cards:

> "I have a huge overdraft, which is my biggest thing which I have to sort out by June somehow. Halifax [bank] let you go up to £3,000. They'll reduce it and I think there'll be a monthly charge that will kick in, so that will be a pain. Some people are telling me to consolidate it and, like, get a credit card to pay it off or something. I just need to borrow £3,000!" (Katie, 23)

> "I have an overdraft, credit card … It's about £2,000 combined. I supplemented my income with my credit card when I was a student, which is the worst thing you can do with a credit card, and that's what kind of got me into the debt." (Steve, 29)

It wasn't just graduates struggling with debt. Phil (30) did not attend university, but had run up a high credit card balance of £5,000 during a period of unemployment. Reinforcing the point that unsecured credit is frequently used to fund necessities, here he describes how his situation rapidly spiralled out of control:

> "It's probably about £5,000 I owe. It fell apart after I stopped working cos I was unemployed for a bit and, at that time, I did have a few credit cards and stuff, and was in quite a bit of debt. I was offered a consolidation loan through this tosser at the bank who paid off a lot of the debt, but then they charged me a massive amount and I ended up owing them twice as much as they paid me out! And then being unemployed made everything worse. Pinging from job to job, I got myself into a bit more trouble. It's been very difficult financially." (Phil, 30)

Craig (28) took out a £5,000 loan immediately after graduation during a period in which he was unemployed, using it to pay off credit cards and store cards acquired during his studies, but quickly faced interest charges that resulted in him seeking help from a debt consolidation agency. The use of loans and credit cards as a form of wage replacement, or to supplement benefit payments and low incomes, was common among all our participants. This raises a number of difficult questions about the accessibility of credit to those who are in a vulnerable financial position, as well as the inadequacy of unemployment benefits, particularly in the UK's enduring era of 'austerity'.

Faced with a need to obtain more money than they were able to earn, in order to manage rapidly escalating debts, one participant had resorted to an even riskier way of attempting to increase his income:

> "I also play online poker to support my income! On average I make about £20 a day, so that keeps me going. In one day I've lost £200, but I've won £6,000 in a day. That's what paid for my Masters degree actually! I'm not in a very good financial state at the moment and it's one of the only ways I can make money. If I had a full-time job, I wouldn't do it because I wouldn't need to." (Stuart, 23)

Far from being 'flawed consumers' wilfully making bad choices, our participants reported going into debt as an undesirable yet essential mechanism in order simply to survive; or, in the case of higher education, an unavoidable requirement that was heavily marketed as the best way to obtain a more secure economic future. In some senses, it was ostensibly 'rational' decisions that had led to the individual financial crises they experienced.

Housing and mortgages

Increasingly high levels of debt are preventing many young people from affording a home of their own, an aspiration that is culturally normalised and widely shared in the UK. Five of our participants still lived with their parents, or had moved back into the parental home 'temporarily' in order to save money. Others were housed with partners or friends in the private rental sector. None of the participants had managed to take that mythical 'first step onto the property ladder'.

For our participants, qualifying for a mortgage to secure home ownership represented more than a simple consumer purchase. Katie (23) stated that she would "like the security of a house", echoing the idea of an owned home as a 'bedrock of certainty in an uncertain world' (Howker and Malik, 2010: 65). This statement also echoes those messages of 'good economic sense' that sees housing as the essential asset for financial security and marketed as providing a stake in the economic success of the country (*The Guardian*, 2012). In 2015, however, the average deposit required for a first time buyer stood at £42,505 (English Housing Survey, 2016: 13), an exorbitant amount far beyond the realms of possibility for most young people, especially those on low incomes and who lack basic job security.

The Conservative government's recent 'Help to Buy ISA', which was promoted by banks and building societies as helping young people to save for a house deposit, has recently been revealed to be accessible only when the exchange of properties is complete. As a saving mechanism that cannot be used as a deposit, this flagship policy is 'technically useless' for securing a mortgage (Morley, 2016). The absence of any tangible support for young people meant most participants felt that home ownership would be beyond their reach for some considerable time, another dimension of their *deferred* lives:

> "I don't know how I'll be able to buy a house. The thought is dwindling a little bit because I don't know if it will ever be possible. You certainly hear that it might not ever be possible; this is what the newspapers are telling you everyday. I was trying to work it out the other night how many years I would actually have to save before I could afford it." (Jennifer, 25)

> "I would love to buy a house, but I dunno whether we'll ever get a deposit. We went to try and get a mortgage – must've been about two years ago – and they were like, yeah, we can give you a mortgage, but we'd need to come up with £25,000 for a deposit. I felt like saying, 'yeah I'll just get that out my back pocket'! I mean, where are you supposed to get £25,000 from? I'll never ... unless there's some inheritance or something to come from my parents. Until that day, I'll never be able to get a house. Houses should be more affordable and people need to own homes cos it's basically your assets, isn't it? And in the future, you've got that to fall back on if you get into trouble. And I think you need that. It's security and stability." (Nick, 28)

Saving the hefty sums required for a house deposit while being a temporary worker seemed so unrealistic that many participants had resigned themselves to being forever a part of 'generation rent', a group with zero prospect of ever owning a home (Blackwell and Jessop, 2014).

Pensions

Similarly, paying into a pension was something that interviewees hoped would happen 'one day' in the future, once they obtained permanent employment. Presently, most of them had little to no spare income that could be put aside for their retirement:

> "At the moment, I couldn't afford to pay into a pension. It's something I will consider when I'm back in permanent employ and I'm sorted with my debts and stuff." (Phil, 30)

> "That would be the best thing about not working for a temp agency. It sucks that I don't have a pension scheme to pay into. I had intended to start paying in from the age of 22, when I got my first proper job, set up a pension and start paying into it early. And now it looks like I might end up being 30 before I can actually make a contribution, so it will be worth considerably less." (Ross, 25)

With irregular, low-paid work providing only a modest income, most of the money our participants earned was spent on either living costs or repaying debts. Any 'surplus' cash that could be saved was usually earmarked for a housing deposit. Consequently, paying into a pension was at the bottom of the list of financial priorities. This is largely attributed to more prolonged transitions to adulthood, with broader financial strains such as unaffordable housing, student debts, stagnant earnings and employment uncertainty reducing the time (and money) available for retirement planning (Berry, 2011). Inadequate pension saving among young people is being increasingly recognised as a pressing social and economic problem. Research by workplace pension provider NOW Pensions (2015) found that 58 per cent of 18- to 35-year-olds are not saving into a pension, with many citing inadequate income, prioritising savings elsewhere (housing deposit) or servicing debts as reasons why.

In October 2012, just after our interviews took place, the UK introduced an 'auto-enrolment' pension scheme to try to arrest these trends. The proportion of UK employees who contribute to a workplace pension increased by almost a quarter, with around 73 per cent of UK employees having an active workplace pension scheme in 2017, up from less than 47 per cent in 2012, according to the ONS (2018). While encouraging, individuals like our participants who are stuck in fixed-term, rolling, or 'zero-hours' employment continue to face difficulties in being eligible for the scheme.

Not beginning to save for retirement until well into one's thirties raises concerns about saving for a long enough period to enable an adequate standard of living in retirement. Research by the ILC in

2017 found that young people today need to save around 18 per cent of their salary to have an 'adequate' income (defined as 70 per cent of average earnings) in retirement, but just 12 per cent are managing to put away anywhere near this amount – five years after the 'auto-enrolment' scheme was introduced. With the 'baby boomer' cohort now all entering retirement, sustained by a smaller and less financially secure generation below, there are warnings of a pensions 'time-bomb' with today's young people likely to work well into their mid-seventies as they simply cannot afford to retire (Willetts, 2006).

Financialised futures

The position of precarity that the participants occupy extends much further than the temporary nature of their employment status. It impacts considerably on their ability to build a coherent life narrative. Chronic insecurity and uncertainty are not conducive to 'long-term thinking, planning, or acting' (Bauman, 2007: 3) with linear ideas of personal 'maturation', 'development' and 'progress' often no longer applicable to biographies lived around such short-term and unstable projects. Standing (2011: 18) refers to this 'precariatised mind' as a 'mass incapacity to think long-term, induced by the low probability of personal progress or building a career'.

The participant's thoughts and plans for the future were strikingly short-term and centred upon finding permanent employment to settle existing debts. Only then could they conceivably plan for the future and make provisions for the longer term, such as buying a house and paying into a pension:

> "In five years time I want to be in a better financial situation, so I don't want to have this bloody Career Development Loan hanging over me and I don't want any, like … the only thing that's an imperative at that point is that I'm financially stable, because I think I'll just be sick of it by then. I don't wanna be pushing 30 and be working full-time and still be struggling." (Beth, 23)

> "At this present time, my main concern is to get a full-time job. The next plans are to clear off the debts and then I'll take it from there… short steps, yeah." (Phil, 30)

> "I would like to be permanently employed with a wage that covered my rent, and gives me enough to have a decent

> standard of living, but whether that's plausible or not at the moment, I don't know." (Gavin, 24)

Throughout our interviews, participants repeatedly spoke of their desire to be 'debt free'. A curious idea in the light of their shared aspiration for home ownership, we propose four ways of interpreting this desire.

First, the notion that a 'debt-free' future awaits this group of young people is highly improbable as understood on their own terms. What the participants appeared to mean by the idea of being 'debt free' was shifting from unsecured 'bad' debts to secured, asset-based 'good' debts, as appropriate to their life stage in the transition to adulthood. In other words, this is a desire to progress along what we call the 'debt *removal* career'. Second, in spite of their present financial vulnerabilities, participants continued to aspire to a better future that, while still heavily financialised, nevertheless revealed a latent sense of hope that they would 'one day' realise their objectives. Third, that while debt might be 'normal' and 'permanent', as Adkins (2017) has recently argued, different types of debt are understood in very different ways. They are negotiated, repositioned, resisted and transformed to reveal a greater sense of agency in financialised lives that might be immediately apparent. Finally, our participants had not fully identified with the guilt and shame they were expected to feel at still being 'in debt'. While they might rebuke themselves for having 'made mistakes', they nevertheless found some solace in the fact that they had done what appeared 'rational' and what was seemingly required of them by mainstream societal norms: namely, graduated from university, obtained career development support, and sought employment. There was a (latent, sociological) sensibility that it was the wider system that had let them down through the provision of 'lousy' jobs, as opposed to them being simply 'lousy' debtors. In all four of these ways, it appears the disciplinary tool of debt is not as totalising as Lazzarato (2011; 2015) and others have suggested.

And yet, despite their hopes and ambitions for the future, participants were unable to foresee a time when their 'debt free' aspirations would be realised. Consequently, the significant commitment and responsibility required to get married and start a family were seen by most participants as just an additional financial burden that would be most unwelcome given current uncertainties:

> "I don't mind kids. I don't think I would want any. Not at the minute. It's a lot to take on. I truly can't afford it. I struggle looking after myself, but having something that

> needs all of your attention just so it doesn't starve or hurt itself … it's a huge responsibility and I don't think I could deal with that." (Gavin, 24)

> "One day I'd like to get married and start a family. One day, yeah. That's the thing, when all my debts are cleared." (Dave, 25)

Only one participant was married (Nick, 28) and none had children, although at the time of interview Natalie (30) was pregnant with her first child. Most revealed that they did expect to get married and have children 'one day', but this was envisaged to be very far away into the future. Existing evidence demonstrates that the average age for (first-time) marriage for men and women in the UK has been increasing over the past forty years, with the average man now getting married at 37 (up from 24 in 1970) and women at age 34 (up from 22 in 1970) (ONS, 2017: 7). Similarly, the age of first-time mothers has risen from around 26 in 1975, to 29 in 2016 (ONS, 2016: 5). Such trends are often said to be largely indicative of women's increased participation in both higher education and the labour market since the 1970s. This may be true, but for the participants in our study, it was the absence of job (and consequently financial) security that was cited as the main reason for deferring such commitments:

> "I guess getting married, in my late twenties I guess, and then starting a family, sort of, around 30 … cos I'd wanna make sure I was in a job and secure and making sure I can provide." (Rose, 18)

> "I think I want what most people want really … marriage, kids, mortgage, that kind of thing; probably much earlier than is realistic. I always thought I'd get married at like 25, kids at 28, mortgage by 30, or whatever, but it seems like it's getting later and later because I'm not on the employment path that I thought I would be on." (Stuart, 23)

Attempting to plan for the future was felt to be a futile exercise given the continued insecurity of their position. There was a shared feeling that the future represented an 'unknown', and that it was impossible to predict in five or ten years what job they would be doing, where they would be living, and whether they would have managed to pay off their 'bad debts' (and presumably transition to their idea of 'good debts', such as mortgages, rather than being literally 'debt free').

Bauman (2007: 26) argues that it is the 'insecurity of the present and uncertainty of the future' that can give rise to feelings of anxiety and passivity. Individuals, exposed to the vagaries of the market in almost all aspects of their financialised lives, no longer feel in control of shaping and directing their own life-course, leading to a sense of 'collective impotence'. Given the sustained efforts of the participants in their attempts to obtain a secure and rewarding career, and the repeated defeats they had subsequently endured, they felt that despite their best efforts they had little meaningful control over the future direction of their lives. Such apprehension and anxiety about 'what may happen' is endemic in the environment of 'constant risk' (Beck, 1992; Sennett, 1998) that precarious workers inhabit. Two of the participants said of the future, "no matter what you do, it's all about luck" (Jess, 25) and simply "being in the right place at the right time" (Danny, 27). Faced with an unpredictable and uncertain future, participants admitted that they were fearful about where life might take them:

> "I'm worried that I won't be able to break even. I've still got a student overdraft … it's getting near the bottom now and it's definitely really worrying. It's just not being in full-time work really. I'm just worried that nothing's gonna come up and I'm gonna have to go back and live with my parents. It's like falling back on old ground." (Stuart, 23)

> "(I worry about) money and whether I'll be able to afford a life that's, 'a good life'. I just think that's quite scary. I do think about the future often, yeah. Sometimes I feel positive, but it depends on what's happening. This job might lead on to something else and, y'know, I'll be in full-time work and in a stable job and able to save up and get a car and stuff. But there's a chance that I might not and I'll just be back where I was." (Rose, 18)

A report by the Resolution Foundation found a generally pessimistic and negative outlook on the future among the British public, with 46 per cent of those surveyed feeling that the next generation in the UK will do worse than their parents (Shrimpton et al, 2017: 17). The growing numbers of young people who are now finding themselves in poverty (Milmo, 2014), and the apparent collapse of the 'intergenerational contract' in which each successive generation will do measurably better than the last, is putting pressure on public policymakers to intervene in order to secure the economic future of so-called 'millennials' (Gardiner, 2016).

'Adulthood' as a social category has historically 'meant the opposite of flexibility' (Blatterer, 2007: 783) and is traditionally defined in terms of family, savings, stability, security, commitment and responsibility. Crucially, it implies a coherent biographical narrative that makes sense of how each of these stages is interconnected (Howker and Malik, 2010:12). The absence of a progressive life narrative and the inability of the participants to reach those (still greatly anticipated) biographical milestones within the prevailing social and economic condition (nor to foresee a time in the future when they could) was robbing participants of hope. Ultimately, they sought what they themselves defined as 'a good life' of relative financial stability, but the immediacy of dealing with debt and job insecurity seemed to defer this life perpetually into the future.

Conclusion

Young adults are now expected to shoulder the burden of unprecedented levels of financial risk as they navigate the increasingly complex transition to a form of adulthood that has debt as a fundamental part of social life. 'Being in debt', as often the only available means of supplementing low income, is therefore unavoidable.

> For young adults, current debt levels undermine the promise that borrowing to buy a home or get an education is a 'sound' investment in the future, because the amount of debt now required to do so has the potential to seriously damage future financial security. (Montgomerie, 2011: 17)

It is this 'future-orientation' that we argue is significant. Although often feeling as if they are 'locked' into a perpetual present of managing their immediate finances, our analysis reveals that *the present* is devalued because it is always positioned unfavourably in relation to so many potential futures, some more benign than others. Risks are assumed on the basis of making the more felicitous futures manifest, acting in the here and now to try to increase the likelihood of their realisation. The present thus has a dual obligation as both the 'future's past' (a chance to correct and alleviate those problems to come) and as the 'past's future' (a chance to realise all of those previous ambitions expected to have been achieved 'by now'). This 'future-orientation' is significant in understanding the rationalisation made in distinguishing between 'good' and 'bad' debts.

> … credit is regularly lived as a kind of catalyser, as an opportunity to reorient one's sense of the future, whereas debt is inhabited as a drag on the immediate present and its future, continually exerting a gravitational pull-of-the-past on one's sense of aspiration and mobility. (Deville and Seigworth, 2015: 619-20)

In conclusion, we highlight two main findings from our study. The first finding regards the distinction between 'good' and 'bad' debts. In a formal economic sense, good debts might be assumed to be those that are secured through an asset that is likely to appreciate in value over time; bad debts might be those that are unsecured or run the risk of significant depreciation in value. In a sociological sense, however, our analysis identifies another way of understanding this distinction.

'Good' debts appear to be those that, although likely to be far higher in quantity (that is, total mortgage debt), are rationalised as culturally appropriate to a given stage of the 'debt accrual career' as dictated by shared social norms. In other words, 'good' debts are those that imply satisfactory social mobility has been achieved, and that one's financial decisions in transitioning to adulthood have been successful in the eyes of others.

'Bad' debts, on the other hand, are those that may be far lower in quantity (that is, total of credit card, payday loan or student loan debts), but which are rationalised as culturally inappropriate to the next stage of the life-course and so actively frustrate attempts to transition. Being 'dragged back' towards one's youth and thus further away from adulthood by the burden of student debt while no longer a student, or by still paying off a bill for once essential goods and services that are now no longer required, serves to anchor individuals in a past that prevents social mobility and thus defers the financial independence traditionally associated with full adulthood.

The second finding is in tension with the first and problematises the quest for social mobility. A cherished value of young adults, to assume ever more financial risks in the expectation of transitioning to full adulthood, nevertheless conflicts with the openly stated desire to escape the constant pressure of transition by 'settling down' with home, marriage and family. This was expressed by all participants in our study. There are a range of moral and affect-laden assumptions about the anticipated 'financial career' of individuals, with the goal of a 'typical family unit' still seemingly tied to popular imaginaries of economic success and stability.

Clearly, we have not provided here a universal account of debt in terms of how it may be differentially experienced, or in terms of its effects. There is scope for a further investigation of the sociology of debt in relation to the wider financialisation of young adults, especially given the limitations of our non-representative sample. As well as temporal dynamics, for example, debt and credit are classed, gendered and racialised in all sorts of ways, and relations of indebtedness do not always simply destroy social relationships but also actively produce them (Deville and Seigworth, 2015: 626; Zelizer, 2005). We intend to pursue these lines of enquiry in later research. While acknowledging the significance of these factors, there nevertheless appears also to be a commonality of lived experiences among those young adults who are indebted. This could give rise to a politics of debt resistance capable of challenging the inequities and injustices of a vividly asymmetrical financial system, which continues to rely upon individuals being willing to tolerate living deferred lives.

Note

The research presented in this chapter was funded by a Frank Stell Scholarship facilitated by the University of Leeds, UK.

References

Adkins, L. (2017) 'Speculative Futures in the Time of Debt', *The Sociological Review*, 65, 3: 448-62.

Ahmed, K. (2017) 'Financial Regulator Warns of Growing Debt Among Young People', *BBC News*, accessed at: http://www.bbc.co.uk/news/business-41627238 on 31 January 2018.

Barr, C. and Malik, S. (2016) 'Revealed: The 30-year Economic Betrayal Dragging Down Generation Y's Income', *The Guardian*, accessed at: https://www.theguardian.com/world/2016/mar/07/revealed-30-year-economic-betrayal-dragging-down-generation-y-income on 30 January 2018.

Bauman, Z. (1998) *Work, Consumerism and the New Poor.* London: Open University Press.

Bauman, Z. (2000) *Liquid Modernity*. Cambridge: Polity.

Bauman, Z. (2007) *Liquid Times: Living in an Age of Uncertainty*. Cambridge: Polity.

Beck, U. (1992) *Risk Society: Towards a New Modernity*. London: Sage.

Berry, C. (2011) 'Resuscitating Retirement Saving: How to Help Today's Young People Plan for the Future' accessed at: http://www.ilcuk.org.uk/index.php/publications/publication_details/resuscitating_retirement_saving_how_to_help_todays_young_people_plan_for_la on 1 February 2018.

Blackwell, A. and Jessop, C. (2014) 'Generation Rent: Perceptions of the First Time Buyer Market', *NatCen*, accessed at: http://www.natcen.ac.uk/our-research/research/the-reality-of-generation-rent on 31 January 2018.

Blatterer, H. (2007) 'Contemporary Adulthood: Reconceptualising an Uncontested Category', *Current Sociology*, 55, 6: 771-92.

Boltanski, L. and Chiapello, E. (2007) *The New Spirit of Capitalism*. London and New York: Verso Books.

Brignall, M. and Collinson, P. (2016) 'Government Under Pressure over Student Loan Change', *The Guardian*, accessed at: https://www.theguardian.com/money/2016/jun/04/government-under-pressure-over-student-loans on 31 January 2018.

Brown, W. (2015) *Undoing the Demos: Neoliberalism's Stealth Revolution*. Cambridge, MA: MIT Press.

Chartered Institute of Personnel and Development (CIPD) (2015) 'Over-qualification and Skills Mismatch in the Graduate Labour Market', accessed at: https://www.cipd.co.uk/Images/over-qualification-and-skills-mismatch-graduate-labour-market_tcm18-10231.pdf on 31 January 2018.

Crouch, C. (2011) *The Strange Non-Death of Neoliberalism*. Cambridge: Polity.

De Benedictus, S., Allen, K., and Jensen, T. (2017) 'Portraying Poverty: The Economics and Ethics of Factual Welfare Television', *Cultural Sociology*, 11, 3: 337-58.

Deville, J. and Seigworth, G. J. (2015) 'Everyday Debt and Credit', *Cultural Studies*, 29, 5-6: 615-29.

Dorling, D. (2014) *Inequality and The 1%* London: Verso Books.

DTI (Department for Trade and Industry) (2005) *Over-indebtedness in Britain*, accessed at: http://webarchive.nationalarchives.gov.uk/+/http:/www.berr.gov.uk/files/file18550.pdf

DWP (Department for Work and Pensions) (2007) *Financial Capability: The Government's Long Term Approach*, accessed at: https://webarchive.nationalarchives.gov.uk/+/http:/www.hm-treasury.gov.uk/d/fincap_150107.pdf on 3 February 2018.

Earle, J., Moran, C. and Ward-Perkins, Z. (2016) *The Econocracy: The Perils of Leaving Economics to the Experts*. Manchester: Manchester University Press.

Edmiston, D. (2018) 'The Poor "Sociological Imagination" of the Rich: Explaining Attitudinal Divergence Towards Welfare, Inequality, and Redistribution', *Social Policy and Administration*, 52: 983-97.

English Housing Survey 2014-15 (2016) *Department for Communities and Local Government Report*, accessed at: https://www.gov.uk/government/uploads/system/uploads/attachment_data/file/501065/EHS_Headline_report_2014-15.pdf on 31 January 2018.

Flaherty, J. and Banks, S. (2013) 'In Whose Interest? The Dynamics of Debt in Poor Households', *Journal of Poverty and Social Justice*, 21, 3: 219-32.

Froud, J., Johal, S., Montgomerie, J. and Williams, K. (2010) 'Escaping the Tyranny of Earned Income? The Failure of Finance as Social Innovation', *New Political Economy*, 15, 1: 147-64.

Gardiner, L. (2016) 'Stagnation Generation: The Case for Renewing the Intergenerational Contract', *Resolution Foundation*, accessed at: http://www.resolutionfoundation.org/app/uploads/2016/06/Intergenerational-commission-launch-report.pdf on 1 February 2018.

Green, F. and Zhu, Y. (2010) 'Over-qualification, Job Dissatisfaction, and Increasing Dispersion in the Returns to Graduate Education', *Oxford Economic Papers*, 62: 740-63.

Hartlep, N. and Eckrich, L. (2013) 'Ivory Tower Graduates in the Red: The Role of Debt in Higher Education', *Workplace: A Journal for Academic Labour*, 22, accessed at: http://ices.library.ubc.ca/index.php/workplace/article/view/184428 on 31 January 2018.

Houle, J. (2014) 'A Generation Indebted: Young Adult Debt across Three Cohorts', *Social Problems*, 61: 3, 448-65.

Howker, E. and Malik, S. (2010) *The Jilted Generation: How Britain has Bankrupted its Youth*. London: Icon Books.

ILC (2017) 'The Global Savings Gap', accessed at: http://www.ilcuk.org.uk/index.php/publications/publication_details/the_global_savings_gap on 1 February 2018.

IPPR (2010) 'Trends in Part-time and Temporary Work', accessed at: http://www.ippr.org/assets/media/uploadedFiles/pressreleases/Part-time%20and%20temporary%20work%20technical%20briefing.pdf on 28 January 2018.

Irwin, S. (2018) 'Lay Perceptions of Inequality and Social Structure', *Sociology*, 52, 2: 211-27.

Langley, P. (2008) *The Everyday Life of Global Finance: Saving and Borrowing in Anglo-America*. Oxford: Oxford University Press.

Lapavitsas, C. (2013) *Profiting Without Producing: How Global Finance Exploits Us All*. London: Verso Books.

Lazzarato, M. (2011) *The Making of Indebted Man*. London: Semiotext(e).

Lazzarato, M. (2015) *Governing by Debt*. London: Semiotext(e).
Macdonald, D. and Shaker, E. (2012) 'Eduflation and the High Cost of Learning', *Canadian Centre for Policy Alternatives*, accessed at: https://www.policyalternatives.ca/sites/default/files/uploads/publications/National%20Office/2012/09/Eduflation%20and%20High%20Cost%20Learning.pdf on 31 January 2018.
Mellor, M. (2016) *Debt or Democracy: Public Money for Sustainability and Social Justice*. London: Pluto.
Milmo, C. (2014) 'The Young Are The New Poor: Sharp increase in number of under-25s living in poverty, while over-65s are better off than ever' accessed at: http://www.independent.co.uk/news/uk/home-news/the-young-are-the-new-poor-sharp-increase-in-the-number-of-under-25s-living-in-poverty-while-over-9878722.html on 1 February 2018.
Mirowski, P. (2013) *Never Let a Serious Crisis Go to Waste: How Neoliberalism Survived the Financial Meltdown*. London: Verso.
Montgomerie, J. (2007) 'Financialization and Consumption: An Alternative Account of Rising Consumer Debt Levels in Anglo-America', *CRESC Working Paper Series*, accessed at: https://www.escholar.manchester.ac.uk/api/datastream?publicationPid=uk-ac-man-scw:181191&datastreamId=FULL-TEXT.PDF on 1 February 2018.
Montgomerie, J. (2011) 'The Age of Insecurity: Indebtedness and the Politics of Abandonment', *CRESC Working Paper Series*, accessed at: https://www.escholar.manchester.ac.uk/uk-ac-man-scw:181055 on 1 February 2018.
Moore, S. (2012) 'Instead of Being Disgusted by Poverty, We Are Disgusted by Poor People Themselves', *The Guardian*, accessed at: https://www.theguardian.com/commentisfree/2012/feb/16/suzanne-moore-disgusted-by-poor on 30 January 2018.
Morley, K. (2016) 'Help to Buy Isa Scandal: 500,000 first-time buyers told scheme cannot be used for initial deposit on homes', *The Telegraph*, accessed at: http://www.telegraph.co.uk/news/2016/08/19/help-to-buy-isa-scandal-500000-first-time-buyers-told-scheme-can/ on 31 January 2018.
NOW Pensions (2015) 'Generation Y Expect £100,000 Pension But Over Half Haven't Started Saving', accessed at: https://www.nowpensions.com/wp-content/uploads/2015/04/Generation-Y-expect-%C2%A3100000-pension-but-over-half-havent-started-saving.pdf on 1 February 2018.

ONS (2016) 'Births by Parents' Characteristics in England and Wales: 2016', accessed at: https://www.ons.gov.uk/peoplepopulationandcommunity/birthsdeathsandmarriages/livebirths/bulletins/birthsbyparentscharacteristicsinenglandandwales/2016 on 1 February 2018.

ONS (2017) 'Marriages in England and Wales 2014', accessed at: https://www.ons.gov.uk/peoplepopulationandcommunity/birthsdeathsandmarriages/marriagecohabitationandcivilpartnerships/bulletins/marriagesinenglandandwalesprovisional/2014 on 1 February 2018.

ONS (2018) 'Pension participation at record high but contributions cluster at minimum levels', ONS.

Oxfam (2017) 'An Economy for the 99%', accessed at: https://policy-practice.oxfam.org.uk/publications/an-economy-for-the-99-its-time-to-build-a-human-economy-that-benefits-everyone-620170 on 30 January 2018.

Packman, C. (2014) *Payday Lending*. London: Palgrave Pivot.

Purcell, K., Elias, P., Atfield, G., Behle, H., Ellison, R., Luchinskaya, D., Snape, J., Conaghan, L. and Tzanakou, C. (2012) 'Futuretrack Stage 4 Report: Transitions into Employment, Further Study, and Other Outcomes', accessed at: http://www.hecsu.ac.uk/assets/assets/documents/Futuretrack_Stage_4_Final_report_6th_Nov_2012.pdf on 30 January 2018.

Sandel, M. (2012) *What Money Can't Buy: The Moral Limits of Markets* London: Penguin.

Sayer, A. (2016) *Why We Can't Afford the Rich*. Bristol: Policy Press.

Sennett, R. (1998) *The Corrosion of Character*. London: Norton.

Shrimpton, H., Skinner, G. and Hall, S. (2017) 'The Millennial Bug: Public Attitudes on the Living Standards of Different Generations', accessed at: http://www.resolutionfoundation.org/app/uploads/2017/09/The-Millennial-Bug.pdf on 1 February 2018.

Standing, G. (2011) *The Precariat: The New Dangerous Classes*. London: Bloomsbury.

Standing. G. (2014) *A Precariat Charter: From Denizens to Citizens*. London: Bloomsbury.

Stanley, L., Deville, J. and Montgomerie, J. (2015) 'The Moral Economy of the Twenty-First Century Debtor: Revisiting E.P. Thompson in an Online World', *New Left Project*, accessed at: http://www.newleftproject.org/index.php/site/article_comments/the_moral_economy_of_the_twenty_first_century_debtor on 1 February 2018.

Stiglitz, J. (2012) *The Price of Inequality: How Today's Divided Society Endangers Our Future.* London: Penguin.

The Griffiths Commission on Personal Debt (2005) 'What Price Credit?', accessed at: https://www.centreforsocialjustice.org.uk/core/wp-content/uploads/2016/08/WhatPriceCredit.pdf on 30 January 2018.

The Money Advice Service (2014) 'It's time to Talk: Young People and Money Regrets', accessed at: https://www.moneyadviceservice.org.uk/files/mas_money_regrets_online.pdf on 17 January 2018.

The Money Charity (2018) 'The Money Statistics', accessed at: http://themoneycharity.org.uk/money-statistics_on 2 February 2018.

TUC (2013) 'Involuntary Temporary Jobs Driving Rising Employment', accessed at: http://www.tuc.org.uk/economic-issues/labour-market/labour-market-and-economic-reports/involuntary-temporary-jobs-driving on 30 January 2018.

TUC (2016) 'Britain in the Red: Why We Need Action to Help Over-indebted Households', *Economic Report Series*, accessed at: https://www.tuc.org.uk/sites/default/files/Britain-In-The-Red-2016.pdf on 30 January 2018.

Walker, C. (2012) 'Personal Debt, Cognitive Delinquency and Techniques of Governmentality: Neoliberal Constructions of Financial Inadequacy in the UK', *Journal of Community and Applied Social Psychology*, 22: 533-8.

Walker, I. and Zhu, Y. (2013) 'The Impact of University Degrees on the Lifecycle of Earnings: Some Further Analysis', *Department for Business, Innovation, and Skills: Research Paper 112*, accessed at: https://www.gov.uk/government/uploads/system/uploads/attachment_data/file/229498/bis-13-899-the-impact-of-university-degrees-on-the-lifecycle-of-earnings-further-analysis.pdf on 30 January 2018.

Webley, P. and Nyhus, E.K. (2001) 'Lifecycle and Dispositional Routes into Problem Debt', *British Journal of Psychology*, 92, 3: 423-46.

Weeks, J. F. (2014) *Economics of the 1% How Mainstream Economics Serves the Rich, Obscures Reality and Distorts Policy*. New York: Anthem Press.

Wilkinson, R. and Pickett, K. (2009) *The Spirit Level: Why Equality is Better for Everyone.* London: Penguin.

Willetts, D. (2006) *The Pinch: How The Baby Boomers Took Their Children's Future, and Why They Should Give It Back*. London: Atlantic.

Winterton, M. T. and Irwin, S. (2012) 'Teenage Expectations of Going to University: The Ebb and Flow of Influences from 14 to 18', *Journal of Youth Studies*, 15, 7: 858-74.

Women's Trust (2016) 'No Country for Young Women', accessed at: https://www.youngwomenstrust.org/assets/0000/4258/No_country_for_young_women__final_report.pdf on 30 January 2018.
UKCES (2014) *Precarious Futures? Youth Employment in an International Context*, accessed at: https://www.gov.uk/government/uploads/system/uploads/attachment_data/file/326119/14.07.02._Youth_Report_for_web_V3.pdf on 30 January 2018.
Zelizer, V. A. (2005) *The Purchase of Intimacy*. Princeton, NJ: Princeton University Press.

5

'Choose your moments': discipline and speculation in the indebted everyday

Samuel Kirwan, Leila Dawney and Rosie Walker

Introduction

From conversations overheard on the bus or in the gym, to warnings voiced by macroeconomists and major financial institutions (Keen, 2017; Brazier, 2017); everything is, it seems, about debt. Looming behind the formidable spectres haunting Europe (ecological catastrophe, resurgent nationalisms) is a rising tide of indebted households. This chapter focuses upon the United Kingdom, where a perfect storm of measures has caused not only a ballooning of overall private debt levels, but moreover a fundamental change in the very meaning of 'household debt'.

Yet, if everything is about debt, from our experience, debt is (almost) always about something else. This chapter is an attempt to make sense, as debt researchers also involved in advice work and housing activism, of the individual narratives of debt that we encounter and how they relate to shared experiences of benefit reductions, rising housing costs, and insecure work. It is as such an attempt to understand the broader implications of debt; how debt burdens seep into, and reshape, everyday experiences and intimate relationships.

We do this by focusing upon the *temporal frameworks* of debt. In this sense our work follows a series of prominent texts in the field of debt studies – most prominent among which are those of Lazzarato (2012, 2013) – in which it is the recompositions of past, future and present, the twistings of rhythms and habits, that are the key dynamics explaining what it means to be in debt. This emotio-temporal framing can serve, we argue, to uncover what is otherwise hidden in quantitative indications of rising debt burdens,[1] suggesting as they do a linear expansion in the country's demand for credit, namely that the shifting dynamics of debt in the UK are fundamentally recomposing the 'indebted everyday'.

Taking our cue from the work of Adkins (2016) and Konings (2015; 2018), this chapter challenges the dominant understanding of debt as imposing a 'disciplinary' framework of time upon the subject. Across two bodies of fieldwork – with the advice sector and with debtors – we trace not only the imposition, management and varied narratives of 'disciplinary' structurings of time, but also the 'moments' in which they crack, fragment or are suspended. We show how the ways in which debt is sold, managed and collected, as well as the practices through which debtors consider multiple futures in their negotiations of debt, which weave other forms of time into the indebted everyday. We show also how the stagnation and irregularity of household budgets renders the disciplinary edifice of debt increasingly unstable. Following Adkins, we bring these non-disciplinary 'moments' under the remit of 'speculative time'.

Fieldwork

This chapter explores findings from two sets of interviews.[2] The first are six interviews, conducted in the summer and autumn of 2017, with senior managers in the debt advice sector. Building on extensive fieldwork in the debt advice sector carried out in 2014-15 (Kirwan, 2018), these focused upon: how the types of debt (and debtor) faced by the advice sector are changing, the key challenges facing the sector in 2017, and observations on how advice practice is changing to meet these dynamics. The interviews focused also upon the role played by budgeting – the management of household finances through a monthly 'budget sheet' – within the advice interview. They were conducted at a time in which the key budgeting tool – the Common Financial Statement (CFS) – was being replaced by the 'Standard Financial Statement' (SFS), and as such the interviews examined in detail the role played by the CFS/SFS within advice work.

The second are in-depth interviews with eight debtors across the country, conducted in the summer of 2016. These explored: how debts are intertwined with intimate relationships, the different emotional connections individuals held with separate debts, and how participants considered their shared futures in light of these debts. Recruited through a combination of personal contacts and snowballing, with the exception of one participant, the individuals all fit in to the 'just-about-managing' category: all carried multiple debts that were being serviced at a cost that, while affordable, was having a significant effect upon their lives.

Bringing together these two bodies of fieldwork allows us to observe from different angles the varied temporal dynamics in the lived experience of debt. We explore the different roles played by budgeting practices, noting their role in fostering, imposing, or enticing households into a 'disciplinary' management of time. We explore also the broader performativity of budgeting tools and practices: what role they play in forming, managing and demarcating relationships and households; and how they act as a form of communication between debtors, creditors, the advice sector and the insolvency service. Yet we explore also the ways in which, at both the household and societal level, these dynamics break down. We argue that the cracks in the 'disciplinary' edifice of time, which we describe in two specific registers, are informative as to how the experience of debt is changing. On this basis, we argue that the crisis of debt is less about a quantitative expansion of debt levels, but rather about a widespread inability to believe in a stable and predictable future of debt repayment.

Debt in the UK: the view from the advice sector

The framework for discussion of debt in the United Kingdom remains shaped by the 'great financial crisis', or 'credit crunch', of 2007-8. Thus the situation of rising levels of consumer debt in 2017 has been interpreted primarily in terms of its resemblance to the lending conditions seen to have triggered the 2007 crash, namely excessive consumer credit and high levels of 'toxic' or 'distressed' debt – debts sold without reasonable expectation of repayment (Elliot, 2017). The near-collapse of the Provident loan company[3] in August 2017, triggered by a failure to collect debts, was thus presented by some financial observers as the canary in the coalmine of household debt (*The Economist*, 2017).

Despite the different conclusions they draw from the available statistical data, there is broad agreement between debt charities, the financial services industry and the Bank of England that household debts, across all areas, are rising. This means that individuals in a broader set of situations and income brackets are falling into debt, that those who are in debt are finding those debts more difficult to service and repay, and that any raising of interest rates, broadly expected following the 0.25% rise in the official bank rate enacted in November 2017, will push an increasing number of households into serious difficulty. It also means that the *type* of debts faced by households is changing.

This latter point was a consistent theme in our interviews with the advice sector, being most pronounced for services assisting clients on low incomes and those based in Universal Credit rollout areas.[4] For such services, the conditions and experience of household debt in 2017 bear very little resemblance to the situation a decade previously. One manager describes a situation that would have been unthinkable before 2007:

> "The credit industry have moved an awful lot in my time in terms of being a lot easier to talk to … they're writing off debts, they've accepted the Standard Financial Statement. And yet for most of us the problem is Local Authority enforcement agents, HMRC, DWP. And for the client group that I was dealing with in [city] that was nearly every debt." (Leslie, Manager in a debt advice service)[5]

As Leslie notes, for the low-income debtor in 2017, debt is characterised primarily by the startling shift towards what are termed, within the advice sector, 'priority debts', and elsewhere termed 'frontline debts' (Bailey, quoted in Inman and Treanor, 2017). Thus, for clients of advice services, the key debts faced by clients are no longer credit cards and loans, but rent arrears, council tax arrears, court fines and fuel debts.[6] These are debts for which the consequences of non-repayment, namely eviction, prison, or losing access to utilities (as we have argued elsewhere) are typically misunderstood by clients, who will prioritise 'those who shout the loudest' (Kirwan, 2018).

Joseph Spooner has characterised this divide less by the consequences of non-repayment than by the position of the creditor. He uses the term 'the austere creditor' to capture the approach through which, for example, a local authority revenues team or a DWP enforcement team will seek to collect a council tax liability or benefits overpayment. In contrast to the varied practices of lenders and collectors in the consumer sector (see Deville, 2015), the implication is that 'austere creditors' act with the intensity and focus proper to debtors (Graeber, 2011): driven by narratives of moral right and the necessity of shoring up public finances in times of austerity, they use the significant legal powers at their disposal to intimidate debtors into repaying or secure deductions from income or benefits. In such procedures there is relatively little consideration of the lived reality of the debtor and their capacity to repay.

As we demonstrate, the very different ways in which these debts are *lived* have led to significant changes in the indebted everyday. The risks are greater, the threat and cost (if not the physical presence) of bailiffs[7] more significant (Advice UK et al, 2017); and deductions from income more frequent and severe (Gustaffson, 2017). Even 'consumer debts', creating an image of reckless expenditure or rampant consumerism – hence the prevalence with which newspaper articles depicting spiralling consumer debt are illustrated with women holding shopping bags (Ramsay, 2009) – are more likely to be payday loans making up shortfalls in income than financing excessive spending (StepChange, 2017).

While the shift to 'priority' or 'frontline' debts was already an established theme in our 2014-15 research (Kirwan, 2018), a new site of concern ran through our interviews in 2017. This was that of the 'deficit budget sheet': the situation in which, for households either in debt, or veering into debt (in particular after an insolvency procedure), there is no possibility of working out a balanced budget. Or moreover, no matter how much maximising of benefit income is possible, the only way to produce a balanced budget is to present unworkable, or imaginary, figures in key areas of household expenditure. The deficit budget sheet presents significant problems for advisers, as they require a balanced budget to make arrangement with creditors. Balancing the immediate need to present balanced budgets has become a key challenge for many services:

> "I mean it hasn't ever been a problem before, because you'd always want to present a balanced budget sheet. But it's a problem now, because of the fact that people don't have enough money to live on. … But I think, fundamentally, I don't like putting things like fifteen a week down for food, that doesn't feel right to me, so my gut feeling is that it should be a budget sheet of this is what you've got coming in and this is what you've got going out." (Leslie, Manager of a debt advice service)

The key consequence of a deficit budget is that *there will be no way out of debt.* As Leslie continues, the 'deficit budget sheet' leads to "ongoing conversations where there's no resolution, it just feels that debt relief order is the only answer, and then do another one again in five years for some people". As we discuss later in this chapter, there is a growing sector of debtors for whom there is no debt-free horizon, only a cycle of escalating arrears and debt relief.

The calendrics of repayment

In the moral economy of debt relations, a clear space is reserved for the 'good' debtor. This is the working adult who, taking responsibility for their actions, accepts the need to restrict their spending and direct their wages towards debt repayments. They stop going out, or insist on buying their own drinks if they do. They holiday at home and instil the virtues of frugality and patience in their children.[8] Most importantly, they make a budget. They continue making and remaking it, discuss it, work on it and amend it in line with their needs and finances until the day they return, 'debt free', their lives ready to begin again. They gear their lives to the temporal schema of debt repayment. They accept the need to be *disciplined*, on the agreement that this period will come to an end. Life is structured by a dual temporality of rhythm and promise: a life held to predictable, punctual events, held in place by the distant horizon of future freedom (Adkins, 2015: 3; Jasarevic, 2014: 264).

An investigation of the role played by this disciplining mechanism is central to Maurizio Lazzarato's two-part investigation (2012; 2013) of the role of debt in shaping class structures and inequality, focused in particular upon 'Euro-America', principally the United Kingdom, Germany, Italy and the United States. Following Foucault, Lazzarato's central argument is that debt, or more precisely the debt relationship, forms the fulcrum for an arrangement of power; no longer should inequality be explored in terms of class structures, but rather in variegations of the debtor/creditor relationship. While other key texts offering new schema and typologies for understanding the contemporary class landscape, notably Guy Standing's (2011) characterisation of the 'precariat', focus upon changing material conditions, Lazzarato focuses upon a two-way power relationship characterised by the temporal structure of discipline. Faced with the creditor, the debtor must promise to adhere to a stable and predictable behavioural rhythm:

> Granting credit requires one to estimate that which is inestimable – future behaviour and events – and to expose oneself to the uncertainty of time. The system of debt must therefore neutralize time, that is, the risk inherent to it. … By training the governed to 'promise' (to honor their debt), capitalism exercises 'control over the future', since debt obligations allow one to foresee, calculate, measure and establish equivalences between current and future behaviour. (Lazzarato, 2012: 45)

Such calculations and measurements of the future, extrapolated from the present, find their formal representation in the calendar. The need to repay submits the time of experience to the ordered time of monthly deadlines and payments, a temporal schema described by Jane Guyer as 'the calendrics of repayment' (Guyer, 2012). As Lazzarato identifies, granting credit, inasmuch as it imposes the 'calendrics of repayment', constitutes the *theft* of time; no longer is the debtor able to experience the present as the possibility of something new or unexpected – their life has been laid out in advance. In a nation of debtors, the principal line of power concerns the capacity of the creditor to *neutralise* life in all its variety and unpredictability. Lazzarato does not comment upon the significant expansion of this logic with the new capacities of monitoring and surveillance afforded to collectors and, more importantly, credit rating agencies (Deville, 2015; Deville and Van der Velden, 2015). As the latter sector improves the two-way flows of information between itself and, to name a few actors, landlords, Local Authorities, and employers, the demand to regularise one's life is set to become all-consuming. The 'creditor', taken broadly to refer to the assemblage of agencies with an interest in regulating the behaviour of debtors, knows where you have been, what you have done, and how to use this information as leverage for ensuring good conduct.

One does not need to look far to find the 'calendrics of repayment' to be the organising temporal schema in 'austerity' Britain. Seeking to raise the scale of the household debt problem in the UK in 2013, Johnna Montgomerie (2013) emphasises the simple statement 'I'm broke', meaning not necessarily that one is penniless or bankrupt, but rather that one must respond to an invitation of expenditure with an emphasis upon frugality, prioritising financial obligations over relationships to friends and family. As Montgomerie argues, this statement is key to ongoing economic stagnation under the 'balance sheet recession'. Levels of consumer spending will continue to contract so long as available income is locked into paying down household debt.

In few spaces is the 'calendrics of payment' more important, and its role more multi-dimensional, than the advice sector. While the 'success' of the advice process is a deeply contested concept in an era of target-based funding, one can observe at least that the key achievements advice can make – whether enabling someone to manage their own finances, making agreements with creditors to reduce repayments or write off debts, or enabling insolvency (Atfield et al, 2016) – are each reliant upon working out with a debtor a structure of regularised payments and expenditure (Kirwan, 2018). Across the sector, this is carried out through the approved budget sheet, the Common Financial Statement.[9]

Advice and the Common Financial Statement

The CFS is a monthly budget sheet, compiled on an Excel spreadsheet, consisting of five sheets: general information, income, expenditure and debts, all of which are collated in an outline sheet which can be sent to creditors. The CFS, put together by key partners in the advice, charity, debt management, credit and insolvency sectors, presents a stark case of the regularisation of time, and the precluding therein of time as unexpected. It presents also the broader role played by the 'calendrics of repayment', most notably its role in allowing a certain form of communication between different actors.

While there is pressure on some services, in certain situations, to complete a financial statement very quickly (Walker et al, 2015; Davey, 2017), most notably for face-to-face services seeking to address an immediate problem, others will focus on giving the client time to complete an accurate and reflective statement:

> "From our point of view what it's about doing is encouraging them to think more broadly about their actual expenditure, rather than what they *think* is their expenditure. And one of the things we often do, is to do a CFS with them, send it as a draft, get them to review it and maybe sit on it a week, maybe makes some notes through that week of what they've actually spent, and then maybe review it further down the line so we come up with a more realistic budget." (Roger, Manager of a debt advice service)

As other advisers noted, this opportunity to give a client time to compile a CFS is also time for them to reflect upon, and regularise, their own spending (see Kirwan 2018). If the goal is not only to alleviate the effects of debts, but also to reform the debtor so that they might be able to deal with them in future, key to the *success* of advice is the loop between the actions of the client and their ongoing negotiation and interpretation of the budget sheet. Thus, as a household budget sheet to be used in the everyday life of the client, it also plays a key role in *formalising* the household (Davey, 2017); debtors must consider the role of others within (and without) their household, notably the joint responsibility of partners and ex-partners for certain debts, and also the role of non-dependents, for example older children still living in the family home but not contributing to it financially.

The CFS also contains 'trigger figures', visible to the adviser but not the client, which define permitted levels of expenditure in key areas, as well as a distinction between essential and additional expenditure. Thus, if enjoyment is to be included in a financial statement, it must fit within a formal category and not exceed a pre-defined figure. Echoing the internal debates advisers have over how best to deal with practices and pleasures that fall outside 'essential' categories, one manager describes the difficulty with the overly formal approach taken by many advisers:

> "So, I think the difficulties come with financial statements where, if you look at it sort of blindly, without looking at the broader circumstances for that guy in particular, you could look at it, 'well he's spending all that money on beer', which he is. But it's all the things that come with that few hours that he has, where he might see people and talk to people, and ultimately, by having that social interaction, it might actually make his debt solution in the longer term more successful, because he's happier in his own mind. Because often I think when it does fail, so when the things like DMPs [debt management plans] fail, it's often because a person feels a little bit too constrained by the plan, and that pressure's on them really, so if you can remove the pressure and make it easier for them, I think it has a greater chance of success really." (Roger, Manager of a debt advice service)

By bringing this narrative back to the theme of the 'success' of a budget sheet, Roger emphasises the belief that the budgeting *could* work if it could be more flexible and better incorporate the need for social interaction and enjoyment. Yet also, lurking at the edges of his account, is a recognition that the need to break out of the disciplinary structure of the budget sheet will always be a driving force undermining their utility. It is this intrinsic crack in the disciplinary edifice that we explore below through the concept of 'speculative time'.

This negotiation between advisers over how to compile a budget sheet nonetheless reiterates the importance of the CFS; all of our participants agreed that fixing a stable, workable budget should be the goal of the sector. Yet there was also agreement that in the context in which regular payments, whether of income or benefits,[10] is becoming a distant dream for many, maintaining this role has become a significant challenge for services. Participants described the difficult task of seeking to fit the constraints of a predictable monthly budget sheet when the grounding condition of a workable budget, namely a reliable income, was no longer available. How a budget sheet can accommodate fluctuations and gaps is as such a pressing issue within the sector (Bolton, 2017; Van Rooyen, 2017).

Amid such discussions, it is clear why the 'deficit debtor' carries such a threat for the advice sector. Fixing a budget is as much about negotiating repayments as it is about fixing the client to a stable plan (Kirwan, 2018); to send a client away with a budget sheet that promises only to get them into further debt is seen as an admission of failure. Again, we explore further this fragmentation of the 'calendrics of repayment' below through the concept of 'speculative time'.

Relationship budgeting

In our interviews with debtors the 'calendrics of repayment' not only plays a key role in managing household finances, it also had varied and complex roles to play within intimate and familial relationships. A first indication of this appears in Amy's account of the role played by debt repayments in her current relationship. Amy and her partner had a mix of loans, Personal Contract Purchase (PCP) agreements for their cars, and overdrafts. She had accrued significant debts following the breakdown of her previous relationship, and her new relationship was still defined by the attempt to pay these off. Amy emphasised the importance of repayment schedules, particularly the strain of these, to how she and her partner related to each other and understood their future together:

RW: Do you think the debts you have affect your relationship with your partner now?

Amy: Only that I moan at him that we've got too much of it. I think his loan is about the same as mine per month, and his car is a bit more than mine. So it works out at about £700 pounds a month that goes out on debt. I always say to him if we didn't have that we could have a lot more fun. I'm really looking forward to two-and-a-half years' time when we have paid everything off. It does really affect your life. Like, we're trying for a baby at the moment and I think all that money each month would make a massive difference.

In Amy's account, knowing that they are paying their debts and that this period will pass, is important to the couple. Yet she makes clear her frustration with their life, noting that they would be living fuller lives were this restriction not upon them. She articulates feeling that it is only the future horizon – the moment in 'two-and-a-half years' time', that allows them to function; lurking behind this is a fear that this horizon may never appear.

Claire and Simon had multiple secured and unsecured debts, most of which were related to decisions they had made in order to improve their lives in the long term, such as returning to university. Significantly, in times of difficulty they had borrowed money from Simon's parents, and managing these repayments played a key role in their account of the changing role of debt in their lives. Interviewed together, what emerges from their discussion is the importance of shared budgeting – of joining bank accounts and jointly negotiating debt repayments – as a signal of the strength of their relationship:

Simon: Claire has always been good with money and she could see what I was doing and wouldn't be able to deal with it all. So it was about 2011 when she took the reins and started doing all the budgeting.

Claire: I would go on online banking every day and check everything was okay.

Simon: And give me a telling off sometimes! [Laughs] but it was fine. We know some couples who are married and they still keep it strictly separate, money wise. That feels a bit alien to us.

Claire: My brother and his girlfriend have a daughter and we asked them not very long ago whether they had a joint bank account or separate and it started off a really big argument between them about who pays for what. It was clear that we had made the right decision to join our bank accounts.

Claire and Simon's playful negotiation of their different spending habits and budgeting arrangements displays how important the agreement to follow a disciplinary arrangement was to their learning to recognise and live with each other's boundaries and habits. Yet, following Viviana Zelizer (2000), it displays also the way in which shared budgeting practices enable couples to demarcate the *form* of relationship they hold. That is, shared budgeting, in providing a response to how the difficult intertwining of money and intimacy will be negotiated, allows couples to identify and present their own relationship and differentiate themselves from other forms of being together.[11]

For Shelly, recounting a similarly positive narrative of the importance of shared budgeting for her current relationship, this 'other' form of relationship was that in which it is the male partner who makes the financial decisions. Indeed, the significant level of debts she held were related to her previous marriage, to which her husband had both brought debts and continued to accrue them in their joint names.

Interestingly, Shelly and her partner had used budgeting software to facilitate this shared approach to household finances:

> "But now it's all fine, we've been in this flat for nearly two years and we love it. So that £10,000 ... there was a point where we had to dip into it little bit, but because of what happened with [ex-husband], my approach to finances with [new husband] is completely different. All of our money comes into one account and we have this program called 'You need a budget' to manage our finances. It's incredible. I feel so much happier now I know that I've got ... we are always two months ahead, so I know we've got a buffer." (Shelly)

Shelly articulates here the extra form of stability given by the 'calendrics of repayment', namely that, by regularising their finances and moving away from spontaneous and unexpected actions, they are more ready to deal with spontaneous and unexpected shocks. This 'buffer' forms a mobile horizon as a counter to the permanent horizon – which for Shelly appears so remote as to be impossible – of being 'debt-free'.

The form of relationship that Shelly and Claire and Simon were defining themselves against, namely that in which it is the man who makes the financial decisions for the household, was taken by Martin, who was the closest of our respondents to the image of the 'noble' debtor central to the moral economy of debt relations. Martin displayed a heightened degree of vigilance regarding the management of what was a complex debt portfolio, including mortgages, loans and hire-purchase contracts. Yet, similarly, the way in which he had taken on the role not only of budgeting but of cutting back on spending in order to service debts becomes a way of marking out roles and boundaries within the household:

> "But me personally, I've never spent money on clothes. I just wear the same clothes until they fall off me and I get given them for birthdays and Christmas. My wife likes to buy the odd bit of clothing here and there and sometimes

> she'll be wearing something and I'll say 'Oh, where is that from?' and she'll say 'Oh, it's been in my wardrobe for a long time', and I know she's blatantly kidding herself. But it's nothing crazy and I wouldn't say we've been forced to cut back on anything. We don't really get anything to cut back on. We buy food and basics. I don't really think that question is applicable to us." (Martin)

Despite his confidence in the wisdom of the decisions he has made, like Amy, Martin continues to describe the weight of certain debts and his attachment to the promise that they will be relieved. Martin describes one particular debt as "a bit of a ball and chain hanging around our necks", noting how much he is looking forward to the specific date on which it is paid off. These holding horizons appear throughout our debtor interviews; they punctuate reflections on the difficulty of managing in the present, providing future memories of how things will change on these single, or multiple, dates. Yet also running through the interviews, though not explicitly voiced, is a suspicion that this date might never come. We can trace across these accounts a recognition that life will intervene – that new purchases or restrictions on income will push this date back, and back.

As we have argued, managing debt and budgeting are key practices through which partners negotiate their differences and connections: how they learn to live with each other. While this presents a positive view of the role played by the disciplinary structuring of life proper to indebtedness, these accounts also articulate a way of being together in the world described by Lauren Berlant (2011) as one of 'cruel optimism'. That is, in these negotiations, what is at stake is a tension between the optimism for 'a good life', located on a horizon that may never arrive, and the practices for drawing close to this good life, which, while playing important symbolic roles for partners, are also experienced as distinctly *cruel,* in particular inasmuch as they impose restrictions on the fulfilment of a relationship (see also Dawney et al, 2018). Articulated most clearly in Amy's account is the feeling that, while the promise that life will be better is what allows them to believe in their relationship, in continuing to live in conditions of restriction, the practices of achieving that good life are slowly destroying them. Attached to a future in which the promises of life will be fulfilled, the ways in which they manage this attachment produce simmering tensions and a sense of a life not being lived.

However, to focus only on practices of budgeting, and the disciplinary framework it brings, is to miss the broader temporal palette through which credit and spending are experienced in the everyday. That is, despite the centrality of budgeting and the 'calendrics of repayment' in these accounts, each narrative (as indicated by Martin's description of his wife's minor deceptions) is punctuated by moments in which they act outside of their budgeting commitments. Rather than seeing these as anomalies, as momentary disruptions in the calendrics of repayment, we see these as central to an understanding of the temporal structure of debt. Indeed, we argue that the disciplinary structures of debt repayment form a canvas, or background, to the varied moments in which debtors act otherwise.

Exploring speculative time

Thus far we have explored the temporality that, following Lazzarato, is imposed by the creditor upon the debtor: a disciplinary structuring of the everyday in which newness and the unexpected are impossible. We can see how the virtues of the disciplined subject sit at the heart of the moral economy of debt; witness the steadiness, stability and patience of the debt collector or housing officer on daytime television as they negotiate the chaotic lives around them.[12] Time as it is supposed to be lived defines a life in which time, as the arrival of the new, is impossible.

As Adkins (2016: 5) argues, however, there is reason to dispute that the 'calendrics of repayment' constitute a 'theft' of time. The above interviews show the ways in which couples negotiate their differences and reconcile former lives, demarcating and stabilising a shared life, through budgeting practices; they show the *generativity* of discipline. Budgeting is not only an intimate practice, it is a way that couples identify and demarcate the forms of intimacy they enjoy. Yet it is important not to valorise this experience: as noted above, this generativity can be defined by a 'cruel optimism' – the maintenance of conditions that wear away at the present in order to stay close to the promise of a better future.

Yet Adkins takes this critique further. Like Martijn Konings (2015, 2018), through a focus upon the 'speculative' she rejects the notion that this disciplinary structuring of life is *all there is*. As such, we emphasise that our fieldwork is also rich with moments in which the 'calendrics of repayment', while seemingly all-consuming, fall apart, are suspended, or are so severely attenuated they can be quickly cast off.

Adkins' interest in the speculative begins from the observation that, while Lazzarato and others are focused upon the disciplinary structure organised around the repayment of debts, the credit sector is in fact less interested in repayment than it is in *payment*. That is, by focusing upon the defined, predictable profits of individuals regularly paying down their debts until the debts are repaid, key academic studies of debt have missed the key shift within the credit industry, namely that profits are drawn from *irregular* flows of money used to service debts that will never be repaid. Adkins cites the multiple products that allow debtors flexibility over their payments, noting that 'repayment schedules may, for example, be sped up, slowed down, suspended, delayed, rescheduled, reset, restarted, reassembled, reorganized and even reversed' (2016 :8). Adkins traces these changes to the dominance of the securitised debt industry, in which flows of payment are pooled, 'sliced up' in line with key attributes, then repackaged and sold on. In such markets what carries weight is less what is already known, such as repayment timeframes and rates of interest, than what is unpredictable: an unexpected default or full repayment.

The prevalence of such arrangements suggests that 'the calendrics of repayment', premised upon a defined future when the debt is paid off, are less important than a certain 'calculus' proper to the securitisation of debt, in which multiple futures are held in potentiality. The time of debt, ultimately, is subject to constant and ongoing creativity and activity as multiple futures are considered, gambled upon and traded. In this time: 'futures therefore do not unfold from the present, but the present is remediated by futures which have not yet – and may never – arrive' (Adkins, 2016: 10).

As both Miranda Joseph (2014) and Martijn Konings (2015; 2018) have noted, such attempts to engage with the role played by speculative practices in the field of money and debt runs against 'mainstream' thinking within the social sciences, which remain dominated by two beliefs. The first is that debt, and money are necessarily destructive of intimate and communal relationships (Taylor, 2002 cited in Joseph, 2014: 3-4), accounts often sown with a romanticisation of working-class communities in which an aversion to debt was a point of pride. Both academic and journalistic reports of the current rise of household debt have foregrounded the experiences of shame and guilt and the isolating effects of debt as confirmation of this direct and undistorted relationship. The second is that the 'financialisation' of everyday life, in which 'fictitious capital' colonises and distorts an increasing range of practices and objects, represents a dangerous twisting of the 'true value' of money and debt. Such 'Polanyian' perspectives, Konings argues, have become particularly prevalent in the post-financial crisis era as part of calls for increased regulation of the speculative fictions of the financial sector. Such critiques, however, lead to a monetary 'foundationalism' that is at odds with the speculative practices that animate the operation of money and debt in the everyday (Konings, 2018: 24).

In both cases, Adkins' emphasis upon the centrality of the speculative shows the limits – and, moreover, the continual disruptions to – such beliefs. The importance for the social sciences in engaging with the speculative is shown by the fact that 'speculative time' is not only a matter for the securitised debt industry and the credit sector. Given the proliferation of products shaped in the image of this 'calculus', Adkins notes the significant challenge this reorganised temporality poses for the gendered subject of household debt: the woman who is engaged in household budgeting as part of responsibility for the home (Adkins, 2017: 453).

For the relationships we discussed above, it is the importance of speculative practices in managing or disrupting the forms of 'being together' forged through the calendrics of repayment that is of particular importance. Our participants' accounts indicate how credit products promise to *break these constraints*; they offer a moment outside a relationship defined by restriction. To focus only upon how lives are bent to the rhythms of repayment schedules, and how these are attested in the emotional spaces of the everyday, is to miss the multiple moments in which time is experienced in other ways.

Speculative moments: suspending and interrupting disciplinary time

While writing this chapter, the largest high-street provider of hire-purchase goods in the United Kingdom, Brighthouse,[13] launched a marketing campaign entitled 'Choose your moments', illustrated by a woman wearing a virtual reality headset. Facing out from a shop window onto a busy shopping street, the image fills this 'moment' with endless promise; that the borrower can, for this moment, fully escape the life they are carrying with them.

Such observations lead one to consider the potential lending interface the consumer carries with them at all times. While the transformations promised by mobile borrowing remain, for the time being, a site for specular science fiction rather than everyday reality (Seigworth, 2016), our interviews nonetheless illustrate the ways in which mobile banking provides an irruptive presence. As Amy notes:

> "I've got the Barclays banking app and all the time they're saying, get this overdraft of £700 or get this loan for this much, and it's like tempting you." (Amy)

It is, of course, only a short step from here to a banking app that knows where you are, and can calibrate such offers to purchases you might be considering in that moment.

It is important to emphasise in both these examples that credit is not sold as a considered decision, but rather, in a specific embodied moment, as an opportunity to *break out of* a life defined by restriction and stability. What the marketing of credit understands better than the sociologist is the desire to act outside of the 'calendrics of repayment', in particular where those rhythms are experienced as prohibiting a relationship from finding its true happiness and fulfilment, or is inhibiting the desires and capacities of one's children. When life is defined by restriction, by a sense that life is not being lived, it is in such momentary decisions that individuals and couples can feel positive and hopeful about their world.

One frequently cited frustration for advisers is that even clients who recognise the advice and stay within a budget will embark upon expenditure that is, seemingly, entirely unnecessary. A variant of this phenomenon has a name, one that displays gendered assumptions around debt, namely 'the lipstick effect', depicting the upsurge in small luxuries at the expense of deferrable items during an economic downturn (Nickolds, quoted in Butler, 2017).

The two most evocative examples of this frustration correspond to spending on holidays and home entertainment. Leslie described attending court with a woman, only to find that, despite her severely limited budget, she had taken out a television on hire purchase.

> "I said, 'You know your TV that you've got,' I said, 'You'll pay for that for the next two years'. She said, 'Yeah, yeah, yeah, and it's so much a week', but on a weekly basis it didn't seem like very much. I said, 'You do realise that that's gonna be £2,700 by the time you have paid for it?' I said, 'that's exactly the amount of your rent arrears,' and I said, 'and to be honest,' I said, because they'd already got three TVs in the house, I said, 'you don't really need it'. And you know, I mean, we couldn't deal with it there and then because it was all very kind of last minute." (Leslie, Manager of a debt advice service)

What this statement shows is the need for the adviser, and the advice process, to tie expenditure to the rhythms of debt and the financial statement. Expenditure on the television is made meaningful by equating it with the level of rent arrears at stake in the repossession court process. Yet one can imagine that, for the client, the two were entirely separate. The television was purchased in a moment in which she wanted to do something special for her children, despite the household already having several televisions.

In a similar manner, Amy regretted taking a holiday, for which they were still paying, but noted the importance of the holiday for maintaining the image of a functioning family.

> "That's why I ended up running up loads of debt. I had completely cleared my credit card the year before and I ended up having to run it up again to keep saving to go for this holiday. Which we probably shouldn't have booked. But my mum and dad said my [children] were going, a couple of years before we went. They made the plan before we split up." (Amy)

What links these areas of spending is that they are part of an *escape* from a life characterised by debt repayments. Home entertainment systems, Davey (2018) argues, allow debtors to manage the difficulties of 'being in debt'. Sinking into a sofa and immersing oneself within a soundscape or the fantasy world of a computer game allows individuals to create a momentary world in which there are no bailiffs' letters, no phone calls, no realisation that the future is rapidly contracting. The promise offered by Brighthouse's 'moment' is that it will be one of *not* being defined by the disciplinary rhythms of debt.

Against the dominant characterisations of such practices within the social sciences as imaginary, irrelevant or betraying a working-class ethic of restraint, we argue that these forms of spending are important moments in managing relationships, and further that a relationship solely composed by the time of discipline would be unbearable. Each interview articulates the need for such momentary release, beyond the abstract hope of a distant future, for a relationship to stay together and the need to show children that the family is *more than* their being beholden and subjected to discipline. Such moments enact a suspension of the cruel optimism described by Berlant (2011), where the practices necessary for maintaining an attachment to a future 'good life' are wearing the family down in the present.

It is interesting in this respect to raise our final participant, Stuart, who had for a long period operated directly against the disciplinary structures established in the moral economy of debt. For Stuart, debt was a game being played by the credit industry. If they were going to speculate upon scaring him into paying, he was going to speculate upon them not being able to:

Stuart:	After a while, there's a funny thing that happens – if you owe the bank money they'll sell it on, won't they … and then your debt becomes a sort of traded commodity. It becomes a bit more removed, less like a standard borrowing and lending transaction and becomes less of an obligation. And then you start thinking, 'Why should I'? You're getting letters from people who use stronger tactics than the bank – more threatening language. They know that by using more aggressive tactics, they'll get the money. They're gambling too.
LD:	What happened when you got a letter?
Stuart:	Binned it. Occasionally I'd open it just out of curiosity.

While the interviewees above demarcated their relationships in terms of budgeting practices, Stuart's previous relationship was characterised by an ecstatic overspending on credit cards. He and his partner "egged each other on. We were both reckless. But when you get in debt, one option is to go mental. If you go mental, you can't pay it back."

Stuart's previous life presents the flipside of the speculation dynamic described by Konings. While the credit industry embarks upon its own form of speculation, enticing and inviting the subject to privilege a moment of escape in which debts do not matter, it also demands, in the time that follows, a contrary allegiance to the reality of debts (Konings, 2018). It demands that the debtor, as Amy does, take responsibility for fitting these moments into the broader narrative of life. Yet Stuart's account presents the fragility of this arrangement; by staying within the plasticity of value, he was able to float upon a life of immanent, rapid, ecstatic change.

In seeking a critique of speculation, 'heterodox' economics and the social sciences insist that we hold to a 'true' value of debt that is misshaped and misrepresented in the neoliberal valuation of free, unanchored speculation. Yet in so doing we miss the ways in which the subject practises, and is drawn into, their own forms of speculative imagination and decision making, and in which a politics might be drawn from *disrupting* the contrary movement; the fragile demand made by the credit sector to fully submit current actions to previous speculation.

The 'austere creditor' and the deficit debtor

Yet there is another way in which the changing dynamics of debt in the United Kingdom demand that we must go beyond the 'calendrics of repayment'. As identified in our interviews with those in the debt advice sector, there is another line along which the disciplinary time of indebtedness is breaking down, namely the increasing number of debtors with 'deficit' budgets for whom the only debt 'solution' is repeated insolvency.

With the shift to 'priority' debts, the time of debt is increasingly *not* defined by the credit industry. That is, in place of credit companies, who have taken a risk upon a borrower in the calculation of future payment flows, the everyday of indebtedness is increasingly defined by the 'austere creditor': those recouping statutory and other essential liabilities, principally council tax and rent. These are creditors that have a lesser investment in producing a disciplined subject, given the legal and other powers (eviction, committal, removal of regular energy supply, removal of goods) at their disposal.

On the side of the debtor, the 'deficit debtor', as we have termed the emergent subject at the sharp end of benefit cuts and insecure work, poses a distinct challenge to the forces of discipline within the advice sector. Income is simply too unstable and too low for debtors to be able to guarantee that they can meet essential outgoings. (These outgoings themselves rose considerably over the course of our research with the falling value of the pound.) Inasmuch as the sector is reliant upon producing, through a balanced budget sheet, a client who can take their life forwards on a stable grounding, the impossibility of making income meet expenditure takes from the adviser the belief that they can relieve the stress of living with mounting debts, as well as undermining their form of communication with creditors.

Within the schema set by Lazzarato (2012: 51), the levels of poverty faced by those in insecure work or claiming benefits at stagnating levels correspond to his description of a system that places individuals in ongoing deficit to society and the state. They are faced with taking the responsibility for life entirely on their own shoulders, without the support and sympathy of a benevolent welfare state. Yet the ensuing observation, namely that these individuals must be submitted to an even tighter net of discipline and self-regulation, does not fit with the collapse of the disciplinary structure oriented around the 'calendrics of repayment'. For those living in 'deficit time', the only fixed horizon is that of insolvency. The possibilities of bailiffs arriving at one's door or of losing one's home exist in an ever more attenuated relationship to one's own financial rhythms.

It is important to note that, in specific ways, 'deficit time' is also punctuated by 'speculative time'. Amid these changes, two areas of credit have shown remarkable stability and growth: hire purchase agreements and guarantor loans. These are both forms of credit sold to individuals with 'bad credit', as they are secured not on the hope of future income, but rather on the goods themselves or the borrower's relationships with friends and family. Their resilience indicates that, when a future of stable payments is no longer possible, borrowers must be flexible and creative beyond standard forms of debt repayment. The question of debt is as much 'Can I afford this based on my projected future earnings?', as 'What role will this relationship play in my future?', or 'What objects in my life could I do without actually owning?'.

Considering the 'value' of debt, we can again see the need to challenge the assumption that there is any originary 'true value' rendered 'elastic' by the creative, speculative practices which would stretch and distort the true value of a debt (or debtor). As Konings argues, the debtor *lives with* 'plasticity', with fluctuating futures and connections that are running across, or resonating with, the offers and promises of the lending sector.

'Choose your moments': despite terrible living conditions, despite an ongoing eviction process, you might be walking past a shop window, and be able to hold on to the brightest possible future for long enough to walk in and discuss taking on a new television. Credit sells the disciplined debtor a promise to break out of the calendrics of repayment. But, increasingly, in those creative spaces of 'credit for people with bad credit', it resonates also with the subject for whom the temporal dynamics of discipline have already broken down.

Conclusion

What is often missed in accounts of debt are the articulations of hope, regret and love that motivate spending decisions. In being critical of the moralising accounts of profligate spending, of narratives of 'benefit cheats' and 'scroungers' enjoying the fruits of their irresponsibility, accounts become wedded to an idea of the 'noble poor' that sidelines the very practices that are central to ways of interpreting and dealing with debt and to negotiating intimate and familial relationships in times of difficulty.

As Miranda Joseph (2014: 3-4) argues, this is linked to a certain romantic valuation of working-class rejection of debt practices, one that harks to there being a 'true value' of indebtedness muddied by the speculation practices of the debt industry (Joseph, 2014: 2). Speculative practices are seen as destructive inasmuch as the value of a debt travels so far from the initial debt that its meaning becomes over-stretched.

In this chapter, we have followed particular critiques of the over-emphasis upon discipline in the structuring of indebted life. While we noted, with reference to Lauren Berlant, the destructive nature of an attachment to disciplinary time, drawing on Viviana Zelizer, we recognised also the generativity of disciplinary practices, and their role in demarcating the form of a relationship.

Our core argument, however, takes its cue from the work of Lisa Adkins. Where the credit industry and individual lives are in symbiotic relation, bouncing off and resonating with each other, is in the *disruption* of the disciplinary structuring of life. When Brighthouse urges passers-by to 'choose their moment', it recognises two things. First, debtors will make acquisitive decisions based on a desire to break out, for a moment, of the restrictive life framed by debt repayment, to interrupt the 'calendrics of repayment', which are experienced as a burden and as precisely what is holding back a relationship or hopes for one's children. And second, for large numbers of people, there is no future of being debt free, and the only available credit is that formed through speculating upon other zones of life, such as objects themselves (through hire purchase agreements) or relationships with friends and family (through guarantor loans).

As Martijn Konings argues, there is no 'true value' of money or debt, one that would be rendered 'elastic' by the speculative fictions of the financial sector. The need to engage with the 'plasticity' of value is displayed by the fact that debtors already live with and manage the various futures promised by credit, as well as the demands to adhere to previous speculative actions.

Acknowledgements

This work was made possible by a University of Brighton Rising Stars Award and by the Leverhulme Trust under Grant Number ECF-2016-518. We extend our warmest gratitude and best wishes to our participants who gave their experiences and reflections in such a thoughtful and generous manner.

Notes

1 Namely 200bn of unsecured household debt (Inman et al, 2017) and an expected 40bn in car loans borrowed in 2017 alone (Inman and Treanor, 2017).

[2] These were conducted as part of two separate projects. The first is the Leverhulme-funded Early Career Fellowship, for Samuel Kirwan. The second is the project funding by the University of Brighton and led by Leila Dawney and Rosie Walker.

[3] The Provident is a provider of high-cost credit and is the best known 'doorstep lender' in the United Kingdom. A different interpretation of these poor collection rates was that the Provident's attempt to 'pivot' away, in response to greater regulation of high-cost credit, from standard doorstep collection practices (see McFall, 2016), had failed.

[4] Universal Credit (UC) has been 'rolled out' first in certain areas, before a gradual rollout nationwide. The plan to have all areas fully crossing over to UC by 2020 has been held back first by IT delays and subsequently by significant political and popular opposition to the new system.

[5] All names used in the chapter are pseudonyms.

[6] One further consequence is the confusing of 'priority' and 'non-priority', of which two key examples are benefit overpayments and guarantor loans. While a benefit payment would not previously have been considered a 'priority', new powers of collection afforded to the government creditors in 2014 and the rolling together of benefits into Universal Credit, administered by a single agency with far greater powers of deduction, have led to a heightened risk of benefit overpayment recoupment having a significant material impact on everyday finances (Gustaffson, 2017). The primary provider of guarantor loans in the UK is Amigo, offering 'loans for people with bad credit' (Amigo Loans, 2018). While within the field of consumer credit, the presence of a guarantor escalates the seriousness of a guarantor loan; they are nonetheless sold as a form of 'financial inclusion' (DebtCamel, 2017).

[7] Bailiffs are now known as 'enforcement agents'. While changes to bailiff practice introduced in 2014 aimed to restrict harassment by bailiffs, they have resulted in a system in which local authority debtors in particular are hit with rapidly escalating fees.

[8] Each of these examples is drawn from the growing clutch of voices under the banner of 'financial education', from Money Saving Expert's 'three questions' to the lessons and press releases put out by the Money Advice Service.

[9] We focus in this chapter on the CFS. Its successor, being rolled out across the summer of 2017, is the Standard Financial Statement (SFS), which includes a permitted amount for 'savings'. While our interviewees approved of this development, they noted that the vast majority of their clients would have nothing left over to save.

[10] In addition to benefit 'sanctions' for Jobseeker's Allowance, the rollout of Universal Credit, and the six-week waiting time for the first payment, has provided a considerable hardship for claimants.

[11] Zelizer (2000: 818) examines how, in intimate relationships in which men's sexual companionship and staying overnight was explicitly dependent upon them contributing financially to the household, female partners sought to set 'clear distinguishing markers' to differentiate their relationship from that between a sex-worker and client.

[12] Mirroring the more respectable image for bailiffs heralded by the 2014 reforms, bailiff practice has become a significant site of television entertainment. Twin programmes on BBC1 and Channel 5, 'The sheriffs are coming' (2012-present) and 'Can't pay, we'll take it away' (2014-present), follow high court enforcement agents as they execute high court orders to enforce county court judgements. While these concern debts between private parties, typically missold goods or private rent

arrears, the programmes draw their force from presenting a Manichean world of responsible, stable creditors (conducting staged interviews in their homes on the stress and anxiety of being owed money) and irresponsible, chaotic debtors (filmed running from the cameras, shouting, covering their faces), with enforcement agents as the arbiters reluctantly upholding the moral economy of debt relations.

13 Given their importance in the everyday management of money and debt, it is interesting that Brighthouse has received very little attention in academic literature. Formerly known as 'Crazy George's', the brand introduced the 'radical' notion, introduced from America, of providing goods through rent-to-own agreements to those with poor credit histories (Midgley, 1994).

References

Adkins, L. (2016) 'Speculative Futures in the Time of Debt', *0*, 1-16. https://doi.org/10.1111/1467-954X.12442

Allon, F. (2015) 'Everyday Leverage, or Leveraging the Everyday', *Cultural Studies*, 29(5-6), 687-706.

Amigo Loans (2018) 'Guarantor Loans for People with Bad Credit' [Webpage]. Retrieved 17 December 2018, from: https://www.amigoloans.co.uk/

Atfield, G., Lindley, R. and Orton, M. (2016) 'Living With Debt After Advice: A Longitudinal Study of People on Low Incomes'. Available at: https://warwick.ac.uk/fac/soc/ier/publications/2016/atfield_et_al_2016_fp.pdf

Berlant, L. (2011) *Cruel Optimism*. Durham, NC: Duke University Press.

Bolton, S. (2017) 'Points of View', *Quarterly Account*, 44, 28.

Brazier, J. (2017) '*"Debt strikes back" or "The Return of the Regulator"?*'. Presentation at the University of Liverpool, Institute for Risk and Uncertainty. Available at: https://www.bankofengland.co.uk/speech/2017/debt-strikes-back-or-return-of-the-regulator

Butler, S. (2017) '"The lipstick effect": Britons Treat Themselves as Budgets Tighten', *The Guardian*, 15 July. Available at: https://www.theguardian.com/business/2017/jul/15/the-lipstick-effect-britons-treat-themselves-as-budgets-tighten

Dawney, L., Kirwan, S. and Walker, R. (2018) 'The Intimate Spaces of Debt: Love, Freedom and Entanglement in Indebted Lives', *Geoforum*, https://doi.org/10.1016/j.geoforum.2018.11.006

Deville, J. (2015) *Lived Economies of Default: Consumer Credit, Debt Collection and the Capture of Affect*. London: Routledge.

Deville, J. and van der Velden, L. (2015) 'Seeing the Invisible Algorthithm: The Practical Politics of Tracking the Credit Trackers' in *Algorithmic Life: Calculative Devices in the Age of Big Data*. L. Amoore and V. Piotukh (eds). London: Routledge.

Elliot, L. (2017) 'UK's Borrowing Binge is Worrying the Bank of England', *The Guardian*, 27 March 2017. Available at: https://www.theguardian.com/business/2017/mar/27/uks-borrowing-binge-is-worrying-the-bank-of-england

Graeber, D. (2011) *Debt: The First Five Thousand Years*. New York, NY: Melville House.

Gustaffson, J. (2017) 'Universal Credit and Debt – turning non-priority into priority', *Quarterly Account*, 45, 14-17.

Guyer, J.I. (2012) 'Obligation, Binding, Debt and Responsibility: Provocations About Temporality From Two New Sources', *Social Anthropology*, 20(4), 491–501, https://doi.org/10.1111/j.1469-8676.2012.00217.x

Inman, P. (2017) 'Britain's Growing Debt Problem Demands a Fresh Set of Eyes'. *The Guardian*, 24 September 2017. Available at: https://www.theguardian.com/money/2017/sep/24/britains-growing-debt-problem-obr-figures-economy-in-depth-examination

Inman, P. and Treanor, J. (2017) 'Britain's Debt TimeBomb: FCA Urges Action Over £200bn Crisis'. *The Guardian*, 18 September 2017. Available at: https://www.theguardian.com/business/2017/sep/18/britain-debt-timebomb-fca-chief-crisis

Inman, P., Brignall, M. and Monaghan, A. (2017) 'Are Cheap Car Loans the Vehicle Taking us to the Next Financial crash?'. *The Guardian*, 10 June. Available at: https://www.theguardian.com/business/2017/jun/10/car-loans-personal-contract-plans-vehicle-financial-crisis-pcp

Jasarevic, L. (2014), 'Speculative Technologies: Debt, Love and Divination in a Transnationalizing Market', *Women's Studies Quarterly*, 42 (1–2): 261-77.

Joseph, M. (2014) *Debt to Society: Accounting for Life Under Capitalism*. Minneapolis, MN: University of Minnesota Press.

Keen, S. (2017) *Can We Avoid Another Financial Crisis?* Cambridge: Polity.

Kirwan, S. (2018) 'On "Those Who Shout the Loudest": Debt Advice and the Work of Disrupting Attachments', *Geoforum*. https://doi.org/10.1016/j.geoforum.2018.05.005

Konings, M. (2015) *The Emotional Logic of Capitalism: What Progressives have Missed*. Stanford, CA: Stanford University Press.

Konings, M. (2018) *Capital and Time: For a New Critique of Neoliberal Reason*. Stanford, CA: Stanford University Press.

Lazzarato, M. (2012) *The Making of The Indebted Man*. South Pasadena, CA: Semiotext(e).

Lazzarato, M. (2013) *Governing Through Debt*. South Pasadena, CA: Semiotext(e).

McFall, L. (2016) 'What's in a Name: Provident, the People's Bank and the Regulation of Brand Identity', in I. Ertürk and D. Gabor (eds) *The Routledge Companion to Banking Regulation and Reform*. London: Routledge.

Midgley, D. (1994) 'UK: Thorn EMI's Fissile Future' in *Management Today,* 1 August 1994, available at: https://www.managementtoday.co.uk/uk-thorn-emis-fissile-future/article/409882

Montgomerie, J. (2013) 'Household Debt: The Silent Dimension of the Financial Crisis', available at: http://speri.dept.shef.ac.uk/2013/08/28/household-debt-silent-dimension-financial-crisis/

Ramsay, I. (2009) '"Wannabe WAGS" and "Credit Binges": The Constructions of Overindebtedness in the UK"', in J. Niemi, I. Ramsay, and W. Whitford (eds), *Consumer Credit, Debt and Bankruptcy: Comparative and International Perspectives*. Oxford: Hart Publishing, pp. 75-90.

Seigworth, G. (2016) 'Wearing the World Like a Debt Garment: Interface, Affect, and Gesture', *Ephemera*, 16(4), 15-31.

Soederberg, S. (2014) *Debtfare States and the Poverty Industry: Money, Discipline and the Surplus*. London: Routledge.

Standing, G. (2011) *The Precariat: The New Dangerous Class*. London: Bloomsbury Academic.

StepChange (2017) *The High Cost of Credit* [Report]. Available at: https://www.stepchange.org/Portals/0/documents/Reports/stepchange-affordable-credit-discussion-paper-july2017.pdf

The Economist (2017) 'For The First Time Since The Crisis, More Britons Are Going Bust', available at: https://www.economist.com/news/britain/21727077-credit-card-borrowing-has-soared-households-are-squeezed-growing-number-cant-keep-up

Van Rooyen, M. (2017) 'Points of View', *Quarterly Account*. 47, 30.

Walker, C., Hanna, P., Cunningham, L. and Ambrose, P. (2015) 'Parasitic Encounters in Debt: The UK Mainstream Credit Industry', *Theory & Psychology*, *25*(2), 239-56. https://doi.org/10.1177/0959354315574929.

Zelizer, V. (2000) 'The Purchase of Intimacy', *Law and Social Inquiry* 25(3), 817-48. https://doi.org/10.1111/j.1747-4469.2000.tb00162.x

6

Digital subprime: tracking the credit trackers

Joe Deville

> Sure, there is money in credit. But there is so much more growing besides. (Maurer, 2014: 517)

This chapter introduces a particularly ragged edge of debt involving companies seeking to exploit sets of social and technical relations that often, on the face of it, appear to bear quite little connection to finance. I call this assortment of socio-economic practices 'digital subprime'. In introducing this phenomenon, I hope to provide a window into how a small but expanding set of startup businesses, in competition with both each other and the wider credit market, are attempting to refashion monetary ontologies, and in particular the relationship between money and credit.

In the study of money and credit, there is, as Bill Maurer notes in the opening quote, now something perhaps a little quaint about dwelling on their interdependence – that, on the one hand, all money is dependent on relations of credit and, on the other, that there is money to be made in and from credit. This mutually reinforcing relationship is of course not unimportant. Given the degree to which recent histories have been twisted around the relations and obligations of debt, it is hopefully no longer necessary to outline in too much detail its impact on a variety of registers of contemporary life, ranging across the most intimate and embodied to the most global and abstract. Suffice it to say that, alongside their self-evident role in amplifying a diversity of forms of material deprivation and, for far fewer, profit, relations of credit and debt are: pervasive and utterly everyday (Allon, 2010; Deville and Seigworth, 2015; Langley, 2008); powerful, historically deep-rooted and far reaching (Graeber, 2011; Lazzarato, 2012), playing a direct role in destabilising nation states and democratic processes (as recent Greek history has vividly demonstrated; see also Streeck (2011)), undeniably implicated in the amplification of a range of kinds uncertainty and anguish (Davies et al, 2015; Fitch et al, 2011) as well as cruelly misdirected optimism (Berlant, 2011), at least partly responsible for the routine invocation of particular modes of individualised, entrepreneurial subjectivity (Langley, 2008; Marron, 2009), while at the same time, in part through the quasi-alchemy of securitisation and leverage (Allon, 2015a; Montgomerie, 2009), exacerbating social cleavages of various kinds.[1] It is through all these manifestations of debt, and many others besides, that money asserts not just its relevance to experience and social conduct, but its ability to in many cases radically transform life's quality and in some cases its liveability. Simultaneously, modern money is critically dependent on and feeds off a myriad of relations and credit-like social obligations (Allon, 2015b; Grossberg et al, 2014; Ingham, 2004). These are then variously transformed, to a degree via technologies of commensuration, into the relations of credit that shape a myriad of monetary ontologies.[2]

The quaintness Maurer identifies stems from the fact that an overly tight focus on the entrenched relations of money and credit carries the risk of missing the diversity of other practices, devices and processes that are increasingly orbiting around and meshed into contemporary forms of money and that allow them to flourish, including those associated with consumer credit, the focus of this chapter (see also Allon, 2015b, 2015c). There are the infrastructures of payment transfer, whose management, and in particular the management of the streams of data involved, can become a substantial source of profit in its own right (Maurer, 2012a, 2012b), as well as the related payment card industry (Deville, 2013b; Stearns, 2011; Swartz, 2014), infrastructures of cash dispensing (Bátiz-Lazo et al, 2014; Bátiz-Lazo and Reid, 2011), and technologies and techniques associated with the management of credit risk and default, whether on the side of the consumer (Langley, 2014) or the organisation (Deville, 2015b; Lazarus, 2013b; Ossandón, 2014; Poon, 2007, 2009). One could even extend the net to more ephemeral practices, such as the governmental attempts to nurture particular kinds of educated, financially aware monetary citizens (Arthur, 2012; Lazarus, 2013a, 2015; Marron, 2014). Money is self-evidently a social relation. However, it is too easy to make assumptions about what this relation might consist of; money is instead a rather ambiguous assemblage (Allon, 2015b, 2015c).

This chapter uses digital subprime as a way of teasing out some of these relations and showing the surprising sets of actors that are put into dialogue. It begins with an overview of some of digital subprime's key features, moves on to look at some of the methodological challenges involved in studying it, before examining some of the specific forms of data that organisations in this domain may be gathering and could gather in future. As I will go on to discuss, the analysis thus rests in part on a speculative approach, concerned above all with mapping a terrain of possibility.

Digital subprime

Digital subprime is an expanding, global phenomenon, encompassing new and forthcoming ventures spread over a number of countries in Western and Eastern Europe, in Northern, Central and Southern America, as well as in South Africa, Asia Pacific and Australia.

While being broadly concerned with the redefinition of conventional credit scoring practices for online lending, the term encapsulates three more specific interlinked tendencies: first, offering loans that are short term and high cost – what are sometimes referred to as payday loans – with a customer base assumed to have poor or non-existent credit histories; second, the reengineering of forms of online social connectivity and influence-based assessment to determine credit-worthiness; and third, the reengineering of forms of data mining and algorithmic analysis. In this sense, digital subprime can be seen as transferring to the field of credit scoring sets of 'big data' techniques and logics most commonly associated with online marketing but also now inserted into an increasingly diverse set of practices, as far afield as online dating (Mackinnon, 2016), tracing terrorist payment networks (De Goede, 2012) and librarianship (van Otterlo, 2016).

With digital subprime, analogous techniques are used to either supplement third party credit ratings, or to replace them altogether. This is at least partly because, for companies targeting subprime or near-prime borrowers, conventional credit records may be particularly unhelpful guides, given that the simple absence of credit data (a 'thin' credit file as it is often known in the industry) can translate into a poor credit score, while in many countries, credit scoring is not as extensive as in North America and many Western European countries.

The techniques of digital subprime involve collecting an array of information about past, present and future users. As well as information that might be gathered from existing databases, sometimes but by no means always including conventional credit scores, this may include data that users often unwittingly 'leak' about their identity and online behaviour, potentially collected using third-party online tracking devices, which are then used to help determine creditworthiness. What exactly is being collected in these processes and how tends to remain obscure. This may in turn be bolstered by data that users are incentivised to provide to creditors as they build up a relationship with them over time.

In the US, ZestFinance is perhaps the most prominent digital subprime company. It was set up by an ex-Google employee and the former Head of Subprime Credit Cards at Capital One. After initially focusing on providing the infrastructure for short-term lending websites it controlled (SpotLoan and Zestcash), in time it shifted its predominant focus to licensing its services to financial service providers. Recently, for example, it revealed a partnership with the lending arm of car manufacturer Ford, Ford Credit (BusinessWire, 2017). In a TEDx talk given early in the company's life, one of its two founders, Douglas Merrill,[3] provides a summary of the more specific promise that digital subprime companies see in online data:

> It turns out that there are hundreds of sources of data, trivially available on the net. And thousands if you include things like web-crawls etc. And if your view is that all data is credit data, you build a piece of mathematics, or in our case a whole bunch of mathematics, that consumes thousands of data points. And of those thousands many are missing, many are wrong, etc, but regardless you build a score. And suddenly you build a score that allows you to figure out people who are maybe not quite good enough to get a subprime credit card, but are a way better credit risk than the payday loan guys. So instead of offering them a 700% APR borrowing [sic], you can offer them something inbetween. (Merrill, 2012)

While the stated goals of digital subprime companies may differ from one another (whether or not, for instance, claiming that the use of such techniques translates into lower cost credit products), their work is underpinned by a shared promise: that the algorithmic processing of diverse data, potentially with no clear direct relation to an individual's past relationship with financial products, can provide predictive insight into both the identity of that individual and their propensity to behave in a certain manner.

This promise is one that has been highly successful in attracting investors. I will give just a few examples, of what is becoming an increasingly diffuse global marketplace. Let's start with ZestFinance. To date, it has received investments of likely well over $100m (both debt and equity), including from PayPal co-founder Peter Thiel, while also having run tests with a major unnamed US credit card provider and is expanding into China, helped most recently by presumably major, although undisclosed, investment by the Chinese search and web services company Baidu (Lippert, 2014; Lohr, 2015; Russell, 2016). In increasingly moving away from the business of lending directly to borrowers and instead offering its services to others, it mirrors one of its rivals Big Data Scoring, which '[works] with lenders of all kinds – some of the largest banks in the world, payday lenders, P2P lending platforms, microfinance providers, leasing companies, insurance providers, e-commerce platforms and telecoms' (Big Data Scoring, 2018). There is also Elevate Credit, reportedly recipients of $70m debt financing (Glasner, 2016), which has been similarly associated with a reliance on 'big data' in scoring potential borrowers, including drawing on information about users' social media accounts as part of its fraud prevention and credit-worthiness assessments (Adams, 2013; Loten, 2016; Yu et al, 2014). Elevate Credit also has a UK presence as the payday lender Sunny, where until recently it sat in competition with Wonga, a payday lender most commonly known for the controversies around its historically high interest rates (see the end of this paragraph). Wonga attracted early investment of over £70m (Moules, 2011) and expanded its interest to additional operations in Poland, South Africa and Spain, although in 2018 its UK business went into administration, (see 'The uncertain visibilities of algorithmic practice', below). A further global player is German-based Kreditech, which has raised at least $150m, with Thiel surfacing once more as an investor (Anon, 2015; Lunden, 2015, 2016). It has active operations in the Czech Republic, Mexico, Poland, Russia and Spain (Kreditech, 2018). Some notable if smaller members of the group are LenddoEFL, a company resulting from the merger of a Lenddo and Entrepreneurial Finance Lab and with main offices in Bermuda and Singapore, as well as UK- and US-based HelloSoda and LendUp, which operates in various US states. These aim to develop credit-scoring systems which variously combine data on borrowers from a variety of sources beyond just using conventional credit scores to determine credit-worthiness. For those operations that lend directly, the cost of the loans varies. US products tend to range between 250% and 700% APR, a range within which most Kreditech loans also find themselves, while Wonga's UK borrowers currently pay just over 1,500%.[4]

Problems of method

Digital subprime is a component of the credit industry that remains underexplored. The majority of insights in this area stem from broadly journalistic accounts (for example Jeffries, 2011; Lewis, 2011; Shaw, 2011; Pollock, 2012; White, 2012; Cookson and Moore, 2013; Morozov, 2013; Lippert, 2014; Lohr, 2015; Wilhelm, 2018), with some of the most detailed scholarly assessments of such practices being reports by advocacy organisations, focusing broadly on consumer protection issues (Mierzwinski and Chester, 2014; Yu et al, 2014).[5] Recent academic studies have, however, begun to explore the implications of these scoring practices more deeply. This includes their potential impact on how reputation and 'good' character are understood (Rosamond, 2016), how they newly delimit the 'value' of certain unbanked populations, thus instituting new forms of visibility and hence governability (Aitken, 2017), and the implications such techniques have for the regulation of credit scoring (Hurley and Adebayo, 2016).

The continued lack of detailed scrutiny of these practices is no doubt in part due to them presently occupying a niche socio-economic domain. Even if their reach is expanding, they remain a small part of the larger domain of payday lending and microfinance, itself a form of 'fringe finance' (Aitken, 2014). With digital subprime we are then perhaps at the fringes of the fringe.

Perhaps a more significant issue, however, is the double bind facing the researcher interested in such practices. First, there is the imperative not to become swept up by the hype around big data. As much as such techniques promise analytical power, and as much as this promise is drawn on by those looking to sell their analytical services, they can be readily implicated in the revelation of utterly spurious patterns (Boyd and Crawford, 2012). Moreover, as noted above, there is a tendency for online organisations seeking to harness the power of abundant data to rely to a greater or lesser extent on a range of third-party devices and services whose insights are then potentially combined, including with whatever data and analytics the organisation itself has access to. I will come onto the details of this in due course; for now, it is important to simply note that big data analytics in such cases is not a cohesive entity, but rather a highly heterogeneous exercise, involving a distributed combination of technologies and methods (Madsen, 2015; Marres, 2012). Before jumping to conclusions about their scope and power we should, as John Law and Evelyn Ruppert point out, try harder to attend to 'the lives and specificities of devices and data themselves' (Law and Ruppert, 2013: 10-11).

One of the challenges in doing so, however, relates to a second perhaps greater issue confronting researchers interested in the logics of big data analytics: the frequent and deliberately performed opacity of such techniques. As in many such domains, the precise techniques digital subprime companies employ are carefully guarded trade secrets. It is in the interests of the organisations producing these new forms of credit scoring to keep the details of how they are profiling potential borrowers from competitors, to the extent that it has been argued that this characteristic opacity poses significant consumer protection issues (Mierzwinski and Chester, 2014; Schmitz, 2014; Yu et al, 2014). This is a major barrier to understanding exactly what is being done with the data that is collected.

One response is to attempt to retrieve and analyse the sorts of data that digital subprime companies are themselves using, as Persis Yu, Jillian McLaughlin and Marina Levy (Yu et al, 2014) attempted to do in the US. In their case, this involved requesting and purchasing information from data brokers – these are organisations that combine data from various sources, including from the behaviour of individuals who are browsing online and are tracked as they move around different sites (more on this later), and then sell this information to third parties, including to digital subprime customers. Their conclusion was that such information, when compared with conventional credit data, was highly inaccurate. For instance, they looked at the data provided to them by the data broker Spokeo on 15 volunteers, which showed high levels of errors when it came to predictions about postal addresses, the identity of family members, and users' social profiles (see Figure 1).

While the authors of this study are quite right to draw attention to the consumer protection issues involved in making credit assessments using data usually utterly opaque to consumers themselves, I would not be so sure that, from the perspective of lenders, this is 'bad data' (Yu et al, 2014: 33). Not only does Spokeo in fact make good predictions in many of the categories – being right in a large majority of cases when it comes to quite intimate information such as income, home value, education, and occupation – but also wrong information, in isolation, may not in itself be a barrier to prediction. To reprise Merrill: '… And of those thousands [of data points] many are missing, many are wrong, etc, *but regardless you build a score*' (emphasis added). The point is not (necessarily) that such companies are unconcerned with accuracy, but that they *are* concerned first, with *combining* information from various sources as a way to make up for missing/inaccurate data and then, second, with building scores that they can then *test*. A score may be used not just to establish a threshold for excluding potentially unreliable debtors, but also as a benchmark, in which predicted borrower behaviour can be compared with how they behave once they are enrolled, as a basis for refining a score in due course.

Figure 1: Number of study participants (15 total) with mistakes in their data report, by category, using data from Spokeo

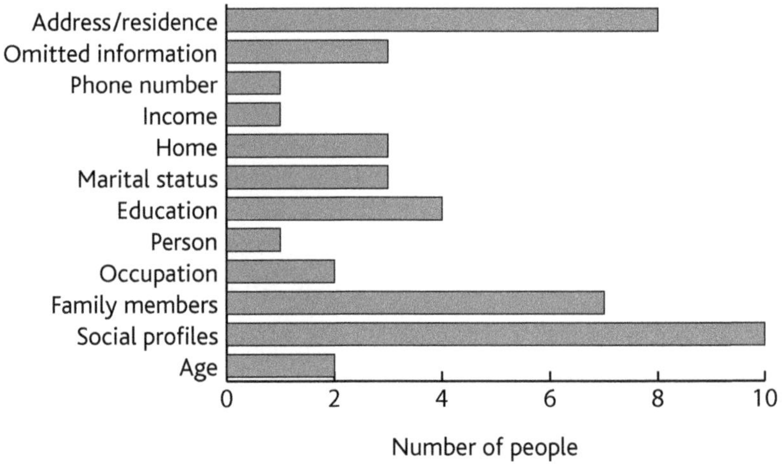

Note: This image has been redrawn. The data it draws on is used with permission of National Consumer Law Center (nclc.org).
Source: Yu, et al (2014: 19)

In the light of both the challenges facing researchers interested in such phenomena and the urgent need to better understand the forms of data that are being collected in such cases, the remainder of this chapter adopts an approach that is at once empirically grounded and speculative. On the one hand, rather than, as Yu et al (2014) do, looking at the tracking and analytical services that such companies could use, it looks at those they do use, using an approach to be explained in the next section. On the other, given the difficulty in knowing exactly what data provided by these third parties are actually fed into the credit scores themselves, the approach is, much like that of Yu et al (2014), speculative, involving outlining the contours of the landscape of data that might, but also might not, be being drawn upon. This form of what could be called 'speculative empiricism' can be seen as one way of responding to some of the problems of the empirical associated with the widespread proliferation of such techniques (Adkins and Lury, 2009; Burrows and Savage, 2014; Marres and Gerlitz, 2016; Ruppert, 2013; Savage and Burrows, 2007).[6] It is also hoped that in simply mapping the state of a rapidly evolving and unstable set of practices, where a new approach is created as quickly as another disappears, this research will be of future historical interest. In presenting this research, I draw in part on a project pursued collaboratively with Lonneke van der Velden.

The uncertain visibilities of algorithmic practice

One response to the opacities of online, big data algorithmic analytics is to seek out moments when what are usually unseen sets of practices become visible. Van der Velden and I have elsewhere explored in greater detail some of the various ways of detecting these often fleeting visibilities (Deville and van der Velden, 2016). I will draw on this for an example, as it provides a particularly helpful way into what may be at stake with such practices. It concerns the now defunct UK payday lender, Wonga. For many UK readers, no introduction to Wonga will be necessary. For others, some context: Wonga is often seen as having stood for everything that has been wrong with the British subprime lending sector (and here it should be noted that subprime lending practices in the UK have been far more restricted to unsecured lending than mortgage lending). Not only were its interest rates of over 5000% APR unusually high – although the introduction of a cap on interest rates in 2015 forced it rates down to just over 1,500% APR – many of its other practices came under scrutiny. Its adverts, featuring a cast of rubber-faced puppets, were deemed by a number of media commentators to be highly problematic because of their purported potential appeal to younger borrowers, while its debt collection practices and specifically its historic use of 'fake' external collections companies led to censure by the regulator (in this respect, however, they were by no means alone within the broader UK credit industry (Deville, 2015a)).

Likely as a result of a combination of these controversies and the impact of regulatory changes on this industry, Wonga, for some time the most prominent and largest payday lender in the UK, went into administration in August 2018. Elsewhere, Liz McFall and I have explored some of the roots of its failures of what we call 'market attachment' (McFall and Deville, 2018). What interests me for now, however, are the infrastructures that it put in place to attempt to secure that attachment. Wonga UK, like many other payday lending companies (whether or not using data scraping techniques), used a particular device to facilitate a borrower's enrolment into its products: two horizontal 'sliders'. The convention in the industry is for the top slider to control a variable loan amount and for the lower slider to control the term of the loan. Through these two devices, users select the characteristics of the loan to be applied for. In Wonga's case, in the early stages of our research in 2013, we noticed these sliders exhibiting some unusual behaviour. Their starting position was not constant. Through the conduct of various tests with the help of volunteers based in different locations, we observed that location – we presume determined via the proxy of a user's IP address – appeared to be a variable that shifted the position of the loan amount slider. We also observed a second significant variable: the browser used to access the site (for example, Firefox, Chrome, Safari, Internet Explorer). We also observed a final variable that had an effect: repeat visits. Over time, after returning to Wonga's homepage on multiple occasions, the starting position of the bottom slider, controlling repayment time, shifted downwards, making the default repayment time being shown shorter.

Although this behaviour was only short-lived (an aborted experiment, perhaps), it is important for what it stands for: first, an interest in collecting information about users from traces they reveal about themselves as they browse and, second, the ambition to use this information to treat potential customers differently.

Why were Wonga doing this? It is possible to speculate that it was doing two things. First, with the shifts in the loan amount displayed, it was potentially examining the efficacy of providing users with different starting 'offers', with higher risk debtors – as measured via this seemly peculiar data – being 'offered' smaller loans and lower risk debtors the reverse. The sliders in this instance were therefore potentially playing a part in Wonga's risk management procedures. Second, it is likely that the repayment time bar was being used as a marketing tool. It is a generic problem for e-commerce sites to convince borrowers to head down what is sometimes called 'the funnel' from browsing to purchase. Indeed, many of the tracking technologies to be discussed are concerned with this. From the perspective of Wonga, it is possible that a user who returns to a site repeatedly but does not proceed down the funnel is seen as in need of enticing. By pushing the repayment slider down over time, a hesitant user is being, in effect, offered an ever-cheaper credit product (given the interest rate is fixed, which is not the case on all such sites). After all, the end goal for most lenders is to elicit not the purchase of a product but an application for one. This, then, would be part of the process of managing the frictions and 'thresholds' that might prevent users applying for credit, very much along the lines explored by James Ash and colleagues (Ash et al, 2018).

It is rare for the results of the behind the scenes algorithmic apparatuses of digital subprime to surface into the domain of the visible in this way – indeed, in Wonga's case it turned out to be quite temporary. In the stead of other such examples are a few tantalising crumbs. In a conversation with the founder of a startup interested in such techniques, I was told that a well-placed source had in turn revealed that, for Wonga, a user's screen resolution had at one point turned out to be a particularly predictive variable. Or there is Douglas Merrill's throwaway revelation in an interview for Bloomberg that 'people who filled out the ZestFinance loan application in capital letters are riskier borrowers than those who write in upper- and lowercase'. Then a punchline: 'Merrill says he doesn't know why' (Lippert, 2014); grist to the mill for those who (prematurely) see the agnostic modelling techniques of big data analytics as marking the end of theory (for example, Anderson, 2008).

While there are certainly challenges in seeing exactly what such companies see, it is nonetheless possible to gain some quite rich insight into their particular 'modes of seeing' (Madsen, 2015), into *how* they see, that is. As will now be discussed, it is possible to clearly demonstrate that such companies routinely deploy an array of third-party tracking technologies to monitor visitors, in which there appears to be a consistent interest in trackers that provide rich real time information about their identity and behaviour. Through the repurposing of existing digital tools for social research (Rogers, 2013), we can begin to track these trackers.

Tracking the trackers

The repurposed tool in this case is called Ghostery.[7] It is a browser plugin designed to enable ordinary website users to understand exactly which third-party tracking technologies might be running in the background of a site and to prevent them from being loaded if desired. Ghostery is in turn put to work in this research via the 'Tracker Tracker',[8] a tool developed by the Digital Methods Initiative at the University of Amsterdam. The Tracker Tracker makes it possible to analyse large numbers of sites at once, using the Ghostery library (see van der Velden, 2014). The digital subprime project used it to analyse which tracking devices these sites are using and, potentially, how this changes over time (the latter is not the subject of this chapter). This involved an initial pilot study in 2013 with eight sites that for various reasons we suspected might be involved in the performance of credit assessments using unconventional data sources and a longer twelvemonth study in 2013-14 of a total of 23 sites.[9]

This analysis reveals, unsurprisingly, a plethora of advertising-focused trackers that are common in the domain of online consumption and information provision, used to monitor the mix of online advertising used to drive users to these sites.[10] Also, it is quite clear that, like many e-commerce companies, digital subprime sites maintain a strong interest in the detailed analysis of the performance of their sites. Take the trackers 'Optimizely', 'New Relic' and 'AB Tasty'. These appeared on a number of the sites in our sample[11] and can be used to test website design and efficiency. This includes providing clients with tools to conduct and analyse so-called 'A/B tests' on a user's experience of different site configurations and the efficiency of software running in the background. A/B tests are commonly concerned with tweaking a user's journey down the funnel towards whatever goal a website owner has – as noted, in the case of digital subprime this is most likely to be towards making an application for credit. It involves the explicit 'real life' testing of website configurations by dividing users into test and control groups and analysing the effectiveness of distinct arrangements and designs. Even if a relatively common practice in e-commerce spaces, this is clearly a crucial part of the mix of digital subprime's particular data-based provision of financial services. Finally, it is also unsurprising to observe the universal use of Google's suite of analytical tracker software. Google provides website owners with an extremely reliable, tried and tested range of real time information, including on information such as predicted location, referral site, device type being used, all of which could potentially be fed into an analysis of user behaviour. It should be noted here that 'real time' is crucial if such data are to be deployed in an algorithmically driven, rapid and automated credit scoring process.

Particularly useful is Ghostery's ability to show the way that many digital subprime sites use more specialised trackers involved in making real time predictions about the identity of users. One tracker of interest is ThreatMetrix, which was for a time deployed on Spotloan, the US based payday lending site set up by ZestFinance.[12] ThreatMetrix is above all a tool for its users to manage the risk of dealing with potentially anonymous online users. Specifically it guards against what it calls 'account takeover' – that is, potentially, an individual employing another user's details, perhaps stolen. Defending against this requires, as they describe it, 'a holistic view of device, identity and behavior of users' (ThreatMetrix, 2015). This is achieved through the construction of 'profiles or personas'. The method is to analyse the way people are interacting with the website in question, comparing 'normal and abnormal usage patterns to distinguish between returning customers and cybercriminals. Furthermore, our solution can detect if botnets are involved by looking at the behavior of activities on actual webpages' (ThreatMetrix, 2015).

So, in the service of screening out potentially risky customers, the tracker on the one hand focuses on trying to provide richer information on the user connecting to the website in question (based on referring to a set of existing and constantly updating data on how users 'normally' behave in particular situations) and, on the other, tries to detect anomalies between who the user is purporting to be and the device (for example, computer, tablet, phone) being used. From the perspective of the credit industry this interest in accessing a potentially 'truer' (sociotechnical) identity makes eminent sense: including in its credit scoring procedures, it, like many other financial services, has a longstanding concern with developing techniques to tie down the identity of its potential users (in its case, potential borrowers). Here we see this concern moving online, where the greater potential for anonymity exaggerates the challenge.

Helpfully, ThreatMetrix has provided some more detailed information on exactly how this is done. It includes working to profile users according to the IP address and ISP (internet service provider), including looking to establish the location of an individual, to establish whether they are connecting to the website using a proxy IP address and, if so, to find their 'true' IP address. It also involves a range of other mechanisms to begin to build up a richer profile of the user. These include (all taken from ThreatMetrix, n.d.):

- *Browser profiling*: 'the use of HTML, JavaScript, Flash or other methods available in the browser in order to profile a device. Information available through the browser includes, but is not limited to, screen resolution, browser type, clock time, time zone, languages and media supported'.
- *HTTP profiling*: 'extracting additional risk information communicated during the HTTP connection between the client and the server. Such information includes, but is not limited to the types of compression supported, proxy support and language.'
- *Operating system fingerprinting*: profiling connection characteristics in real-time 'to accurately determine the operating system, and often version, being used to establish the internet connection'.
- *TCP fingerprinting*: 'provides information about the type of connection being used, connection speeds, and for more sophisticated approaches, can be used to individually fingerprint devices based on the network protocol stack.'

It is not necessary to go into the details of these methods. The key point is simply that a range of what, to an average user, might seem to be highly mundane technical data are transformed into ways of beginning to tie down their identity. Identity in this case becomes partly composed of a range of traces that might be being leaked about the specific configuration of the device in question and the ways this device is establishing a connection to the website in question. The reason that this is particularly important for the present account is that it highlights the *potential* that mundane 'leaked' data affords for those who can access it when it comes to assessing the risk of potential borrowers. We also see screen resolution reappearing as a useful piece of data, the allegedly particularly predictive variable used by Wonga. We can at this point speculate a little further about what function it serves. Screen resolution reveals a lot about the precise type of device being used, while also being a data point whose availability is highly consistent, given that it is universally released in order for websites to scale correctly. When it comes to directly incorporating such data into credit assessment processes, it may be that identifying the device also functions as a useful proxy for information about the 'type' (for example, social class, age) of person applying for credit. As noted earlier, however, data analysts may claim to have little interest in hypothesising about such causal relations.

Wonga themselves in the period of our research used a tool that promises access to some similar information, called Maxymyser. One of the services it provides is again to enable users to optimise the specifics of website design. But it also provides real time information about the type of customers visiting a site. As the company writes in a report (subtitled 'Breaking down the key strategies to better identify & target top customers'), one of the services on offer is to build customer profiles for financial services and to provide information on 'client age range, geo location, single/multiple accounts, account age, account activity' (Maxymyser, 2014). In echoes of ThreatMetrix's method, data points used to inform such analyses include 'Software/hardware (e.g. browser type)', 'Device type', 'Time of visit (e.g. day, hour)', 'most recent conversion action' (in other words, the behaviour of a user on the site itself, potentially as they move towards making a financial purchase/application), and information about how the user arrived on the site ('Traffic source type' and 'referring URL').

Two other US-based sites, Spotloan and CashnetUSA, used the Quantcast tracker. Alongside delivering targeted advertising, one of the services Quantcast offers its clients is detailed information about its users. Alongside the familiar geographic and site behaviour information is the offer to US clients in particular of real time demographic predictions. Take, for instance, Quantcast's case study of the reviews and online booking service Yelp (see Figure 2). What it shows is how Quantcast, acting as a data broker, translates mundane online behaviour into concrete predictions about a range of variables, some of direct use to financial service providers. This includes variables as personal as income, education, and political leanings (as well as age and ethnicity, although under the Equal Credit Opportunity Act, US-based creditors are prohibited from using these as variables in their credit scoring processes (see Consumer Financial Protection Bureau, 2013)).

Quantcast also makes clear that in doing so it relies on the sheer extent of its tracking activities. Its selling point is the potential to turn its vast presence across a large range of sites mostly in its role as the deliverer of targeted advertising,[13] into predictions about the characteristics of its users. As they put it, 'We see the average US online user 600 [times] per month—that's equivalent to having coffee with your friend every hour. This intense visibility into online behavior patterns allows us to draw incredibly detailed profiles, even for small user groups' (Quantcast, 2015b). If such data were to be fed into a credit scoring algorithm – and once again, we remain in the domain of the speculative – then online consumption activities (broadly defined) would be becoming transformed into data points in a credit scoring algorithm, something that a user would unlikely to be aware of.

Part of what such speculative work does, then, is to show, first, the routine presence in this sector of tracking technologies at least designed to deliver this kind of information, and second, the kinds of data that

Figure 2: Yelp case study, using June 2015 data.

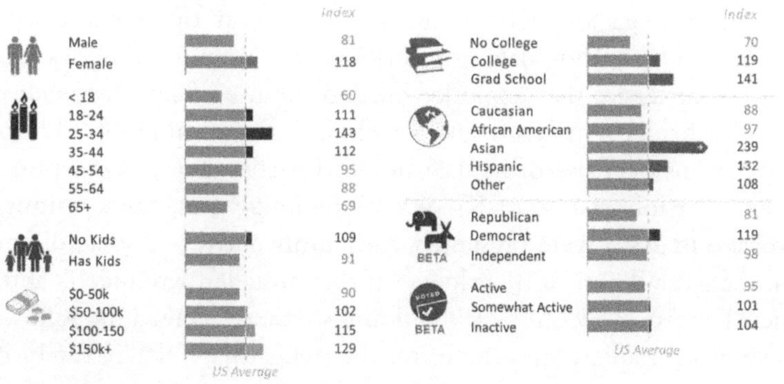

Note: This image has been recreated.
Source: Quantcast (2015a), www.quantcast.com.

it would be at least feasible to access and, potentially, start to integrate into credit assessment processes.

The promise of social ties

There is a further dimension to some such analytics: harnessing the information contained in an individual's social ties. Although using very similar principles to other digital subprime companies, Lenddo specialises in basing credit worthiness at least in part on a user's social networks (alongside other 'non-traditional data', including, it claims, 'telecom data', 'browser data', 'mobile data', 'e-commerce transaction data', 'psychometric data', 'form filling analytics' (Lenddo, 2017)). An interview with Lenddo's founder Jeff Stewart in 2014 gives some insight into the kind of data that it saw as of interest:

> What career profiles do your Facebook friends have? What products or restaurants do you (and your friends) Tweet about? … [S]ays Stewart: 'If you hang out with people who make a lot of money and pay their bills, then you are more likely statistically to do that'. (Balch, 2014)

As suggested by its recent merger with Entrepreneurial Finance Lab, Lenddo is increasingly focused on trying to sell its method and its software protocols to third parties. However, it did lend directly for its first four years of operation, up until 2015 (Balea, 2015). Then it looked to harness the power of social networks more explicitly, by compelling borrowers to obtain references from others in their social network – if the referee was judged positively, this would improve their credit-worthiness, as would taking out loans (Balea, 2015).

Both Wonga and Kreditech, meanwhile, at times expressed an interest in harvesting data from Facebook – although this was before the controversies that exploded around the use of similar techniques by Cambridge Analytica and Facebook's impositions of additional restrictions over use of its data by third parties. For instance, on the Polish version of one of Kreditech's identikit sites, users visiting its website in 2013 were presented with an incentive – a small discount on the overall cost of their loan – if they installed Kreditech's app on their Facebook account. When doing so, they received the following permission request (and thereafter the obligatory 'Okay?' Yes/No):

> Kredito24.pl would like to access your public profile, friend list, email address, custom friends lists, messages, News Feed,

> birthday, chat status, work history, status updates, checkins, education history, groups, hometown, interests, current city, photos, website, personal description, likes and your friends' birthdays, work histories, status updates, checkins, education histories, events, groups, hometowns, interests, current cities, photos, websites, personal descriptions and likes. (Kredito24.pl, 2013)

If granted, these permissions would have included access to data that might have significantly assisted in the enhancement of predictive capacity. This includes information that could be searched to help confirm the identity of a user, including birthday, hometown and location. It might also provide insight into information that could supplement or undermine the income level declared by a potential borrower: educational history, work history, as well as relationship details. Further, information such as an individual's 'likes', and indeed those of their friends, could potentially help build up a rich picture of an individual's characteristics to a far greater extent than Quantcast's by comparison rather rudimentary assessment of political preference. A very similar permissions request was at one point also to be found buried in Wonga's HTML code (Deville, 2013a). In fact, in some respects, the request was more intimately intrusive: alongside requesting 'likes', further permissions requested included the user's listed interests, games activity, religious and political views, any subscriptions they might have, and any groups the user was part of. Although a Facebook connection option was not active at the point in 2013 when this code was observed, it had been the year before, accompanied by the claim that connecting 'helps us to know you better. This will improve your chances of being approved for a loan' (Lewis, 2012).

Kreditech also scaled back its interest in Facebook data. By 2014 the request had changed to a request to view a user's 'public profile', without the offer of a discount. This shift is likely to have been in response to a pre-Cambridge Analytica clampdown by Facebook on the unjustified harvesting of data by third-party apps (Constine, 2015). For Wonga, meanwhile, perhaps its hesitation was due to an early and prescient recognition of the reputational risks involved. In 2012, for instance, a scandal blew up in Germany over a credit agency's plan to scrape just this kind of data (Hawley, 2012). What certainly remains, however, is the promise offered up to digital subprime companies by social media data: that individuals' intimate preferences and social behaviours as well as, potentially, their locations within wider networks of individuals, can be transformed into data for an assessment of creditworthiness (see also: Morozov, 2013).

Conclusion

It is tempting to be bleak in assessing digital subprime's significance, given the potential scope of its tracking activity. It has already been suggested that credit scoring practices represent a form of 'super-panopticism' (Burton, 2008; Leyshon and Thrift, 1999; drawing on Poster, 1995). This would make digital subprime, with its apparently deeper intrusions into the everyday, implicated in a kind of 'super-super-panopticism'.

At present, however, with reference to the digital subprime sites addressed in this chapter, that would be too strong a claim. This is in part because it may be that systems are being developed that use similar logics but that would put the kinds of surveillance being practiced by digital subprime sites in the shade. In particular, it has been revealed that the Chinese government, building on a series of pilot projects, has the ambition to develop a population-wide credit score, involving tracking a wide diversity of domains of everyday life and underpinned by intrusive enforcement and punishment mechanisms. The score would be assembled in part via enhanced data sharing between areas including 'public security, civil affairs, human resources and social security, natural resources, housing and urban construction, finance, banking, taxation, industry and commerce, security supervision, securities, science and technology and other such departments', and by extending its gaze potentially to individuals' online browsing and shopping habits (Anon, 2016; see also: Creemers, 2018; Denyer, 2016). But also, when it comes to digital subprime specifically, while a range of high level investors are being motivated to part with considerable sums to underpin its experiments, we need to know more about precisely how the data that are being accumulated about potential borrowers are transformed into concrete predictions and forms of value. Seeking to understand algorithmic calculation from the outside is likely to open up as many questions as answers. This chapter is thus in part an injunction to further research, while seeking to make a case for methods and approaches that look to map, as accurately as they can, the state of the terrain and the possibilities it might afford.

At the same time, what this exercise has shown are clear ambitions on the part of digital subprime organisations to reshape present and future ontologies of money and debt in their refashioning of credit scoring. Individuals are to be rendered creditworthy far less according to their demonstrable history with credit products and far more according to an assessment of a set of digital proxies of identity and behaviour, the latter of which may have only the loosest connection to credit and finance. Credit scoring thus appears as an alternately more personal and more abstract affair, sometimes turning its attention to the mundane affects and intimacies of contemporary online life, composed of networks of loose social connections and casually expressed preferences of various sorts (the 'like', most paradigmatically), while, in other moments, recomposing behavioural tendencies through sets of technical data that would seem to most – incorrectly it turns out – to be highly impersonal.

Digital subprime clearly, then, adds to that ever-longer list of industries whose success is predicated on highly dispersed mechanisms of value creation, involving turning a profit out of diverse and only tangentially related data, provided by individuals and ostensibly accessible for 'free' (see Allon, 2015b). What is perhaps more interesting though is what it adds to the potential futures of money. Money as relation as credit as consumer credit has just maybe found a way to become yet more tightly entangled in the threads of daily life, to an extent that would be previously unfathomable. This is a monetary future where so-called financialisation extends to a propensity to use one browser or another, or to use devices with a particular screen size, or to CAPITALISE INFORMATION IN APPLICATION FORMS.

How and to what extent all this will come to matter to money, to debt, and to the lives of borrowers remains to be seen. As with all new financial innovations, digital subprime is vulnerable to scandal, to governmental intervention, to consumer resistance, and quite simply to failing to live up to the promises it has been making – we have already seen how a number of its experiments have been shelved or adapted in light of changing sociopolitical realities. Its future is certainly open. What is also certain, is that it needs to be tracked.

Acknowledgements

I would like to offer my thanks to Lana Swartz and Manuel Castells for the invitation to the 'Money as Communication' workshop at University of Southern California in October 2014 where an earlier version of this chapter was presented and to participants for the very helpful discussion that followed. I am also grateful to the participants of the 'Domesticizing Financial Economies, Part II' mini-conference at SASE in London in June 2015 for further feedback, in particular my commentator José Ossandón. Thanks also to Mark Featherstone, Michael Palm, Lana Swartz and Lonneke van der Velden for their insightful comments on earlier drafts.

Notes

1 This is, of course, but a small subset of the relevant work on these various topics.

2 This is, I realise, a reductionist account of the relationship between credit and money. Ingham's detailed account of this is particularly rich, even if it fails to account sufficiently for the processual and materially significant dimensions of monetary becoming (Deville, 2017).

3 My colleague and I (Deville and van der Velden, 2016) draw on the same quote in a chapter looking in more detail at the methodological problematics studying these companies poses. I return to this chapter at a number of points in the chapter here.

4 As I detail later in the chapter, historically the APR of its UK loans was far higher, with rates having peaked at 5,843%. This has now changed, with the introduction of a cap on payday lender interest rates in 2015.

5 There is also Wei et al's (2016) rather eccentric attempt to quantitatively model the future effects on society of the widespread proliferation of a form of credit assessment based on an analysis of friendship quality, inspired by the social-media based techniques of some digital subprime companies.

6 Elsewhere the term 'speculative empiricism' has been used by Didier Debaise to refer to a sociological mode of attention influenced by Gabriel Tarde and Alfred North Whitehead amongst others, who point to the ways in which entities are formed by forces that are not in any straightforward way detectable via empirical registers (there are also parallels here to affect theory). In this instance, I use the term a little more prosaically. That said, given some of my own Whiteheadian leanings (Deville, 2015b), I am happy for this heritage to resonate in the background. I also have in mind Martin Savransky's injunction (influenced by Whitehead) to consider speculation as a 'key … into a certain pragmatics of thought' (Savransky, 2017). I somewhat basely transpose his response to the problems of the theoretical to the empirical.

7 https://www.ghostery.com

8 https://tools.digitalmethods.net/beta/trackerTracker/. The tool was created in a collaborative project by Yngvil Beyer, Erik Borra, Carolin Gerlitz, Anne Helmond, Koen Martens, Simeona Petkova, J C Plantin, Bernhard Rieder, Lonneke van der Velden and Esther Weltevrede at the Digital Methods Winter School 2012.

9 The 23 sites were: cashnetusa.com, dollarsdirect.ca, dollarsdirect.com.au, fairloanfinancial.com, tcsbank.ru, isepankur.ee, kredito24.cz, kredito24.es, kredito24.mx, kredito24.pl, lenddo.com.co, lenddo.com.ph, lendup.com, plaingreenloans.com, mobiloans.com, netcredit.com, poundstopocket.co.uk, quickquid.co.uk, quickquidflexcredit.co.uk, risecredit.com, spotloan.com, sunny.co.uk, wonga.ca, wonga.co.za, wonga.com, wonga.pl, zaimo.ru. For further details on the method and the pilot project see Deville and van der Velden (2016).

10 These are too numerous to detail here. But more common examples include: Appnexus, Advertising.com, Bidswitch, Doubleclick (owned by Google), Google Adsense, IntelliAd, Tribal Fusion.

11 Lenddo, Spotloan, Wonga.

12 I build here on previous analysis of the function of ThreatMetrix in this domain (Deville and van der Velden, 2016), which additionally looks at the QuBit OpenTag tracker. It should be noted that, as far as it is possible to tell, Spotloan stopped using ThreatMetrix in mid-2014.

13 For instance, the targeting of online advertisements based on searches at e-commerce sites – products coming to follow us as we browse is a familiar experience for many of us.

References

Adams, J. (2013) 'Think Finance Turns to Social Media for Clues to Creditworthiness'. Available at: http://www.americanbanker.com/issues/178_12/think-finance-turns-to-social-media-for-clues-to-creditworthiness-1055911-1.html (accessed 5 October 2018).

Adkins, L. and Lury, C. (2009) 'Introduction: What is the Empirical?', *European Journal of Social Theory* 12(1): 5–20.

Aitken, R. (2014) *Fringe Finance: Crossing and Contesting the Borders of Global Capital.* London and New York: Routledge.

Aitken, R. (2017) 'All Data is Credit Data: Constituting the Unbanked', *Competition & Change*, 21(4): 274-300.

Allon, F. (2010) 'Speculating on Everyday Life: The Cultural Economy of the Quotidian', *Journal of Communication Inquiry* 34(4): 366-81.

Allon, F. (2015a) 'Everyday Leverage, or Leveraging the Everyday', *Cultural Studies* 29(5-6): 687-706.

Allon, F. (2015b) 'Money, Debt, and the Business of "free stuff"', *South Atlantic Quarterly* 114(2): 283-305.

Allon, F. (2015c) 'On Capitalism's Emotional Logics' in *Progress in Political Economy*. Available at: http://ppesydney.net/on-capitalisms-emotional-logics/ (accessed 5 October 2018).

Anderson, C. (2008) 'The End of Theory: The Data Deluge Makes the Scientific Method Obsolete', *Wired*. Available at: https://www.wired.com/2008/06/pb-theory/ (accessed 5 October 2018).

Anon (2015) 'Starinvestor Thiel investiert in Hamburger Kreditvermittler Kreditech' in *Manager Magazin*. Available at: http://www.manager-magazin.de/unternehmen/banken/starinvestor-thiel-investiert-in-hamburger-kreditvermittler-kreditech-a-1041770.html (accessed 5 October 2018).

Anon (2016) 'Opinions concerning accelerating the construction of credit supervision, warning and punishment mechanisms for persons subject to enforcement for trust-breaking' in *China Copyright and Media*. Available at: https://chinacopyrightandmedia.wordpress.com/2016/09/25/opinions-concerning-accelerating-the-construction-of-credit-supervision-warning-and-punishment-mechanisms-for-persons-subject-to-enforcement-for-trust-breaking/ (accessed 5 October 2018).

Arthur, C. (2012) *Financial Literacy Education: Neoliberalism, the Consumer and the Citizen.* Rotterdam: Sense Publishers.

Ash, J., Anderson, B., Gordon, R. et al (2018) 'Digital Interface Design and Power: Friction, Threshold, Transition', *Environment and Planning D: Society and Space.*

Balch, O. (2014) 'Lenddo's Jeff Stewart: Making Online Loans to Strangers Make Sense'. Available at: http://www.theguardian.com/sustainable-business/lenddo-jeff-stewart-microfinance-internet-personal-loans (accessed 5 October 2018).

Balea, J. (2015) 'Lenddo Stops Lending, Now Helps Clients Determine Customer Trustworthiness'. Available at: https://www.techinasia.com/lenddo-customer-trustworthiness (accessed 16 July 2018).

Bátiz-Lazo, B. and Reid, R. J. K., (2011) 'The Development of Cash-dispensing Technology in the UK', *IEEE Annals of the History of Computing*. 33(3): 32-45.

Bátiz-Lazo. B., Karlsson, T. and Thodenius, B. (2014) 'The Origins of the Cashless Society: Cash Dispensers, Direct to Account Payments and the Development of On-line Real-Time Networks, c.1965-1985', *Essays in Economic & Business History* 32(0): 100-37.

Berlant, L. G. (2011) *Cruel Optimism*. Durham: Duke University Press.

Big Data Scoring (2018) 'Big Data Scoring: The Leader in Big Data Scoring Solutions'. Available at: http://bigdatascoring.com/ (accessed 13 July 2018).

Boyd, D. and Crawford, K. (2012) 'Critical Questions for Big Data', *Information, Communication & Society* 15(5): 662-79.

Burrows, R. and Savage, M. (2014) 'After the Crisis? Big Data and the Methodological Challenges of Empirical Sociology', *Big Data & Society* 1(1).

Burton, D. (2008) *Credit and Consumer Society*. London: Routledge.

BusinessWire (2017) 'Ford Credit and Zestfinance team up to enhance risk modeling, better serve consumers and lower credit losses'. Available at: https://www.businesswire.com/news/home/20170825005455/en/Ford-Credit-ZestFinance-Team-Enhance-Risk-Modeling (accessed 13 July 2018).

Constine, J. (2015) 'Facebook is shutting down its API for giving your friends' data to apps' in *TechCrunch*. Available at: https://techcrunch.com/2015/04/28/facebook-api-shut-down/ (accessed 5 October 2018).

Consumer Financial Protection Bureau (2013) *CFPB Consumer Laws and Regulations: Equal Credit Opportunity Act (ECOA)*. Available at: http://files.consumerfinance.gov/f/201306_cfpb_laws-and-regulations_ecoa-combined-june-2013.pdf.

Cookson, R. and Moore, E. (2013) 'Wonga Eyes Expansion in US and Spain'. Available at: https://www.ft.com/content/575363cc-6577-11e2-a3db 00144feab49a#axzz2SDwrNcNy (accessed 5 October 2018).

Creemers, R. (2018) 'China's Social Credit System: An Evolving Practice of Control'. ID 3175792, *SSRN Scholarly Paper*, 9 May. Rochester, NY: Social Science Research Network. Available at: https://papers.ssrn.com/abstract=3175792 (accessed 13 July 2018).

Davies, W., Montgomerie, J. and Wallin, S. (2015) *Financial Melancholia*. London: Goldsmiths, University of London / Political Economy Research Centre. Available at: http://www.perc.org.uk/perc/wp-content/uploads/2015/07/FinancialMelancholiaMentalHealthandIndebtedness-1.pdf (accessed 5 October 2018).

De Goede, M. (2012) '"Smart Targeting" and the Meaning of Money', *Cultural Anthropology Online*. Available at: https://www.culanth.org/fieldsights/335-smart-targeting-and-the-meaning-of-money (accessed 5 October 2018).

Denyer, S. (2016) 'China's Plan to Organize Its Society Relies on "Big Data" to Rate Everyone'. Available at: https://www.washingtonpost.com/world/asia_pacific/chinas-plan-to-organize-its-whole-society-around-big-data-a-rating-for-everyone/2016/10/20/1cd0dd9c-9516-11e6-ae9d-0030ac1899cd_story.html (accessed 5 October 2018).

Deville, J. (2013a) 'Leaky Data: How Wonga makes Lending Decisions', *Charisma: Consumer Market Studies*. Available at: http://www.charisma-network.net/finance/leaky-data-how-wonga-makes-lending-decisions (accessed 5 October 2018).

Deville, J. (2013b) 'Paying with Plastic: The Enduring Presence of the Credit Card' in Gabrys, J., Hawkins, G., and Michael, M. (eds) *Accumulation: The Material Politics of Plastic*. London: Routledge, pp. 87-104.

Deville, J. (2015a) 'Inside the World of Debt Collection'. Available at: https://www.opendemocracy.net/ourkingdom/joe-deville/inside-world-of-debt-collection (accessed 5 October 2018).

Deville, J. (2015b) *Lived Economies of Default: Consumer Credit, Debt Collection and the Capture of Affect*. London: Routledge.

Deville, J. (2017) 'Retrocasting: Speculating about the Origins of Money' in Wilkie, A, Savransky, M. and Rosengarten, M. (eds) *Speculative Research: The Lure of Possible Futures*. London: Routledge, pp. 98-110.

Deville J. and Seigworth, G. J. (2015) 'Everyday Debt and Credit', *Cultural Studies* 29(5-6): 615-29.

Deville J. and van der Velden L. (2016) 'Seeing the Invisible Algorithm: The Practical Politics of Tracking the Credit Trackers' in Amoore, L. and Piotukh, V. (eds) *Calculative Devices in a Digital Age*. London: Routledge, pp. 90-109.

Fitch, C., Hamilton, S., Bassett, P. et al (2011) 'The Relationship Between Personal Debt and Mental Health: A Systematic Review', *Mental Health Review Journal* 16(4): 153-66.

Glasner, J. (2016) 'CrunchBase Spotlight: Data hints at down rounds, but not wipeout, for marketplace lending', *TechCrunch*. Available at: https://techcrunch.com/2016/07/06/crunchbase-spotlight-data-hints-at-down-rounds-but-not-wipeout-for-marketplace-lending/ (accessed 5 October 2018).

Graeber, D. (2011) *Debt: The First 5,000 Years*. Brooklyn, NY: Melville House.

Grossberg, L., Hardin, C. and Palm, M. (2014) 'Contributions to a Conjunctural Theory of Valuation', *Rethinking Marxism*. 26(3): 306-35.

Hawley, C. (2012) 'Critique of German Credit Agency Plan to Mine Facebook for Data' , *Spiegel Online*. Available at: http://www.spiegel.de/international/germany/critique-of-german-credit-agency-plan-to-mine-facebook-for-data-a-837713.html (accessed 5 October 2018).

Hurley, M. and Adebayo, J. (2016) 'Credit Scoring in the Era of Big Data', Yale *Journal of Law and Technology*. 18: 148-216.

Ingham, G. (2004) *The Nature of Money*. Cambridge: Polity Press.

Jeffries, A. (2011) 'As banks start nosing around Facebook and Twitter, the wrong friends might just sink your credit'. Available at: http://betabeat.com/2011/12/as-banks-start-nosing-around-facebook-and-twitter-the-wrong-friends-might-just-sink-your-credit/ (accessed 12 August 2013).

Kreditech (2018) 'What we do' in Kreditech. Available at: https://www.kreditech.com/what-we-do/ (accessed 16 July 2018).

Kredito24.pl (2013) Kredito24. Available at: http://www.kredito24.pl (accessed 20 August 2013).

Langley, P. (2008) *The Everyday Life of Global Finance: Saving and Borrowing in America*. Oxford: Oxford University Press.

Langley, P. (2014) 'Equipping Entrepreneurs: Consuming Credit and Credit Scores'. *Consumption Markets & Culture* 17(5): 448-67.

Law, J. and Ruppert, E. (2013) 'The Social Life of Methods: Devices', *Journal of Cultural Economy* 6(3): 229-40.

Lazarus, J. (2013a) 'De l'aide à la responsabilisation. L'espace social de l'éducation financière en France', *Genèses*: 76–97.

Lazarus, J. (2013b) '*L'Épreuve de l'Argent. Banques, banquiers, clients*'. Paris: Calmann-Lévy.

Lazarus, J. (2015) 'A la recherche des normes contemporaines de l'argent: elements pour une analyse de la promotion de l'education financiere'. *Terrains/Théories* 1. Available at: http://teth.revues.org/346 (accessed 21 July 2015).

Lazzarato, M. (2012) *The Making of the Indebted Man: An Essay on the Neoliberal Condition*. Cambridge, MA: MIT Press.

Lenddo (2017) 'Credit Scoring Solution. Lenddo'. Available at: https://www.lenddo.com/pdfs/Lenddo_FS_CreditScoring_201705.pdf (accessed 16 July 2018).

Lewis, J. (2012) 'Wonga Faces Questions Over Borrowing by Children'. Telegraph.co.uk, 14 October. Available at: http://www.telegraph.co.uk/finance/personalfinance/borrowing/loans/9606570/Wonga-faces-questions-over-borrowing-by-children.html (accessed 5 October 2018).

Lewis, T. (2011) 'With Wonga, Your Prosperity Could Count on an Algorithm'. *The Guardian*, 16 October. Available at: https://www.theguardian.com/money/2011/oct/16/wonga-algorithm-lending-debt-data (accessed 5 October 2018).

Leyshon, A. and Thrift, N. (1999) 'Lists Come Alive: Electronic Systems of Knowledge and the Rise of Credit-Scoring in Retail Banking', *Economy and Society* 28(3): 434-66.

Lippert, J. (2014) 'Lender Charging 390% Uses Data to Screen Out Deadbeats'. Available at: http://www.bloomberg.com/news/articles/2014-10-01/lender-charging-390-uses-data-to-screen-out-deadbeats (accessed 5 October 2018).

Lohr, S. (2015) 'Zestfinance Takes its Big Data Credit Scoring to China'. Available at: http://bits.blogs.nytimes.com/2015/06/26/zestfinance-takes-its-big-data-credit-scoring-to-china/ (accessed 5 October 2018).

Loten, A. (2016) 'Online Lender Elevate Taps Fintech Vet as CIO', *The Wall Street Journal*, 25 March. Available at: http://blogs.wsj.com/cio/2016/03/25/online-lender-elevate-taps-fintech-vet-as-cio/ (accessed 31 October 2016).

Lunden, I. (2015) 'Sources: Peter Thiel is investing in Kreditech's $100m Series C round', *TechCrunch*. Available at: http://social.techcrunch.com/2015/07/10/kreditech-2/ (accessed 5 October 2018).

Lunden, I. (2016) 'Online lender Kreditech closes out Series C at $103M after getting $11M from the IFC', *TechCrunch*. Available at: http://social.techcrunch.com/2016/03/23/online-lender-kreditech-closes-out-series-c-at-103m-after-getting-11m-from-the-ifc/ (accessed 31 October 2016).

Mackinnon, L. (2016) 'Love's Algorithm: "The perfect parts for my machine"' in Amoore, L. and Piotukh, V. (eds) *Algorithmic Life: Calculative Devices in the Age of Big Data*. London: Routledge, pp. 162-75.

Madsen, A. K. (2015) 'Between Technical Features and Analytic Capabilities: Charting a Relational Affordance Space for Digital Social Analytics', *Big Data & Society* 2(1).

Marres, N. (2012) 'The Redistribution of Methods: On Intervention in Digital Social Research, Broadly Conceived', *The Sociological Review* 60: 139-65.

Marres, N. and Gerlitz, C. (2016) 'Interface Methods: Renegotiating Relations Between Digital Social Research, STS and Sociology'. *The Sociological Review* 64(1): 21-46.

Marron, D. (2009) *Consumer Credit in the United States: A Sociological Perspective from the 19th Century to the Present*. New York: Palgrave.

Marron, D. (2014) '"Informed, Educated and More Confident": Financial Capability and the Problematization of Personal Finance Consumption', *Consumption Markets & Culture* 17(5): 491-511.

Maurer, B. (2012a) 'Late to the Party: Debt and Data', *Social Anthropology* 20(4): 474-81.

Maurer, B. (2012b) 'Payment: Forms and Functions of Value Transfer in Contemporary Society', *Cambridge Anthropology*. 30(2): 15–35.

Maurer, B. (2014) 'Postscript: Is there Money in Credit?', *Consumption Markets & Culture* 17(5): 512-18.

Maxymyser (2014) 'Do You Really Know Your High Value Customers Online? Breaking Down The Key Strategies To Better Identify & Target Top Customers'. Available at: http://go.maxymiser.com/rs/maxymiser/images/MAXY_MX001_WP_HighValue_final.pdf (accessed 30 June 2015).

McFall, L. and Deville, J. (2018) 'The Market Will Have You: The Arts of Market Attachment in a Digital Economy' in Cochoy, F., Deville, J., and McFall, L. (eds.) *Markets and the Arts of Attachment*. London and New York: Routledge, pp. 108-31.

Merrill, D. (2012) 'Tedx New Wall Street: Douglas Merrill: New Credit Scores in a New World'. Available at: http://www.youtube.com/watch?feature=player_embedded&v=18CyX5sJx5I (accessed 5 October 2018).

Mierzwinski, E. and Chester, J. (2014) 'Selling Consumers, not Lists: The New World of Digital Decision-Making and the Role of the Fair Credit Reporting Act', *Suffolk University Law Review* XLVI: 845–880.

Montgomerie, J. (2009) 'The Pursuit of (past)Happiness? Middle-class Indebtedness and American Financialisation', *New Political Economy*, 14(1): 1-24.

Morozov, E. (2013) 'Wonga, Lenddo, Lendup: Big Data and Social-networking Banking'. Available at: http://www.slate.com/articles/technology/future_tense/2013/01/wonga_lenddo_lendup_big_data_and_social_networking_banking.html (accessed 5 October 2018).

Moules, J. (2011) 'Wonga Raises £73m to Feed Loan Appetite'. *Financial Times*, 16 February. Available at: http://www.ft.com/cms/s/0/1c1fb866-39f3-11e0-82aa-00144feabdc0.html#axzz3gc800R8J (accessed 5 October 2018).

Ossandón, J. (2014) 'Sowing Consumers in the Garden of Mass Retailing in Chile', *Consumption Markets & Culture* 17(5): 429-47.

Pollock, I. (2012) 'Wonga: What Makes Money Lender Tick?' Available at: http://www.bbc.co.uk/news/business-18019272 (accessed 5 October 2018).

Poon, M. (2007) 'Scorecards as Devices for Consumer Credit: The Case of Fair, Isaac & Company Incorporated' in Callon, M., Millo, Y. and Muniesa, F. (eds) *Market Devices*. Oxford: Blackwell, pp. 284-306.

Poon, M. (2009) 'From New Deal Institutions to Capital Markets: Commercial Consumer Risk Scores and the Making of Subprime Mortgage Finance', *Accounting, Organizations and Society* (34): 654-74.

Poster, M. (1995) *The Second Media Age*. Cambridge: Polity Press.

Quantcast (2015a) 'Yelp Network's audience profile on Quantcast'. Available at: https://www.quantcast.com/p-M4yfUTCPeS3vn (Accessed: 30 June 2015).

Quantcast (2015b) 'Quantcast Measure', Quantcast. Available at: https://www.quantcast.com/measure/ (Accessed: 30 June 2015).

Rogers, R. (2013) *Digital Methods*. Cambridge, MA: The MIT Press.

Rosamond, E. (2016) 'All Data is Credit Data', *Paragrana* 25(2): 112-24.

Ruppert, E. (2013) 'Rethinking Empirical Social Sciences', *Dialogues in Human Geography* 3(3): 268-73.

Russell, J. (2016) 'Baidu invests in ZestFinance to develop search-powered credit scoring for China', *TechCrunch*. Available at: http://social.techcrunch.com/2016/07/17/baidu-invests-in-zestfinance-to-develop-search-powered-credit-scoring-for-china/ (accessed 5 October 2018).

Savage, M. and Burrows, R. (2007) 'The Coming Crisis of Empirical Sociology', *Sociology* 41(5): 885-99.

Savransky, M. (2017) 'The Wager of an Unfinished Present: Notes on Speculative Pragmatism' in Wilkie, A., Savransky, M., and Rosengarten, M. (Eds.) *Speculative Research: The Lure of Possible Futures*. London and New York: Routledge, pp. 25-38.

Schmitz, A. (2014) 'Secret Consumer Scores and Segmentations: Separating "haves" from "have-nots"'. *Michigan State Law Review,* 2014(5): 1411-73.

Shaw, W. (2011) 'Could Wonga Transform Personal Finance?' Available at: http://www.wired.co.uk/magazine/archive/2011/06/features/wonga/page/4 (accessed 3 May 2013).

Stearns, D. L. (2011) *Electronic Value Exchange: Origins of the Visa Electronic Payment System*. London and New York: Springer.

Streeck, W. (2011) 'The Crises of Democratic Capitalism' *New Left Review* (71)II: 5–29.

Swartz, L. (2014) 'Gendered Transactions: Identity and Payment at Midcentury', *WSQ: Women's Studies Quarterly* 42(1): 137-53.

ThreatMetrix (2015) 'Multi-Channel, Cross-Application Visibility And Sophisticated Analytics To Protect Against Fraud.' Available at: http://www.threatmetrix.com/solutions/fraud-prevention/ (Accessed: 30 June 2015).

ThreatMetrix (n.d.) 'Device Fingerprinting and Online Fraud Protection Whitepaper'. Available at: http://www.scribd.com/doc/5342718/Device-Fingerprinting-and-Online-Fraud-Protection-Whitepaper#scribd (accessed 28 July 2015).

van der Velden, L. (2014) 'The Third Party Diary: Tracking the Trackers on Dutch Governmental Websites', *NECSUS. European Journal of Media Studies* 3(1): 195–217.

van Otterlo, M. (2016) 'The Libraryness of Calculative Devices: Artificially Intelligent Librarians and their Impact on Information Consumption' in Amoore, L. and Piotukh, V. (eds) *Algorithmic Life: Calculative Devices in the Age of Big Data*. London: Routledge.

Wei, Y., Yildirim, P., Christophe, V. den B., et al (2016) 'Credit Scoring with Social Network Data', *Marketing Science* 35(2): 234-58.

White, M. C. (2012) 'Can a Payday Lending start-up Use Facebook to Create a Modern Community Bank?' Available at: http://business.time.com/2012/11/16/can-a-payday-lending-start-up-use-facebook-to-create-a-modern-community-bank/ (accessed 12 August 2013).

Wilhelm, C. (2018) 'Big data vs. the Credit Gap', *Politico*. Available at: http://politi.co/2E75tOs (accessed 16 July 2018).

Yu, P., McLaughlin, J. and Levy, M. (2014) 'Big Data: A Big Disappointment for Scoring Credit Risk'. March. Boston: National Consumer Law Centre. Available at: https://www.nclc.org/images/pdf/pr-reports/report-big-data.pdf (accessed 5 October 2018).

7

Debt, usury and the ongoing crises of capitalism

Nicholas Gane

Just over ten years since the start of the global financial crisis, many advanced capitalist societies are witnessing the rise of private debt to levels previously seen in 2008, and in some cases (most notably Australia, see Keen, 2017: 67) to levels higher than at any point during the crisis. This has led to a renewed sense of unease among key figures of the central banking community, as a new crisis, fuelled (like the previous one) by indebtedness and the threat of mass default, appears to be edging closer. In the summer of 2017, as unsecured consumer credit in the UK topped £200bn for the first time since 2008, Alex Brazier, the Bank of England's executive director for financial stability, warned the banking and finance sectors that 'Lending standards can go from responsible to reckless very quickly. ... Lenders have not entered, but they may be dicing with, the spiral of complacency' (see Elliott, 2017). This was soon followed by a statement by the UK's Financial Conduct Authority, which warned that consumer credit had risen just over 10 per cent in a year, with 8.3 million people in the UK classified as having 'problem debts' (Inman and Treanor, 2017). While this situation is nothing new, there are worrying times ahead as consumer credit provision is pushing its historical upper limits, and cheap lines of credit look set to end with likely rises in interest rates in the short to medium term. This situation presents a very real problem for the operation and stability of advanced capitalist societies across the globe for, given that the growth of consumer capitalism has only been possible through the mass provision of private and corporate credit from the 1980s onwards, it is unclear what will happen when further debt creation is no longer an option, assuming there are actual limits to this process.

There are two prominent responses to this situation in the post-crisis literature: one, building on the work of Hyman Minsky, is that crisis is endogenous to financialised capitalism, and that governments, in attending to the immediate pressures of a present crisis, have a tendency to introduce measures which stabilise the economy in the short term but which sow the seeds of another crisis further down the line (see, for example, Keen, 2017; Minsky, 1986). In this view, crises are recurrent features of capitalism that follow on from each other and are likely to become ever more acute without any foreseeable endpoint, for capitalism is seen to be a generative system: if more debt is needed, among other things, then a way will be found to create it. A second, more alarming view, is advanced by Wolfgang Streeck (2014). This is that government responses to the ongoing debt crisis have bought time, and in so doing have postponed the collapse of an unsustainable capitalist system to a date that *will* one day arrive. In the meantime, we are destined to live through a period of what Streeck calls 'deep *indeterminacy*'; one in which 'too many frailties have become simultaneously acute while too many remedies have been exhausted or destroyed' (Streeck, 2016: 12-13). In this view, capitalism is finished, but it is unclear how its death will play out, or what (if anything) might come afterwards.

While seemingly mutually exclusive, both these positions have their points of appeal; on one hand, financialised capitalism has proved to be extraordinarily resilient in the face of crisis, largely because the neoliberal state (or what Minsky calls 'big government') has acted as the guarantor of financial markets in the last instance (as predicted, remarkably, by Foucault in his 1978/9 biopolitics lectures, see Gane, 2014), while, on the other, there is something distinct and deeply worrying about the current situation, defined as it is by 'declining growth, growing inequality, and rising debt – public, private and overall' (Streeck, 2016: 17). This chapter will argue, however, against both these positions, that a crisis-bound future is not inevitable, as there are alternatives, and at the very least governmental means through which the structural debt crisis can be tackled. It will do so by looking more closely at the history of government regulation of personal debt in particular (mainly in the UK and US), and will work with a concept that was once central to debates within classical liberal thought but today is largely neglected (with important exceptions, see, for example, Sayer, 2015): *usury*, which in its initial meaning, referred to the freedom to charge interest on money created as credit.

The question of usury divided key figures within the liberal tradition over whether there should be a free market in the provision of credit (one that can and should operate outside of the reach of the powers of government) or rather government policing of the social and moral limits of debt. These divisions resurface in the current post-crisis period in a contemporary debate over whether the short-term loan market should be free to meet the demands of credit supply (the libertarian position) or should be regulated by government agencies to ensure that it works within limits (more of a neoliberal stance). The concept of usury, it will be argued, is a useful device for questioning the role of state and government in relation to private debt, and, in its original meaning, opens the possibility of an alternative politics of debt that centres not on regulating the rate of interest charged on credit (the libertarian and neoliberal positions above), but rather the freedom of banks and other institutions (payday lenders are one key example) to lend money at a price.

In taking an historical approach, however, it will not be assumed that debt itself is something timeless and unchanging. In *Never Let a Serious Crisis Go To Waste* (2013), Philip Mirowski argues that David Graeber (2011) makes exactly this mistake in his book *Debt: The First 5,000 Years*, and that as a result he shares common ground with figures such as Kenneth Rogoff and Carmen Reinhart – who most would assume would sit on the opposite side of the political spectrum to Graeber – because together they accept the 'key notion of the populist right and the neoclassical orthodoxy, that "nothing is substantially different between then and now"' and the belief that 'markets are timeless entities with timeless laws' (Mirowski, 2013: 17). Contrary to such an approach, debt as a form of governance has changed markedly from the 1970s onwards, let alone from the mid-18th century when debates over usury flourished. It has been well documented, for example, that debt is now financialised to its core (Lazzarato, 2011; 2015), and is also something that has changed in quality from an amount to be redeemed at a particular point in the future to a quantity that will be serviced, and in all likelihood rolled over, indefinitely; Lisa Adkins rightly describes this as a movement 'from a logic of repayment to a logic of payment' (Adkins, 2017: 2). This means that debt now has a different rhythm or temporality and is something that is often never likely to be redeemed; as such, it becomes a new 'apparatus of capture' (Lazzarato, 2015: 43) that is constitutive of new forms of neoliberal subjectivity that define and govern our very existence (Brown, 2015). These are all relatively recent developments that have accelerated through the post-crisis period.

Why, then, return to classical debates about usury in order to think again about the governance of private debt in the present? This chapter treats debt as *the* main structural problem for the continued operation and stability of financialised capitalism, and as debt has become more important since the rise of consumer credit in the mid-20th century so has the question of usury. For, as private debt has grown exponentially, small increases in the rates of interest charged on credit now have a geared effect because the quantity of debt is so much greater in relation to individual and household income (which, for most, has been depressed since the recent financial crisis). Put simply, with the leveraging of private debt to unprecedented levels, interest rates become ever more important as small shifts can potentially lead to the inability to pay *en masse,* and with this marks the start of 'new' crisis that to a large extent is a continuation of the one before.

This means that the question of usury has become increasingly important with the rise and acceleration of contemporary finance capitalism. But, as already stated, the concept of usury, historically, has both a descriptive and critical usage, and can be used to raise important questions about the underlying politics of debt, including whether government or state should play an active role in limiting the market in credit provision (and if so what this role should be), and whether the governmental regulation is, in fact, the answer. For these reasons, this chapter will, in the first instance, look more closely at this concept.

Usury: a brief history

The concept of usury has a long and complex history. Geoffrey Ingham (2004: 206) finds an initial expression of this concept in Aristotle's *Politics,* in which it is argued that 'usury is most reasonably hated, because its gain comes from money itself and not from that for the sake of which money was invented. For money was brought into existence for the purpose of exchange, but interest increases the amount of the money itself' (Aristotle, 1999: 17). This idea of usury as the making of money through the provision of credit at a rate of interest also has a long religious history (see Graeber, 2011: 9–13 for an overview). Burton traces the religious prohibition of usury to the Old Testament, in particular to Deuteronomy, in which 'Hebrews were told not to lend to their brethren at interest', and Ezekiel, who took a stronger line and argued for the execution of individuals who engaged in usury' (Burton, 2008: 8; for a detailed analysis of Deuteronomy and the role of usury in ancient Hebrew culture, see Nelson, 1969). A comparable idea of usury can be found in the Islamic term *riba,* which in its earliest sense refers to 'the increase of money in consideration for an extension of the term of maturity of a loan', and is prohibited in the Qur'an through four revelations (Ahmad, 2010: 54). Not all religions, however, share this view. Graeber observes, for example, that in 'mediaeval Hindu law codes, not only were interest-bearing loans permissible (the main stipulation was that interest should never exceed principal), but it was often emphasized that a debtor who did not pay would be reborn as a slave in the household of his creditor – or in late codes, reborn as his horse or ox' (Graeber, 2011: 11). A similarly tolerant attitude towards lenders, he adds, can be found in Buddhism, but that – seemingly across all world religions – moral sympathies tend to lie with debtors rather than creditors. Indeed, he observes that 'Looking over world literature, it is almost impossible to find a sympathetic representation of a moneylender – or anyway, a professional moneylender, which means by definition one who charges interest' (Graeber, 2011: 10).

In the case of England, a biblical view of usury predominated until the mid-16th century, at which point the power to govern creditor-debtor relations began to pass from the church to parliament. This transition was underpinned by the passing of key parliamentary acts that, in turn, formalised the previously moral prohibition of lending at interest, most notably *The Act Against Usury* (1552), *From An Act Against Usury* (1571), and *An Act for Restraining the Taking of Excessive Usury* (1600). Through the course of these acts, the meaning of usury changed: it no longer referred simply to the practice of charging interest on credit, but to a legally acceptable rate of interest beyond which the arrangement became usurious. Burton cites the 1571 Act, in particular, as a turning point as it allowed interest rates of up to 10 per cent to be charged on loans; anything more and the lender would be forced to forfeit the principal amount. As a consequence, she argues, 'there was a prevalent view that not all usury was against God's law. Interest rates at 10 per cent came to be considered legal and normal' (Burton, 2008: 9). Thomas Wilson, who was Secretary of State from 1577-81, considers the 1571 Act in detail in his *A Discourse Upon Usury* (edited and republished by R. H. Tawney in 1925). He notes, however, that the loopholes in this statute were 'not inconsiderable' and that there were still means through which unscrupulous lenders could legally charge more than 10 per cent on loans. One of these, which is of contemporary significance, was that creditors could compress the timeframe for the repayment loans in order to make debtors more prone to default. Wilson explains: 'the lender could get more than ten per cent for his money by stipulating for repayment with a time too short to be practicable, and then charging as a penalty the payment which he could not legally exact as interest' (Wilson, 1925: 169).

The legislation that followed through the 17th century centred on the regulation of the rate of interest that could be charged on a loan, most notably the Usury Act of 1660, which had the full title 'An Act for Restraining the Taking of Excessive Usury'. But the 1571 Act remained of significance as it played an important role in the emergence of the modern banking system; indeed, following this Act seven banks were established as a result of the first bill on usury in 1571 – in London, York, Norwich, Coventry, West Chester, Bristol, and Exeter – that became known as 'banks for the relief of common necessity' (Wilson, 1925: 159). The rationalisation of the banking system gathered pace following the founding of the Bank of England in 1694, and in 1714 the Statute of Usury capped interest rates at five per cent, which became the benchmark for subsequent anti-usury legislation in the US (see Schoon, 2015: 578). But through the 19th century, in particular, usury laws were fiercely contested and were repealed in the UK in 1854, only to be replaced in turn by the Moneylenders Act of 1900, which provided the basic regulatory framework for the governance of consumer credit through much of the 20th Century.

The question of usury, while largely neglected within contemporary economic thought, was central to debates within classical liberal economics. Adam Smith is a key early figure here, and his position, given that he is celebrated by many on the political right as a champion of the free market, is surprising: there should be usury laws to regulate the rate of interest that can be charged on loans. This position, which has been subjected to close scrutiny within Smith scholarship (see Jadlow, 1977; Levy, 1987), is most clearly advanced in *The Wealth of Nations* [1776], where he writes that it should be permissible to charge interest on credit, for 'as something can everywhere be made by the use of money, something ought everywhere to be paid for the use of it' (Smith, 1999: 456). He argues that attempts to prohibit the charging of interest have been counter-productive as 'they increase the evil of usury' by forcing debtors to underwrite the risks carried by creditors who may incur penalties for their actions. But Smith's answer is not to create a free market for the provision of credit. Quite the contrary, he declares that there should be a legal rate of interest which 'ought to be somewhat above, ought not to be much above the lowest market rate' (Smith, 1999:457). Smith's justification for setting the maximum rate at this level is that if interest rates are set too high – he gives the example of eight or ten per cent – then only the riskiest debtors ('prodigals and projectors') would be likely to enter into credit agreements on these terms. And if this were the case:

> Sober people, who will give for the use of money no more than a part of what they are likely to make by the use of it, would not enter into the competition. A great part of the capital of the country would thus be kept out of the hands which were most likely to make a profitable and

> advantageous use of it, and thrown into those which were most likely to waste and destroy it. Where the legal rate of interest, on the contrary, is fixed but a very little above the lowest market rate, sober people are preferred, as borrowers to prodigals and projectors. (Smith, 1999: 457)

The key point of this passage is that usury laws should be embraced because they encourage safe investment by channelling money to the most industrious and responsible debtors. This argument has been questioned by, among others, David Levy, who asks whether aversion to investment risk is necessarily a good thing, and whether it benefits a society as a whole or simply the individuals involved (Levy, 1987: 397-8). Levy questions the economic rationality of debtors and creditors in Smith's account in relation to their perceptions of risk-taking, and draws the conclusion that while it is not clear, for Smith, whether 'prodigals and projectors' should be excluded from credit agreements by usury laws, 'in his writings there is a whiff of the doctrine of socially responsible investment. In this case, where law can improve social well-being, Smith favors it' (Levy, 1987: 400). Indeed, contrary to Smith's commitment to *laissez-faire* economics on other matters, his core argument for the purposes of the present chapter is that usury laws can promote the creation of responsible and serviceable credit arrangements that work for the wider social good.

Smith's position was soon after subjected to a fierce attack by Jeremy Bentham who, in a series of letters written from White Russia (modern-day Belarus) in 1787 (from where he also wrote his famous letters on the Panopticon), made a vocal case for a 'Defence of Usury' (Bentham, 2016: 45-113), by which he meant a defence of the practice of lending money at any agreed rate of interest rather than the introduction of laws to moderate this practice. Bentham's argument is one that might be expected to be found in the work of Smith: that there should be an unregulated free market in the provision of credit, and one that is largely immune to interference by the state. The first of his letters makes exactly this argument: '*no man of ripe years and of sound mind, acting freely, and with his eyes open, ought to be hindered ... from making such a bargain, in the way of obtaining money, as he thinks fit, nor,* (what is a necessary consequence) *any body hindered from supplying him, upon any terms he thinks proper to accede to*' (Bentham, 2016: 47, italics original). From this starting point, Bentham subsequently criticises Smith's argument for usury laws point by point.

Bentham's overriding response to Smith is that it is illogical to believe in the merits of free market exchange in general but to restrict such exchange when it concerns money in the form of credit. From here a number of practical criticisms of usury laws follow, some of which are technical and question the existence of 'natural' or proper rates of interest (implying that the interest rate ceiling imposed by usury laws is largely arbitrary), and others are directed more at the powers of government, and concern who, exactly, should be deemed competent to make the judgement of what counts as usury. Bentham also takes issue with Smith's argument that usury laws benefit society as a whole by ensuring that money is lent to the safest investors or consumers rather than to 'prodigals and projectors'. Bentham argues that there is no evidence to show that this is the case, and responds that usury laws will not stop the actions of 'prodigals', who are likely to turn to the informal economy to borrow money, and risk restricting the actions of 'enterprising' borrowers or (to use a more contemporary term) entrepreneurs who are seen to be key agents of economic growth.

Many of Bentham's arguments continue to inform debates about the governance of debt in the present. Peter Johnson (2009) is right to state that 'It is hard to exaggerate the importance of this work', not least because it 'institutionalises greed and gives it the intellectual form it has today'. For throughout his 'Defence of Usury', Bentham's overriding concern is to protect the interests of creditors rather than debtors. He writes, for example, that:

> … in the case of borrowing money, it is the borrower always who … is on the safe side: any imprudence he may have committed with regard to the rate of interest, may be corrected at any time: if I find I have given too high an interest to one man, I have no more to do than to borrow of another at a lower rate, and pay off the first: if I cannot find any body to lend me at a lower, there cannot be a more certain proof that the first was in reality not too high. (Bentham, 2016: 61)

This position, which wilfully neglects the precarious position of borrowers in the absence of their protection of the law, is in keeping with many of the central tenets of classical *laissez-faire* liberalism, as both creditors and debtors are treated as rational self-interested economic actors who are participants in a market that (without the interference of government) can find its own solutions. But Bentham opposes usury laws on both economic and moral grounds; he argues that usury laws have undesired effects such as preventing the most vulnerable (and thereby the riskier borrowers) from obtaining credit they need, and as a consequence forcing them to use other routes to obtain money by selling goods or property at unreasonable prices in order to subsist. For Bentham, there is a double standard here, for 'Those who cannot borrow may get what they want, so long as they have anything to sell. But while, out of loving-kindness, or whatsoever other motive, the law precludes a man from *borrowing* upon terms which it deems too disadvantageous, it does not preclude him from *selling*, upon any terms, howsoever disadvantageous' (Bentham, 2016: 62). The answer to this problem, he argues, is consistency: there should be no discrimination between a free market for the exchange of property and one for the exchange of money, and on this basis there should be no laws to prohibit usury.

Interestingly, John Stuart Mill, the key figure in British political economy through the latter half of the 19th century and a figure famously reviled by Hayek's mentor, Ludwig von Mises, for corrupting classical liberalism with socialist ideals (see Gane, 2014), later reinforced many of Bentham's views. In *Principles of Political Economy*, which was first published six years before the abolition of British usury laws in 1854, Mill writes that:

> In more improved countries, legislation no longer discountenances the receipt of an equivalent for money lent; but it has everywhere interfered with the free agency of the lender and borrower, by fixing a legal limit to the rate of interest, and making the receipt of more than the appointed maximum a penal offence. This restriction, though approved by Adam Smith, has been condemned by all enlightened persons since the triumphant onslaught made upon it by Bentham in his *Letters on Usury,* which may still be referred to as the best extant writing on the subject. (Mill, 1994: 307)

The irony here is that, on the question of usury, Mill is closer to the classical liberal cause as espoused by Bentham than is Smith (who is so often cited as a touchstone of contemporary neoliberal economics). Indeed, Mill sides with Bentham in arguing that usury laws tend only to protect one partner in credit agreements – the borrower – and that there is no evidence to show that such laws reduce interest rates on loans below that which could be achieved through 'the spontaneous play of supply and demand' (Mill, 1994: 308). He adds that such laws force not only Smith's 'prodigals and projectors' to borrow money at higher rates from disreputable lenders, but effectively 'all persons who are in any pecuniary difficulties, however temporary their necessities may be' (Mill, 1994: 310). Again, the argument is that usury laws do not resolve the problems of exorbitant lending and excessive risk-taking, but in fact increase the vulnerabilities of both creditors (as the law is said to protect only borrowers) and impoverished debtors, who are forced to enter informal agreements with moneylenders that operate outside of the law. The answer, for Mill as for Bentham, is for there to exist a free market in the provision of credit, one that should be regulated in limited ways by the state, if at all. Indeed, in later editions of *Principles of Political Economy*, Mill gives his full support for the repeal of English usury laws, and writes in the seventh edition of 1871 that they have now been 'happily abolished' (Mill, 1994: 310).

The regulation of credit pre- and post-crisis

While the above arguments from Bentham and the Mill might seem to belong in the 18th and 19th centuries respectively, they have been revisited many times since in order to justify the rollback of usury laws and governmental regulation of credit markets more generally. Indeed, it is worth noting that the majority of existing literature on usury (most of which is centred in the discipline of economics) treats the regulation of the interest charged on credit as a regressive step. This literature is, in some cases, historical in outlook. Temin and Voth, for example, treat usury laws as a key instance of the tendency for government regulation to shackle the progress of the financial revolution that took place in England through the late-17th to mid-18th centuries and, on this basis, draw the conclusion that the consequences of usury laws were 'almost entirely negative' (Voth and Temin, 2012: 84). Elsewhere, the arguments of Bentham and Mill have been repackaged many times over in order to justify the deregulation of credit markets that took place through 1970s and 1980s, particular in the UK and US. Christopher DeMuth, then President of the American Enterprise Institute, for example, makes an extended case against credit card interest rate regulation in a 1986 paper that argues for free competition between credit providers on the grounds that this will bring interest rates below those stipulated by usury laws and therefore be beneficial to consumers, adding that usury laws can only be damaging to the economy as they result in an 'artificial contraction in the supply of credit' (DeMuth, 1986: 201). Such arguments, which are neoliberal to the core as they view the market or more specifically market-based competition as a social good, have taken on a renewed significance in the post-crisis situation, in which the supply of credit – of all kinds – has become an immediate priority. This situation is important for the purposes of the present chapter as it provides a stark example of what can happen when the free market arguments of Bentham and Mill are pushed to an extreme, and when the state, through a period of exception during which anything seemingly becomes possible in the name of crisis, absolves itself of responsibility for the governance of personal credit.

One of the most striking developments that accompanied the unfolding of the crisis was the rapid growth of the short-term credit market or what is known colloquially as 'payday lending', for as unemployment soared and traditional lines of credit tightened, a large number of households were forced to find other means of raising money, in many cases just to cover basic living costs (see Kollewe, 2017) or to service the costs of existing debts. While payday lending is nothing new, in the period 2008-15 its market value more than trebled in value in the UK (Szilagyiova, 2015), and by late 2017 had a total worth of over £2.5bn. This situation is by no means unique to the UK. In the US, while there are regulations that outlaw payday lending in some states (many of which have a religious history), in 2012 an estimated 12 million adults used payday loans each year, mainly to cover the costs of 'ordinary living expenses', including recurring expenses such as 'utilities, credit card bills, rent or mortgage payments, or food' (Pew Institute, 2012).

With the expansion of payday lending came many stories of usury in its modern sense (the charging of excessive rates of interest), particularly in cases where the recipients of loans were unable to service their debts. In the US, for example, it became headline news that in Missouri, a state with more payday lenders than McDonalds restaurants, one client of a payday lender ended up owing a sum that was 36 times the $100 she originally borrowed (Kendzior, 2015). In the UK, it was commonplace to see television adverts advertising short-term loans at well over 1,000% APR, and in one case that made headline news a borrower was charged at an extraordinary rate of 16,734,509% APR (Jones, 2013). The morality of such credit arrangements was brought sharply into public focus in the UK when in 2013 a teenager - Kane Sparham-Price - committed suicide after a prominent payday loans company emptied his bank account in order to take payments to satisfy the terms of a short-term credit agreement. The coroner, in his report on this suicide, made a strong case for tighter regulation of such loans: 'Whilst I accept that the various payday lenders are legally entitled to 'clear out' someone's bank account if money is owing to them, it struck me that there ought to be a statutory minimum amount which must be left in an account (say £10) to avoid absolute destitution…' (quoted by Khomami, 2015). This call for regulation was echoed elsewhere by a wide range of political and third sector organizations, including trade unions, charities, religious groups, and even Occupy.

The regulation of contemporary credit markets, however, has a complex history. If we take the global financial crisis as the central point of focus, then, as Pettifor argues (2017: 49–53), a line of continuity can be drawn from the deregulation of credit markets in the 1970s through to the bursting of the credit bubble in 2007, and the emergence of a new bubble subsequently as the memory of causes of the financial crisis has slowly faded. This said, however, the regulation of credit, and in particular short-term credit, is not straightforward and policies and practices vary widely across different nation-states and political and religious cultures.

In the UK, regulation of the credit industry, at least in its modern form, can be traced to the Moneylenders Act of the early 20th century, which centred on whether interest charged on loans was excessive and the terms of credit agreements 'harsh and unconscionable', and later to the 1974 Consumer Credit Act, a landmark attempt to protect consumers from extortionate credit agreements by ensuring, among other things, that demands for early payment could not be made and that basic information about credit arrangements, such as the Annual Percentage Rate, be communicated to customers in writing. As in the US, however, the 1980s witnessed the wider deregulation of the UK banking sector, starting with the abolition of exchange controls and ending with the mass provision of new forms of consumer credit that largely outmaneuvered the regulatory framework previously put in place. Private debt grew exponentially through this period, seemingly never to return to previous levels: in 1980 the ratio of household debt to GDP stood at 30%, by the early 1990s this had risen to 60%, and at the point of the crisis hit nearly 100%.

While minor amendments were made to the Consumer Credit Act in 2006, a more serious attempt to impose a tighter regulatory framework on the credit industry emerged in response to the financial crisis. In April 2014, responsibility for the regulation of consumer credit passed from the Office of Fair Trading (OFT) to the Financial Conduct Authority (FCA). This regulatory body, in turn, introduced a new consumer credit 'sourcebook' ('CONC') that led to the capping of interest on payday loans at 0.8% per day, and the imposition of new rules on the rolling over of debts and ability for payday lending companies to take payments from their customers, in some cases without warning, through the use of 'continuous payment authority' (CPA). Similar regulations were applied to the credit card industry, and the FCA moved to prohibit certain surcharges on credit card transactions and encouraged card providers to do more to provide 'further assistance' to customers in 'persistent debt' (see https://www.fca.org.uk/news/press-releases/fca-proposes-new-rules-help-customers-persistent-debt-credit-cards). While these measures tempered some of the excesses of the credit industry, a number of key advisory bodies, most notably Citizens Advice, argued that they did not go far enough as many borrowers continue to struggle to with the conditions of their payday loans (https://www.citizensadvice.org.uk/Global/CitizensAdvice/Debt%20and%20Money%20Publications/Payday%20Loan%20Report%202.pdf), while credit card companies still actively target customers who are struggling with existing debts (see Partington, 2017).

In the US, rules on high-cost short-term credit (HCSTC) agreements (which include payday loans), many of which date back to the attempt to tackle usury at the outset of the 20th century through the Uniform Small Loan Law, vary considerably from state to state. Today, payday lending is outlawed in some states, while others place limits on APR, fees charged and the rollover of credit arrangements. Other forms of credit – such as credit cards and mortgages – have an equally complex history. Johnna Montgomerie (2006) traces the deregulation of the credit card industry to the collapse of the Bretton Woods Agreement at the outset of the 1970s, and to a succession of laws that followed which opened up, first, interstate credit card use, and, later, the creation of asset-backed securities that enabled the credit industry 'to expand virtually unabated' (Montgomerie, 2006: 312).

A key development came in 1978, when a Supreme Court ruling (*Marquette National Bank vs First of Omaha Service Corporation*) broke with previous usury laws by declaring that limits on credit card interest rates could now be determined by the state in which the card provider was located rather than that of the consumer. As Zinman explains: 'the *Marquette* decision gave banks the authority to "export" the bankcard interest rates permitted by their home state to customers in other states' (Zinman, 2003: 8). For this reason, a number of major credit card companies based themselves in states such as South Dakota, Nevada or Delaware, where a cap on interest rates did not apply. This deregulation of credit markets continued apace through the 1980s and 1990s, starting with the Depository Institutions Deregulation and Monetary Control Act signed by President Carter in 1980 which, among other things, gave banks greater freedoms to determine their interest rates.

This push for a free market in credit provision was maintained through to the global financial crisis in 2007, following which there was an attempt to re-regulate credit markets, particularly through the 2009 Credit Card Accountability Responsibility and Disclosure Act, which introduced a range of new consumer protections for credit card holders (see https://www.creditcards.com/credit-card-news/help/card-act-12-consumer-protections-6000.php), and the more sweeping 2010 Dodd-Frank Act, which established a Bureau of Consumer Protection and sought to tackle 'predatory' mortgage lending. Following the election of Donald Trump, however, much of this new regulatory framework (the success of which has been hotly contested) looks set to be rolled back, particularly after the passing of the Financial Choice Act by Congress in June, 2017. As its name implies, this act seeks to give consumers and credit providers greater 'choice' outside of the powers of 'Washington bureaucrats'. This struggle over the governance of credit continues to rumble on, with those on the political left and neoliberal right calling for tighter regulation and those on the libertarian right seeking the further rollback of such regulation in the name of consumer choice and freedom. The question this leaves us with is whether regulation is indeed the answer.

Where now?

The question of usury divided key figures within the classical liberal canon with, on the one hand, Smith arguing for government regulation of interest that can be charged on loans and, on the other, Bentham and Mill declaring that there should exist a free market in the creation of credit, one largely exempt from governmental interference. While the question of usury was central to debates within classical liberal economics and political economy, it almost completely disappeared from view following the death of John Stuart Mill (and at the same time political economy) in 1873. With the emergence of neoclassical economics in the latter stage of the 19th century, such political concerns largely evaporated, and for the most part the concept of usury barely featured in the social sciences of the 20th century (a notable exception is Nelson, 1969).

It is only following the 2007 financial crisis that the concept and practice of modern usury has returned with a vengeance, most notably in the form of payday lending, which (as shown in this chapter) serves as an important reminder of the human costs that can result from the deregulation of credit markets, and, more particularly, from the absence of government-enforced limits on the rates at which interest (and fees) can be charged on loans. Indeed, while (as noted at the outset of this chapter) the nature of debt has changed since the mid-19th century, the immediate post-crisis situation illustrates the potential consequences of following Bentham and Mill on the question of usury, of the continuing influence of their ideas within policy and industry circles. Indeed, as regulation of payday lending has tightened in the UK since 2014, there have been warnings from organisations such as the Consumer Finance Association that could come straight from the pages of Bentham and Mill, in particular that in the absence of such credit, debtors 'risk of falling into the hands of illegal lenders' (Peachey, 2015). In this sense, while the nature of debt has changed since the 19th century, many of the arguments that seek to legitimate it have not.

The simple option is to call for the further regulation of the conditions of debt as an answer. But in addressing the question of regulation, one of the key points to be drawn from this chapter is that this cannot be done in the abstract: regulatory frameworks are both place-specific and subject to subtle but important policy changes across time. The recent move, for example, by the Trump administration to 'empower' the consumer and credit industry by emphasising the value of individual choice is in keeping with a libertarian commitment to the withdrawal of the state from intervening in the workings of the so-called free market. This is quite different from attempts to place limits on the workings of credit markets through the Dodd-Frank Act in the US and consumer credit laws introduced by the FCA in the UK.

The push for such laws in the immediate post-crisis situation, while often well-intended, were in keeping with a neoliberal (rather than libertarian) response to the crisis as they positioned the state to improve the operation of credit markets rather than call into question, more fundamentally, the role of debt as a key mechanism of power within a broader landscape of advanced financialised capitalism. In this sense, although for different reasons to those suggested by Bentham and Mill, it might be argued that the regulation of credit is part of the problem, rather than a potential solution to the ongoing debt crisis. In a key piece on neoliberalism and the crisis, Martijn Konings develops this line of argument: 'the current Crisis is not a product of politics and regulation having let the market spin out of control, but precisely a product of contradictions internal to the operation of power and control, of financial power having gone beyond its own conditions of possibility' (Konings, 2010: 29).

A key part of the problem is that the state itself has changed since the heyday of classical liberalism for, as Foucault observed in his lectures on biopolitics, under conditions of neoliberalism it has been reprogrammed to serve the interests of 'the market' while itself becoming marketised to its core. In keeping with this view, Konings

(2010) rightly argues that the common belief that neoliberalism is characterised by deregulation is a myth: it is rather that it has introduced regulatory policies that have worked in the service of the market and to the benefit of elite groups. Indeed, in the wake of the recent crisis, it is clear that heightened regulation of credit markets has neither solved the acute problems of mass indebtedness nor addressed the stark social inequalities generated by financialised capitalism. Quite the contrary: debt remains *the* key apparatus of capture for the many, while guaranteeing the unprecedented social and political power of the few.

This does not mean, however, that financialised capitalism is without its problems. For neither libertarian arguments for the further deregulation of credit markets on the grounds of empowering individual choice, nor neoliberal attempts to improve the working of credit markets by introducing enhanced regulatory frameworks offer any way out of the ongoing structural debt crisis. Moreover, high-profile cases that illustrate the human and social costs of this ongoing crisis (such as the case of Kane Sparham-Price already discussed) disturb neoliberal and libertarian positions alike: first, they draw public attention to the underlying morality of the debt economy and to the human and social costs of mass indebtedness (even if regulation itself does not solve this problem, it is often framed to address such concerns); second, such cases demonstrate the problem of treating markets, in this case credit markets, as entities that can be governed through forces of competition that, to some extent, can themselves be the drivers of regulation; and third, they raise the related question of whether the limits set by new regulatory frameworks can be established and enforced in any progressive way by state agencies that themselves are increasingly market-oriented in basis.

The important point raised by Konings (2010) is that there is nothing inevitable about having to choose between the existence of freer credit markets, on one hand, or tighter regulation of the loan industry on the other, or between the cyclical crises of capitalism (Minsky, 1986) and 'death from a thousand cuts' (Streeck, 2014: 13) for that matter. For while regulation might look like the preferable option, there are alternatives. One is concealed within the history of idea of usury itself: that the problem lies not in agreeing a legitimate rate at which interest on credit may be charged, but rather, and more fundamentally, whether it is legally and morally acceptable to charge interest at all. This presumption, which unites Smith with his critics Bentham and Mill, is questioned by the recent writings of, among others, Andrew Sayer, Mary Mellor and Ann Pettifor. In a key chapter of his book *Why We Can't Afford the Rich*, entitled 'Interest … for What? *Or* We

Need to Talk About Usury' (2015), Sayer, for example, argues that there is merit in returning to pre-modern critiques of usury (as the practice of charging interest on credit), for while it is 'common to think that charging interest on loans is only fair, and also a good way of encouraging people to lend … in many ways it's economically dysfunctional, and arguably socially unjust…' (Sayer, 2015: 59). One of the attractions of such ideas of usury, he adds, is that they do not privilege the interests of the creditor (as in the classical liberal texts considered in this chapter), but instead treat debt as a form of power relation that is fundamentally unequal on the basis that it enables the creditors to profit from borrowers' poverty (Sayer, 2015: 66).

Sayer's attack is targeted primarily at a banking system that is able to create money freely and loan it at interest purely for the purpose of profit-making (Sayer, 2015: 73-6). This practice is placed under close critical scrutiny by Mary Mellor in her recent work *Debt or Democracy*. She questions why the power of money creation lies with central banks rather than with 'states more generally', and why, given that the money created by central banks is 'debt free at the point of its creation', public money is then circulated in the form of debt (Mellor, 2015: 3-4). These concerns are shared by Pettifor, who, in *The Production of Money: How to Break the Power of Bankers* (2017), argues that usury has become normalised in Western societies within which 'monetary systems have been weakened by the parasitic grasp of finance capital' (Pettifor, 2017: 44), and that what is needed, by way of response, is a new politics of money (and with this also of debt) that seeks further democratic control over the money supply by restoring many of the governmental powers lost through processes of deregulation. Here, she takes a position against thinkers such as Sayer and Mellor by arguing that money by definition cannot be debt-free (Pettifor, 2017: 111). Indeed, rather than making a wholesale case against debt *per se*, her aim is a more moderate one, namely: 'The creation of a socially just monetary system – one that promotes widespread prosperity by acting as servant, not master of society and the economy; a monetary system that enables us all – including the public sector – to do, and be what we can be' (Pettifor, 2017: 112). The first step towards this goal, she adds, is to promote a better public understanding of what money is, how it is created, and how the modern financial system works more generally.

While it is not possible to discuss what Pettifor aptly calls the 'price of money' in any detail here, the above positions are useful as they demonstrate the ongoing significance of the concept of usury, and beyond this the lines of political contestation that remain open and which offer potential alternatives to the theories of crisis offered by

Minsky and his followers on one hand, and Streeck on the other. For, regardless of their individual conclusions, Sayer, Mellor and Pettifor are right to argue for a new politics of money and debt, one that is informed by attention to historical debates such as those over the right to charge interest on credit, and concerned with larger-scale questions about the role played by banks, as well as smaller-scale private agencies such as payday lenders, in creating money to satisfy and fuel a profit motive.

The current chapter has sought to contribute to this endeavour, if only in a minor way, by using the concept of usury to think about the role of government in regulating the supply and conditions of private debt, and to argue that regulation, ultimately, is not enough. Indeed, new ideas, politics and practices are urgently needed to tackle the debt crisis, as regulation can only temper the extremities of financialised capitalism rather than tackle the root causes of the crises it produces. The argument of the present chapter is that the question of usury, and more specifically of the right to charge interest on credit, is an important starting point for a politics that seeks to move beyond the tightening or loosening of a regulatory framework.

References

Adkins, L. (2017) 'Speculative Futures in the Time of Debt', *Sociological Review*, 65, 3, pp.448-62.

Ahmad, A. (2010) *Developments in Islamic Banking Practice*, Boca Raton: Universal.

Aristotle (1999) *Politics*. Kitchener: Batoche.

Bentham, J. (2016) *Writings on Political Economy Volume I*. Oxford: Oxford University Press.

Brown, W. (2015) *Undoing the Demos*. New York: Zone.

Burton, D. (2008) *Credit and Consumer Society*. London: Routledge.

DeMuth, C. (1986) 'The Case Against Credit Card Interest Rate Regulation', *Yale Journal on Regulation*, 3, 2, article 2. Available at: https://pdfs.semanticscholar.org/07b1/73896eb1038f5cbb7b886ef5f15e26ebce71.pdf

Elliott, L. (2017) 'Bank of England Warns of Complacency Over Big Rise in Personal Debt', *The Guardian*, 24 July. Available at: https://www.theguardian.com/business/2017/jul/24/bank-of-england-household-debt-bank-credit-card-car-loans

Foucault, M. (2008) *The Birth of Biopolitics*. Basingstoke: Palgrave.

Gane, N. (2014) 'The Emergence of Neoliberalism: Thinking Through and Beyond Michel Foucault's Lectures on Biopolitics', *Theory, Culture and Society*, 31, 4, pp.3-27.

Ingham, G. (2004) *The Nature of Money*. Cambridge: Polity.

Inman, P. and Treanor, J. (2017) Britain's debt timebomb: FCA urges action over £200bn crisis, *The Guardian*, 18 September. Available at: https://www.theguardian.com/business/2017/sep/18/britain-debt-timebomb-fca-chief-crisis

Jadlow, J. (1977) 'Adam Smith on Usury Laws', *Journal of Finance*, 32, 4, pp.1195-1200.

Johnson, P. (2009) 'Brodbeck on Bentham', *openDemocracy*, 9 October. Available at: https://www.opendemocracy.net/article/openeconomy/brodbeck-on-bentham

Jones, R. (2013) 'The Payday Lender that Charged 16,734,509.4%'. *The Guardian*, 16 March. Available at: https://www.theguardian.com/money/2013/mar/16/payday-lender

Keen, S. (2017) *Can We Avoid Another Financial Crisis?* Cambridge: Polity Press.

Kendzior, S. (2015) 'The US Payday Loans Crisis', *The Guardian*, 9 May. Available at: https://www.theguardian.com/us-news/2015/may/09/us-payday-loans-crisis-borrow-100-to-make-ends-meet-owe-36-times-that-sum

Khomami, N. (2015) 'Teenager Killed Himself Hours after Wonga Cleared Out His Account', *The Guardian*, 25th September. Available at: https://www.theguardian.com/business/2015/sep/25/teenager-killed-himself-wonga-cleared-out-account

Kollewe, J. (2017) 'Young People Are Borrowing to Cover Basic Living Costs Warns City Watchdog', *The Guardian*, 16 October. Available at: https://www.theguardian.com/business/2017/oct/16/young-people-are-borrowing-to-cover-basic-living-costs-warns-city-watchdog

Konings, M. (2010) 'Rethinking Neoliberalism and the Crisis' in M. Konings and J. Sommers (eds) *The Great Credit Crash*. London: Verso.

Lazzarato, M. (2011) *The Making of Indebted Man*. New York: Semiotext(e).

Lazzarato, M. (2015) *Governing By Debt*. New York: Semiotext(e).

Levy, D. (1987) 'Adam Smith's Case for Usury Laws', *History of Political Economy*, 19, 3, pp.387-400.

Mellor, M. (2015) *Debt or Democracy*. London: Pluto.

Mill, J. S. (1994) *Principles of Political Economy*. Oxford: Oxford University Press.

Minsky, H. (1986) *Stabilizing An Unstable Economy*. London: McGraw-Hill.

Mirowski, P. (2013) *Never Let a Serious Crisis Go To Waste*. London: Verso.

Montgomerie, J. (2006) 'The Financialization of the American Credit Card Industry', *Competition and Change*, 10, 3, 2006, pp.301-19.
Montgomerie, J. (2007) 'The Logic of Neo-Liberalism and the Political Economy of Consumer Debt-Led Growth' in S. Lee and S. McBridge (eds) *Neo-Liberalism State Power and Global Governance*. Dordrecht: Springer.
Montgomerie, J. (2010) 'Neoliberalism and the Making of Subprime Borrowers', in M. Konings and J. Sommers (eds) *The Great Credit Crash*. London: Verso.
Nelson, B. (1969) *The Idea of Usury*. Chicago, IL: Chicago University Press.
Partington, R. (2017) 'Credit Card Lenders "Targeting People Struggling with Debt"', *The Guardian*, 30 August. Available at: https://www.theguardian.com/business/2017/aug/30/credit-card-lenders-debt-citizens-advice
Peachey, K. (2015) 'Loan Shark Fear Amid Payday Lending Crackdown', *The Guardian*, 30 August. Available at: http://www.bbc.co.uk/news/business-33592180
Pettifor, A. (2017) *How to Break the Power of the Banks*. London: Verso.
Pew Institute (2012) 'Nationwide Pew Survey Challenges Conventional Wisdom on Payday Loans', 18 July. Available at: http://www.pewtrusts.org/en/about/news-room/press-releases-and-statements/2012/07/18/nationwide-pew-survey-challenges-conventional-wisdom-on-payday-loans
Sayer, A. (2015) *Why We Can't Afford the Rich*. Bristol: Policy Press.
Schoon, N. (2015) 'Islamic Finance as Social Finance', in A. Nicholls et al (eds) *Social Finance*. Oxford: Oxford University Press.
Smith, A. (1999) *The Wealth of Nations: Books I-III*. Harmondsworth: Penguin.
Streeck, W. (2014) *Buying Time: The Delayed Crisis of Democratic Capitalism*. London: Verso.
Streeck, W. (2016) *How Will Capitalism End?* London: Verso.
Szilagyiova. S. (2015) 'The Effect of Payday Loans on Financial Distress in the UK', *Procedia Economics and Finance*, 30, pp.842-7.
Voth, H.-J. and Temin, P. (2012) *Prometheus Shackled: Goldsmith Banks and England's Financial Revolution*. Oxford: Oxford University Press.
Wilson, T. (1925) *A Discourse Upon Usury*. London: Frank Cass.
Zinman, J. (2003) 'The Impact of Liquidity on Household Balance Sheets: Micro Responses to a Credit Card Supply Shock'. Available at: https://www.dartmouth.edu/~jzinman/Papers/PortChoiceUnderLiquidityConstraints_Zinman_OldVersion.pdf

8

The art of unpayable debts

Max Haiven

This chapter provides a reading and a contextualisation of three recent performative public artworks to map the way unpayable debts manifest across politics, economics, culture and society under the global order of financialised capitalism. By unpayable debts here I have in mind both, on the one hand, the proliferation of financial debts that cannot be repaid and, on the other, the subterranean collective moral or political debts that, though they cannot be quantified, are no less real or important for that. Starting with a brief consideration of the power and materiality of the imagination as a key dimension of capitalism's financialisation, I then turn to a reading of UK artist Darren Cullen's 'Pocket Money Loans' (2012-present), Argentine artist Marta Minujín's 'Payment of Greek Debt to Germany with Olives and Art' (2017), and Anishinaabe artist Rebecca Belmore's 'Gone Indian' (2009). I am in search of two parallel counter-currents: first, the way dominant systems and structures of financialised power impose unpayable financial debts as a methodology of domination that secures exploitation, extraction, oppression and/or inequality; second, the way that these same systems and structures of financialised power depend upon the disappearance, denial or diversion of the unpayable debts owed to or claimed by the dominated and exploited on which they are, ultimately, based. My effort here is not to provide a comprehensive theorisation of the topic of unpayable debts, but rather to map some coordinates that, between them, triangulate the particular ways that, in the current financialised global order, a dialectics of unpayability plays out.

The imaginable and the unimaginable

The bulk of my previous studies have been dedicated to the question of the relationship between financialisation and the imagination, including the ways in which various forms and formats of contemporary debt both depend on and also help hold in place a set of materially expressed tropes, ideas, images, behaviours and relationships in the realm we typically call 'culture' (Haiven, 2014; 2011; 2017). After all, while debt may be inscribed on contracts, manifested on computer screens, held in databases, or experienced in the form of worry, privation and austerity, it is, to a large extent *imaginary*. I mean this both in the sense that it has no material presence and also in the sense that, were all those who imagine a debt to perish or disappear or lose their memories, the debt would, ultimately, vanish.

But this definition of 'imaginary' as something that 'doesn't exist in the material world' can become deceptive and unhelpful because it describes most of the important things in our societies, too. Nation states and their borders, for instance, or fiat currencies, or ranks or hierarchies among human beings – all are obviously 'real' but at the same time deeply imaginary. A border is a line on a map, a fiat currency is just a token, and a king is just a man, that is, until and unless their power, authority and value are consolidated through a kind of orchestration of the collective imagination, usually backed by the implicit or explicit threat of violence, expulsion or privation (see Graeber, 2007).

This approach to the imagination is inspired by the work of dissident Marxist and psychoanalytic thinker Cornelius Castoriadis (1997a), whose original and radical theories of the imagination aimed to highlight the importance of autonomy and collective struggle. For Castoriadis, the radical imagination was not (as the term is often mobilised today) simply a euphemism for left-wing activist ideologies. Instead, it was a tectonic force at the core of both the subject and their society. The radical imagination (radical here deriving from the Latin origins of the word, referring to roots) was an ever-unsettled and unsettling force at the core of social life, and also one from which subjects and social institutions are formed (see Haiven and Khasnabish, 2014). Castoriadis likens the radical imagination to magma, which erupts through the earth's crust in molten, liquid form before, with exposure to surface elements, cooling and solidifying into seemingly durable rock formations (Castoriadis, 1997b). His decidedly anti-Lacanian approach sees human development as the dialectic play of an open, protean eruption of desire, curiosity and creativity which, in various forms and various ways, solidifies into stable subjects and relationships, only to be unsettled in various ways and at various times (Urribarri, 2002). Likewise, Castoriadis theorised society as the solidifications of the radical imagination, the petrification of imaginative and imaginary structures into hardened institutions (material and cultural). These, in turn, shape and channel the future flows of the radical imagination, though in times of great change they, too, can be swept away by new, violent eruptions, including – notably – revolutions.

From this angle, naming debt as a structure of the imagination is not aimed at discrediting it as 'unreal', for it is just as 'real' as any other social institution. But it is to say, in a way that is echoed in David Graeber's (2011) magisterial anthropological comparison of dozens of different civilisations, that the forms debt takes will always have a great deal to tell us about the relations of social power at play. For this reason, Graeber cautions that our current association of debt with quantifiable monetary measures is both recent and potentially misguiding. We ought to look deeper than the particularity of the number and, instead, take a more properly anthropological view of how these relationships, symbols and (in our terms) imaginary structures are both reproduced by power and reproductive of it. The numbers matter to the extent that they have their own tale to tell about the integration of debt into a capitalist economy of labour exploitation and alienation superintended by money, and because it helps us identify the particular way capitalist forms of debt braid together both political-economic and moral/cultural power with such devastating effects. Miranda Joseph (2014), drawing on interlocutors in the field of critical accounting studies, has framed this as the way regimes of quantification mediate between capitalism's abstract and concrete registers of power.

Other chapters in this book explore these tensions in much more depth and rigour. My desire here is simply to frame the role and importance of art when it comes to debt. This importance stems from a certain dialectic which I have explored in more detail in my book, *Art after Money, Money after Art: Creative Strategies Against Financialization* (Haiven, 2018). On the one hand, as numerous art historians have shown, within the worldview from which today's forms of global, debt-driven capitalism grew – which is to say a Western European, patriarchal, Protestant and colonial framework – art has become perhaps the sole sphere of sanctioned activity where society is permitted to, for lack of a better term, self-consciously 'work' on the structures of the imagination. Due in large part to the way that the sphere of activities we today associate with 'art' also historically produced rarified, unique artefacts for bourgeois consumption and social reproduction, it has, throughout modernity, signalled a certain space of relative autonomy from direct subordination to capitalist reason, and also a certain freedom from conservative social or religious forces (Bürger, 1984). This has bestowed on art an almost revered status, and also offered artists a limited latitude, always historically specific, to explore social and human questions and problems in uniquely incisive and challenging ways. But, by the same token, this has equally meant that this thing we call 'art' has had an uncomfortable proximity to money in ways that should put to rest any high-minded moralism or sanctimony about its transcendental potentials (Bourdieu, 1993). As long as there has been such a thing as 'art' (as distinct from craft, religious iconography or ornament) it has been inscribed in a tangled relationship with money and, indeed, with debt (Wolff, 1984; Groys, 2011).

It is not only the case that artists are always poor and in debt: it is that the *myth* that artists are always poor and in debt participates in, and helps mask, a deeper set of beliefs that art and money are fundamentally opposed. But it is precisely this mythical opposition that guarantees art's unicorn-like economic value within capitalism, and its other (social, cultural, symbolic) values within capitalist societies (see Velthuis, 2007; Beech, 2016). My efforts, along with others, have been to argue that it is not art's critical distance from and innocence of capitalism that makes it such an important vantage point to examine capitalism; it is precisely art's weird proximity to and collusion with capitalism that makes it so interesting when it turns its gaze on phenomena like economics, money or debt (Malik, 2008; Vishmidt, 2013; La Berge, 2015; Fraser, 2012).

This is, I have sought to argue, all the more so in an age of financialisation, when debt, credit and seemingly more abstract forms of money come to rule. Surely art, that sphere of activities historically and institutionally associated with the work of the imagination, should have something to offer us as capital appears to become more imaginary and imaginative, for instance in the supremacy of increasingly arcane derivatives contracts, or the gladiatorial battle of trading robots, or simply in the sublime alacrity with which nearly every human good, from basic food to education, is transformed into an object of speculation (Sholette and Ressler, 2013). More importantly, in an age when artists represent some of the most precarious and indebted workers in the brave new 'creative economy' of 'first-world' cities, might artists' proximity to debt mean that, even beyond any residual autonomy art may have, these workers might have something to teach us, not so much by what they produce but how they produce (see La Berge and Hannah, 2015; Rosler, 2013)?

Unpayable debts

My curiosity is stimulated here because I am trying to understand a sort of meta-phenomenon of debt which otherwise can't quite be named, and which certainly can't be admitted by the technicians and defenders of the financialised neoliberal model of global capitalism: the growth and proliferation of unpayable debts. By unpayable debts

I mean those that are, either by design or by contingency, impossible to close, but which nonetheless continue to function in a disciplinary way over the debtor. My curiosity here is in line with the inquiries of Graeber (2011), Maurizio Lazzarato (2012, 2015) and Joseph (2014) who investigate the powers of debt in an age of financialisation. But it is also particularly drawn to the question of when debts are widely acknowledged to be unpayable, as explored in the case of Puerto Rico by Columbia University's Unpayable Debts Working Group.[1] In these cases, the tangled ropework of ideology that conventionally legitimates debt begins to fray, revealing the frictions, stress lines and contradictions that have always been present in the global debt order.

We might here think of the archetypical subprime loans that were power-sold to poor and working-class North Americans in the first decade of the 21st century, the 'toxicity' of which led to such dramatic consequences in 2007 and 2008. As has been extensively catalogued, these loans, many of them made to so-called NINJA borrowers (No Income, No Job or Assets), were from the outset sabotaged with quickly rising interest rates that seemingly everyone involved (from the salespeople to the mortgage lenders they represented to the banks that securitised the loans to the rating agencies that gave them the stamp of approval) knew would fail (Aalbers, 2012; Dymski, 2009; Wyly, 2010). While we cannot know the motivations of the borrowers – elsewhere I have suggested, at least at the level of class struggle, such loans may represent an unconscious attempt to reclaim a share of wealth (Haiven, 2013) – the lenders clearly did not believe the debts would ever be repaid: the business model relied on selling access to revenue streams from these securitised debts in tranches to investors, thus on some level the hope was that they would never be repaid, and they would simply continue to produce revenue (see Taibbi, 2010). As Andrew Ross (2014) notes in his cross-sectional analysis of the US debt economy, the ideal for the sellers of debt today are not 'deadbeat' clients who do as they think they ought and pay down their loans on time or early but, rather, 'revolvers', who barely pay the interest each month, without affecting the outstanding principle. This is a condition that many people can relate to in an age when a forty-year stagnation in real (inflation adjusted) wages for the poor and working class has been accompanied by rising fuel and housing prices, and the gradual privatisation or marketisation of many necessities (education, transportation, healthcare, child- and elder-care, and so on), causing a massive increase in consumer debt, defaults and bankruptcies (Aitken, 2015; Dienst, 2011).

On the world stage, of course, unpayable debts have been a staple of the global political economy for some time. On the one hand, powerful G8 nations perpetually roll over and indeed increase their debt loads in order to finance the operations of governments parched for revenue thanks to decades of corporate tax cuts (see Soederberg, 2014). When talk of balancing budgets or paying off the debt is mobilised, it is usually as a punitive measure aimed at cutting social spending (see Stanford, 2008; Pettifor, 2017). On the other hand, it is impossible to ignore that the contemporary world system is structured by the patently unpayable debts of many of the world's poorest nations who, in the post-colonial moment, were offered (frequently usurious) loans to assist with capitalist modes of development (see Bello, 2013; Ndikumana and Boyce, 2011). Yet still these debts persist, even when the promised development never materialised, or when the money was stolen by dictators or corrupt officials, or when it is patently obvious that the debt imposes a disastrous impediment to the kind of economic growth it would require to actually pay off the debt, let alone improve the living standards of the population (Toussaint, 2015; George, 1990).

On some deeper level still, my interest is in the deeper, unpayable debts on which the global capitalist system is based, but which cannot be admitted or accepted within the prevailing economic logic. Here I am thinking, for instance, of the debts owed to African and Caribbean nations for the burden of colonialism and the transatlantic slave trade, and also owed to the Black descendants of those enslaved people in Brazil, the US and elsewhere who still today suffer the consequences and endure the regimes of racial capitalism built on top of slavery (see Beckles, 2013; Coates, 2014; Feagin, 2014; Salzberger and Turck, 2004; Feagin, 2014). I am thinking of the unpayable debts owed to the world's Indigenous peoples for the theft of land and for the genocidal policies of settler-colonial governments that, to this day, seek to eliminate autonomous Indigenous presence on land in the name of capitalist extraction and exploitation (Coulthard, 2014; Wolfe, 2016; Simpson, 2014). I am thinking about the notion of climate debt owed largely by wealthy (once-imperialist) carbon-intensive nations to those billions of poor people around the world who will disproportionately suffer the impacts of global warming, desertification, the acidification and pollution of the ocean and so many other ecological ills (Klein, 2015). And more deeply I am thinking about the deep debts, or 'social bonds' that hold societies together, but that are systematically invisiblised within the capitalist economy, for instance the debts of current generations to the past, or the sort of reciprocal bonds of obligation that bind together communities and families, the *sine qua non* of social reproduction (Dienst, 2011; Federici, 2013; Graeber, 2011; Ross, 2014).

The three artistic projects analysed here each, to my mind, take up the question of unpayable debts in different frameworks, and in each case I want to draw out and contrast two modalities of the unpayable debt. Each piece, on the surface, engages with a manifest form of unpayable debt that signals the way debt is used as a weapon or tool of oppression and exploitation in this economic moment. But each piece also signals towards an unspoken, perhaps unspeakable structure of a deeper, more profound debt. Indeed, my curiosity here leads me to seek, beyond the stated or probable intention of each artist, the deeper currents of debt at work, the rumbling of the radical imagination below, that animates these works in a moment of unpayable debts.

I have selected these three artists in part because, thematically, their three respective works triangulate the field I am trying to understand: how unpayable debts become an infrastructure for the reproduction of financialised capitalism. But I have also opted for these artists and projects because each engages the topic through a combination of participation, spectacle and performance, as opposed to more conventional visual methods of expression. For reasons I have explored in some detail elsewhere, and that have been brilliantly explained by critics Marina Vishmidt (2015; Stakemeier and Vishmidt, 2016) and Leigh Claire La Berge (La Berge and Hannah, 2015; La Berge, 2019), these participatory and performative art practices offer particularly important vantage points to examine financialisation, again, not because they stand so far outside of it, but because they are ultimately wrought of the same material (Haiven, 2018). The participatory turn in contemporary art signals a moment not only when art becomes more fully integrated into the circuits of global capitalism, but when those circuits become more art-like in their operations (Davis, 2018).

My effort here is not to provide any sort of comprehensive thesis: it is valuable to engage with (good) art precisely because, in spite of everything, it touches the unknown. One of art's enduring values is that it holds open a potentially critical space where one might, for a moment and as if from the corner of one's eye, catch a glimpse of the systems, structures, patterns and pressures that are otherwise too fast, too contradictory, too intimate or too uncanny to be systematically observed. As Randy Martin (2015) shows, this is not because of some residual tenacity of the autonomous, romantic imagination but, rather, because art reserves a space to explore the way economic systems – especially financialisation – recalibrate the field of sociality. My conjecture here is that the fantasmatic structure of unpayable debts that haunt our planet and our lives today are so ubiquitous, so familiar and so alien that it may only be in this sort of art that we can fathom their ectoplasm, and the way that they are connected structurally, historically and in ways that connect the social, the economic, the aesthetic, the political and the inter-subjective. Here I have in mind to read these artworks for how they help reveal what Avery Gordon (2008), drawing on Jacques Derrida (1994), calls the *hauntology* of power (see also Gilman-Opalsky, 2016; Fisher, 2014) and, in the terms offered by Stevphen Shukaitis (2016), offer resources for thinking through the rebellious strategies of movements-yet-to-come.

Pocket Money Loans

North London, circa 2014, is a silent war zone. Once home to a diversity of ethnicities trying to make a living and a life in the capital of the British Empire, gentrification and rampant housing speculation in the neoliberal period have profoundly transformed the social fabric (Hubbard, 2017; De Verteuil, 2018). It is important to see this as one of the ways financialisation acts as a mechanism through which capitalism further infiltrates and recalibrates the field of social reproduction. (see Haiven, 2014, especially Chapter 2) Whereas once capitalism seemed content to exploit the time of workers in the factory for a wage, today the mechanisms of debt, the acceleration of consumerism, the financialisation of housing and the commodification of 'service' labour all conspire to make everyday life a field for the exploitation of labour and the extraction of rents (Federici, 2012; Bhattacharya, 2017). Nowhere is this more clearly seen than in the emergence of the 'metropolitan factory', the way that the social fabric of global cities are transformed into zones for speculation and the ratcheting-up of a kind of ambient capitalist discipline (Shukaitis, 2015). Perhaps the most recognisable geographic symptom of these ills are manifestations of 'fringe finance' institutions: payday lenders, cheque-cashing outfits, pawn shops and other businesses who prey upon the urgent needs of the poor and so-called 'unbanked', who are disproportionately migrants, people of colour and members of the working class squeezed by the financialised recalibration of cities (Aitken, 2007; Deville, 2015; Servon, 2017).

For this reason, when a small independent art gallery in North London's rapidly gentrifying neighbourhood of Stoke Newington appeared to have been replaced by a new payday loan shop, it is unlikely anyone paid much attention. Those who did were horrified. With a design palette and cutesy icons reminiscent of children's Saturday morning cartoon advertisements, the boutique offered 'Payday loans 4 kids!' at a mere 5,000% Annual Percentage Rate (APR) interest. The interior of the gallery/store featured a comically austere environment surrounded by posters encouraging children to take out a loan backed by toy cars, or for a tooth fairy offering 'cash 4 teeth', or mortgages on bouncy castles, and 'pro-aging cream'. 'We help you buy the things you can't afford!' reads a speech bubble emanating from a decal of the shop's mascot, a cartoon coin, plastered at toddler height on the gallery's front door.

Darren Cullen's 'Pocket Money Loans' immediately drew harsh criticism from those who, understandably, had been so habituated by the unscrupulousness of the fringe finance industry and the ubiquity of increasingly invasive advertising targeting children that they failed to note the satire (loans to children, while entirely plausible, are illegal in the UK). The artist would receive a similar backlash – which he leveraged into widespread media attention – at subsequent iterations of the installation at galleries, exhibitions (including Banksy's widely visited *Dismaland* temporary theme park) and outdoor music and performing arts festivals (including Glastonbury, the largest such event in the world).

The success of Cullen's projects rests on aiming the double-barrelled capitalist threat of extortionate debt and hyper-consumerist marketing at the fetishised figure of the child. Even as early as the mid-19th century, Marx and Engels (1848), writing in *The Communist Manifesto*, derided the cynical way in which bourgeois morality revered the nuclear family and especially the innocence and purity of (middle-class) children while, at the same time, supporting a capitalist system that conscripted millions of proletarian children to life (and death) in factories or poverty (Engels, 1884). In the mid-20th century, Walter Benjamin, among others, focused his attention on the ways in which children's play was already infected by the logic of capitalism, but also escaped and exceeded it (Benjamin, 2006). A whole range of theorists of education have noted the way that formal schooling systems inscribe children into capitalism depending on social and class background and expectation (Bourdieu, 1990). Others including Jack Zipes (2002), Henry Giroux (2001; Giroux and Searls Giroux, 2004), and bell hooks (1994) have noted the educative and indoctrinating character of popular culture in reinforcing class, race and gender hierarchies. This is to say nothing of advertising itself, which, especially since the widespread adoption of television, targets children explicitly and unrelentingly, both in order to have them 'nag' their parents to make purchases but also to train them for a lifetime of consumerism (see

Langer, 2002; Zelizer, 1994; Barber, 2007). More recent theorists, including Lee Edelman (2004), have identified the way the child under capitalism, and particularly under neoliberal capitalism, becomes the icon of a deeply heteronormative 'reproductive futurism' that is used to justify conservative and austere politics today in the name of better tomorrows for our children. Meanwhile, Zygmunt Bauman (1999), among others, has noted the ways that far-right and reactionary imaginations and movements congeal around real or perceived threats to the child, especially when that child is associated with ethnic, national or religious ideals.

Leigh Claire La Berge (2019), in her deeply insightful study of financialisation, labour and contemporary social practice (or participatory) art, focuses on the way such artists have engaged with children in the last decades, 'employing' children in roles ranging from hairdressers to financial consultants, creators of art to destroyers of art. La Berge's overarching argument here is that, because children (in the 'global North', at least) are legally prohibited from working for a wage (thanks to generations of working-class struggle), their employment by artists is a method to reveal a broader shift in the capitalist economy towards what she terms the increased decommodification of labour: the fashion in which labour which was once waged ceases to be remunerated, even though it remains subject to the discipline of capitalism. So, for instance, artists themselves increasingly 'work for free' or for 'exposure', but so too do many aspirants to what were once imagined to be 'middle-class' jobs: it is common and understood that an un(der)paid internship or zero-hours contract is a necessary (but by no means sure) stepping stone to a career in journalism, finance, law or academia (Cederström and Fleming, 2012; Berardi, 2009). Indeed, it has become obligatory for even aspirants to what are imagined to be working-class jobs, even those considered menial, to secure debt to afford training and credentials, or to endure un(der)paid apprenticeships (see Ross, 2014).

For La Berge (2018), all of these are signals of a deeper shift in capitalism germane to financialisation, and towards neoliberalism as a policy and a cultural/ideological hegemony. In the same book, she explores the work of artists Cassie Thornton and Thomas Gokey who have recast debt (specifically student debt) as a medium of creative expression, arguing that in an era of decommodifcation of labour going into and managing debt becomes a work-like activity. In Cullen's 'Pocket Money Loans', the two come together: the hypothetical child borrower works on two fronts, as artist and as debtor.

For our purposes here, we can observe the play of two unpayable debts in 'Pocket Money Loans'. First, the fear and concern generated by the gimmick revolves around the notion that children, who have not yet developed a fully mature neoliberal economic subjectivity, will be scammed into taking out loans to support profligate purchases and enter adulthood with a massive if not unpayable debt. Yet this begs a number of questions. First, arguably the reason we, as a society, forbid children from taking out loans in the first place is because we (rightly) want to protect them from the predation of the market so they might live out their tender years in relative peace. But this high-mindedness seems not to extend to doing much for the 30 per cent of children living in poverty in the UK, a number that has increased dramatically with neoliberalism and austerity (Elliott, 2017; Cantillon et al, 2017). Indeed, in a horrendous sort of way, a small loan, repayable in adulthood, might actually facilitate children's access to some elements of what we conventionally associate with a decent childhood. Nor does it address the reality that, in spite of the fact children are forbidden from borrowing money from financial institutions, their childhoods are still financialised both at the level of the family, where parents are exhorted to go into debt to upgrade children's human capital through expensive curricular or extracurricular education (see Martin, 2002), and of the state, which is increasingly encouraged to see education, pediatric public health and child-centred civic infrastructure or programming as investments in the future workforce or taxbase (see, for instance, Wietecha, 2016; Karoly, 1998).

As ever, the innocence and protection of the child here appears precisely as a means to distract from and normalise the presumed untrustworthiness and economic abandonment of poor and indebted adults. Why would it be unacceptable to use the latest advertising arsenal to offer predatory loans to children when we have based our entire economy around doing so to adults, as the subprime loan debacle illustrated? Indeed, in a society where the fate of most adults is to spend their lives in debt, and where the first major adult economic experience most children have is going into debt to pay for a university education, the protection of children from debt is pyrrhic at best.

This latter point leads us to a second general point about unpayable debt at work in this piece. While many debts that children of poor and middle-class families will incur when they become adults are individually payable, it is more than likely that those children to whom Cullen's projects offers predatory loans will come of age in a society that will see them indebted unto death (see Ross, 2014). Certainly, if present trends continue, a larger and larger number of people in the UK will retire indebted and never repay what they owe (Rupert Jones, 2017). Declining real (inflation adjusted) wages for working- and middle-class workers, as well as rising costs for housing, transportation, fuel, food and education promise a future where debts pile atop one another in cascading waves (Ross, 2014). Even if one is lucky enough to pay down the first, the next is not far off. This is the existential condition that awaits the majority of children and of which they are already implicitly aware, as I have argued in my study of children's financialised engagement with the popular Pokémon brand (Haiven, 2012a). Ultimately, the figure of the debt-free child helps normalise the pernicious subjectivity of the hopelessly debt-encumbered or entrapped adult that the child is destined to become.

Ultimately, this is the nature of the society 'we' have created for our children. Put otherwise, this is the modality of social reproduction 'we' have orchestrated, one based on and reproductive of unpayable debts. Here financial debt serves to supply, co-opt and pervert one of the most primordial unpayable debts that has guided human evolution: that which undeniably exists between past, present and future generations (see Dienst, 2011; Federici, 2013). While it may be more hopeful to name these relationships as gifts, rather than debts, there is something about the notion of intergenerational *bonds* that speaks to the obligations and expectations of care, nurturance and cultivation that are the *sine qua non* for any society, not only as they exist between kith and kin, but also more broadly as they are expressed by social institutions (see Graeber, 2011). The critical impact of Cullen's work relies on revealing to us the way this fundamental set of qualitative and generative unpayable debt relationships has been commodified, financialised and weaponised in ways that, ultimately, advantage the short-term reproduction and accumulation of capital.

Payment of Greek Debt to Germany with Olives and Art

In a large gallery overseen by a mezzanine in Athens' National Museum for Contemporary Art, a stylish senior Latin American woman in designer sunglasses sits back to back with a middle-aged European woman in a red blazer who looks and acts unnervingly like German Chancellor Angela Merkel. They are seated in swivel chairs in front of a shallow tank brimming with black olives; the smell of brine saturates the space. As the performance begins, the two use their feet to pivot their stationary chairs as if in an awkward dance: the two women seem unable to face one another, always careening in the opposite direction, as if seeking and avoiding one another's eyes. Eventually (awkwardly, as if unrehearsed) the two women stand and the Merkel lookalike delivers an earnest address to the audience in German, the gist of which is that she has realised that Greece's debt has already been paid, thanks to the seminal contributions made by ancient Greek civilisation to the founding of the Western world. This performance ends with the artist in the sunglasses, Argentina's celebrated pop and performance artist Marta Minujín, gifting the Merkel *doppelgänger* a slimy handful of olives from the tank to seal the deal. Cue applause.

The work was the kick-off event for the Documenta 14 Festival and its title, 'Payment of Greek Debt to Germany with Olives and Art', succinctly explains the conceit. At this iteration of the festival, which occurs once every five years and hitherto exclusively in Kassel, Germany, Minujín also erected a massive, skeletal replica of Athens' famous Parthenon in Friedrichsplatz, Kassel's main square, and invited the public to donate banned or censored books to cover the exterior (see Fetter, 2017; Francis, 2018). This was significant as Kassel was a key location where the Nazis had burned books some seven decades earlier. Minujín's 'The Parthenon of Books' (2017) was a remake of the same piece, '*El Partenón de Libros*' installed in Buenos Aries in 1983, in celebration of the fall of the censorious military *junta* that year ('"Parthenon of Books" Constructed from 100,000 Banned Books Rises at Nazi Book Burning Site in Germany' 2017). 'Payment of Greek Debt to Germany with Olives and Art' was also a restaging of a past work, in this case Minujín's 1985 performance (captured in a series of photographs) 'Payment of the Argentine Foreign Debt to Andy Warhol with Corn, The Latin American Gold', where the two artists began seated back to back against a white backdrop, surrounded by semi-peeled ears of corn, before Minujín hands several of the specimens to an idiosyncratically befuddled Warhol, who presumably accepts the payment on behalf of the US (to whose Wall Street banks Argentina owed the debt) (Larratt-Smith, 2010). Minujín also repeated the performance, in a way, in her 1996 'Solving the International Conflict with Art and Corn', where she presented the staple crop to a Margaret Thatcher impersonator (though why Thatcher is unclear: the Iron Lady had by then been out of power for six years) (see Verlichak, 2010).

Minujín's series of performances quite explicitly encourage audiences to reimagine debts and how and if they ought to be repaid. Many of the debts that Minujín was seeking to dissolve in her 1985 piece with Andy Warhol stemmed from the kleptocratic and militarist machinations of the (US-backed) *junta*, such that when Argentina emerged as a capitalist democracy it was already on its financial back foot, a situation that would, by the 1990s lead to massive neoliberal restructuring and, in

2001, a major economic crisis (see Roos, 2019). In 1985, Minujín's gesture rightly fathomed international debt not as an objective eternal criterion but something held in place by the orchestration of power, relationships, performance and ritual. Collaborating with Warhol, one of the US's most prominent (and commercially successful) contemporary artists, Minujín's work questioned if and how debts so onerous as to be fiscally unpayable might be repaid otherwise, in this case by symbolically offering corn, a traditional staple of Latin American agriculture (though not one, it would seem that originated in Argentina). Beyond Minujín's appropriation of Latin American Indigenous traditions, where gifts of corn might ameliorate a conflict or pay a blood-debt, this work had the virtue of both revealing and reframing debt as, ultimately, a matter of the weaponised imagination, beyond the particular quantitative figures in which it might typically be denominated.

Whatever critical dimension the piece may have had in 1985 was almost completely evacuated in its 2017 reprisal at Documenta 14, though to understand why we must first sketch its context. Documenta has never been without controversy. Tasked with, in some fashion, capturing and representing 'the contemporary' in a global sense, the festival's origins stem from an attempt to grapple with and transcend the dark legacy of the Nazis, whose antipathy to cosmopolitan, 'degenerate' modern art was well known and who enjoyed widespread political and economic support from Kassel and the broader region of Hesse of which Kassel is the capital (see Papadopoulos, 2018). With such a mandate and such a history to contend with, it is no surprise that the festival is one of the global art world's most significant, anticipated and (therefore) vexed. The 2017 edition of the festival, curated by Adam Szymczyk and an all-star team of international art-world luminaries, was no exception to this trend, thanks to at least two unique historical factors.

First, following criticisms of previous iterations of the festival which had tended to associate 'the contemporary' with Western Europe and North America (following a tacitly white-supremacist and colonial logic), the 2017 edition dedicated itself to 'learning from the South' and opted, for the first time, to split its activities between Kassel and another city, Athens. While Greece is typically associated with the antiquity of 'Western civilisation', this choice came in the context of the catastrophic paroxysms of debt-driven austerity and social collapse forced on the small nation in the wake of the 2008 financial crisis, which Greek commentators from across the political spectrum have likened to a form of financial and political colonialisation by the Troika (the informal name given to the European Central Bank, the European Commission and the International Monetary Fund [IMF]) (Lapavitsas, 2012; Varoufakis, 2016). It is far from insignificant that the first two of these institutions are widely understood to be dramatically influenced (if not controlled) by Germany, the European Union's largest economy and a major source of investment/speculation in Greek private and public debts since the 1990s (Roos, 2019).

Documenta's appearance in Athens came three years after the historical showdown between the Troika and Greece's left-wing Syriza party which in 2015, following a decisive electoral victory and unsuccessful negotiations to write off the debt or reduce the austerity that was destroying the country's social fabric, called a national plebiscite to gauge if the Troika's bailout package (and dramatic austerity agenda) should be accepted (Varoufakis, 2018). Implicit though ambiguous in the referendum was the broader question of Greece's further participation in the European Union (EU). The 'όχι' or 'no' vote was decisive, but days later, in a shocking about-face, the Syriza government ended up accepting the bailout package when faced with the moralistic recalcitrance of hardliners in the Troika (notably representatives of Germany and other 'Northern European' states) (Flassbeck and Lapavitsas, 2015). As the then-finance minister Yanis Varoufakis (2018) (who quit Syriza following the referendum) illustrates, the message was clear: the social and economic life of Greece would be sacrificed in order to shore up the precarious state of the international banking sector, notably Germany's hegemonic Deutsche Bank.

For our purposes, one of the most remarkable dimensions of this debacle was the reports issued by the IMF (one third of the Troika) even before the referendum that indicated that, in spite of so much high-minded moralism insisting Greece had to answer for its profligate borrowing in the 1990s and 2000s, further austerity was almost certain to fail in its stated aim of creating the conditions of debt repayment: without significant economic growth that could only be catalysed through massive government stimulus spending, the Greek economy would weaken and weaken (see Roos, 2019). Beyond the very significant question of whether the debts Greece owed were in fact legitimate in the first place (the subject of a provisional report of a commission of international experts struck by the Syriza government in the lead up to the referendum, and dissolved shortly after their capitulation: see Preliminary Report, 2015), a deeper conundrum emerged here: what does it mean for the Troika to insist on the repayment of a debt that even they realise can never be repaid, a debt that, in fact, fatally undermines the debtor's ability to *ever* repay?

While various national stereotypes have been trotted out to make sense of the German and 'Northern European' self-defeating hardline approach (stereotypes that, at least in Greece itself, recall the officious viciousness of the Nazi occupation of that country), a broader look at European and global political economy is more revealing (Elliott, 2015). Allowing Greece to default on its debts, or debt reduction, or an easement of austerity, would, from the perspective of Germany and other financially powerful nations, send a dangerous signal to other debt-encumbered states in Europe and around the world (see Bello, 2013). While Greece itself represents an almost insignificant economic player within the EU and global economy, its martyrdom was calculated to demonstrate to other nations – including Spain, Portugal, Ireland and Italy (now reclassified as the 'European periphery') – that they would receive no sympathy from the Troika or global markets, and that austerity was obligatory (Flassbeck and Lapavitsas, 2015). Meanwhile, beyond Europe, there were significant fears that, if Greece were given any quarter, it would soon also be demanded by nations in the global South who have been ensnared in neocolonial debt peonage for generations (thanks in large part to the machinations of the IMF) (Roos, 2019; Ndikumana and Boyce, 2011).

This is the first factor that helps explain the curatorial and artistic context of Documenta 14. The second is the so-called 'refugee crisis' that 'began' in the summer of 2014 as millions of people fled the ravaged war zones of Syria, Iraq, Afghanistan, Pakistan and Libya as well as the economic privation and political repression of nations in northern Africa, daring extremely risky crossings over land and sea to seek asylum in Europe, in particular in wealthy 'Northern European' nations (see Reece Jones, 2017; Woznicki, 2018). Let us set aside the important question of how these 'wealthy' nations derived their wealth and stability, in part, from the histories and legacies of the same imperialism and colonialism that led to the instability and poverty from which the refugees fled (a kind of debt we shall return to in the final section of this chapter). For now it is significant to note the fanfare, both within and beyond Germany, when, in 2015, Chancellor Angela Merkel declared (somewhat deceptively) that the Federal Republic would have an open-door policy towards Syrian refugees, eventually admitting nearly one million (see Bergfeld, 2016). Never mind that Lebanon, Jordan, Turkey and Egypt had accepted many times this number. Never mind that the specification of Syrian (and not Afghan or Libyan) refugees aimed to attract generally highly skilled, well-educated, middle-class asylum seekers who could make an important contribution to Germany's economy and ageing workforce (in a long tradition of German exploitation of foreign 'guest workers') (Bergfeld, 2017). Never mind that this arrangement eventually would necessitate a deal between the EU and the notoriously punitive and authoritarian regime in Turkey to deny refugees access to Europe, and also the stranding of over 60,000 refugees in the austerity-ravaged Greece ('After 16 Refugees Drown, Greeks Rally Against EU-Turkey Swap Deal', 2018).

What is significant for our purposes here is the way that Merkel's move was arguably calculated to in some sense repay or amortise Germany's historic and moral debts of the Nazi period. It is not only that this move came shortly after Germany's ugly leadership on the question of the Greek debt. It was also that, in such a monumental gesture of liberal humanism, Germany was perhaps encouraged to imagine itself as finally liberated from the profound collective guilt owing to the Nazi Holocaust (not insignificantly, German speakers use the same word, *Schuld*, for guilt, shame and debt) (Wintour, 2016). As Horst Bredekamp[2] has noted, widely broadcast and shared videos of refugees arriving *en masse* at German train stations and greeted by thousands of German well-wishers, almost seemed to be a magical reversal of the apocryphal image of Jews, Roma people, queer people, communists and others deported to death camps by train by the Nazis, with the enthusiastic support of the (proverbial and literal) grandparents of today's well-wishers. While Germany paid (and continues to pay) economic reparations to Jewish Holocaust survivors and their families, and to the state of Israel, for the debts germane to the world-historic crime of the Nazi Holocaust, Merkel's would-be world-historic gesture was arguably in part aimed at repaying that debt on another set of levels. It should be noted that this explanation for Merkel's refugee policy was also widely propounded by Germany's far right as part of a campaign to suggest that it was high time for the nation to let go of its ideologically stifling and (to their mind) ethno-nationally 'suicidal' guilt complex (see Schwartz, 2017; for an English equivalent, see Murray, 2018).

In any case, by Minujin's 2017 performance, the success of Merkel's policy was widely questioned. The conflict in Syria had escalated and unleashed one of the most terrifying spectres yet seen: the so-called 'Islamic State', a monstrous manifestation of fascistic vengeance cloaked in Muslim fundamentalist garb, that not only imposed a grotesque legal code on the territories it controlled but also coordinated and inspired freelance acts of political violence targeting civilians in Western nations like Germany. In those nations, far-right and neofascist groups greatly profited from these attacks, using them to whip up xenophobic fear, resentment and antipathy towards refugees (Crawford, 2017). Immediately following Documenta 14, Germany's Alternative für Deutschland party (AfD) would go on to enjoy 14 per cent of the popular vote in the 2017 German Federal elections. Indeed, a local Kassel AfD candidate, a lawyer, took it upon himself to launch a lawsuit against the festival, nominally due to its significant budgetary deficit (incurred, in part, because of the logistical challenges of splitting the festival between two cities) (Neuendorf, 2017). The lawsuit was a key example of the kind of right-wing populist political *resentiment* that has made the AfD and similar parties so successful: Documenta was framed (in ways eerily reminiscent of the Nazi's popular castigation of 'degenerate art') as the appropriation of hard-working Germans' tax dollars as a give-away by liberal 'elites' to haughty cosmopolitan internationals for inaccessible and insulting art (Müser, 2017). In this context, Minujín's over-budget, aesthetically awkward skeletal 'Parthenon of Books' in Kassel's main square was lambasted by the AfD and their allies in the right-wing German press as a particularly egregious example of the art world's conspiracy to both rob and mock the *Volk* ('Documenta 14 Artists Pen Second Open Letter Defending Exhibition', 2017).

These contextual factors help explain why Minujín's reheated performance of 'Payment of Greek Debt to Germany with Olives and Art' in Athens was such an artistic and critical failure. First, even if the analogy between Argentina's debt in 1985 and Greece's debt in 2017 were accurate (it's not), it simply does not make sense either that Merkel would replace Warhol or that Minujín would stay in her role, as opposed to, say, a prominent Greek artist (though perhaps no prominent Greek artist agreed to take part). Second, Minujín's half-baked concept had much more to say as a symptom of the international art world's ill-informed and condescending pity towards Greece than it did about the crisis of austerity (see Papadopoulos, 2018). This condescension and ignorance was well represented in a few dimensions of the piece. The first is that, while in the 'speech' given to Merkel and in later interviews Minujín waxed eloquent about the unpayable debt that 'Western civilisation' owes to ancient Greek culture, within Greece practically the only parties that use this hyper-nationalist, atavistic rhetoric are far-right actors, notably the murderous neofascist Golden Dawn party (see Dalakoglou, 2013; Koronaiou et al, 2015). Second, while olives are indeed a key and celebrated part of Greek cuisine and a notable (though not particularly lucrative) export, during the crisis Greece was often saddled in the international arena with the accusation of a kind of cultural and economic backwardness tied to racialised myths about a

Southern culture of leisure emblematised by olives and wine (Mylonas, 2018). Apparently blithely ignorant of these and other resonances and contradictions, Minujín's ill-informed attempt to unsummon Greece's debt and create a cathartic spectacle could rightfully be said to have been an expression of a kind of patronising hubris that critics charge characterised the festival's Greek experience as a whole.

Space does not permit a full explication of all the dimensions of this hubris or its origins and implications, but it does help us to understand a few things about the question of unpayable debts. Minujín's obvious gambit is that she can excavate an unpayable cultural debt of Europe to Greece which trumps the (also unpayable) financial debt owed by contemporary Greece to Europe (mostly to Germany, its banks and their global clients). In the first place, this manoeuvre reifies not only the contemporary financial debt (the piece declares it repaid, not illegitimate in the first place), but also the categories of 'Greece' and 'Europe' that are at the core of the financialised imaginary of nation states that is arguably the source of the problem in the first place. There is, of course, an element of critical truth to the idea that a debt to culture, philosophy and art *ought* to be more important than mere money, especially when that money is itself the hallucination of unanswerable financial institutions or a weapon of geopolitics. But this point is pedestrian and unactionable except to the extent it can call together some sort of common political-economic agency or collectivity. 'We' (the international art world) all get the joke, but no one wants to do anything about it, because the joke is on us: we are the beneficiaries of that same system, as represented by the (professionally ambivalent) institution of Documenta.

To be clear, I do not think Documenta's value is exhausted by these complicities and contradictions: there were many other fine works at the festival, and some of them addressed the political-economic moment of unpayable debts with critical sophistication and aesthetic acuity. However, Minujín's piece, which was also the keynote opening performance of the festival's presence in Athens, reveals that even work that seeks to make some of the dimensions of an unpayable debt visible can, in the end, reinforce or reinscribe the relationships and symbolic infrastructures that allowed for the unpayable debt in the first place. If we wish to find art that can help us envision a different approach, we must look elsewhere.

Gone Indian

It was after midnight and a million people, many of them inebriated, ramble through downtown Toronto's financial district on a warm September night (Fisher and Drobnick, 2012). As they make their way between the charismatic art installations of the 2009 edition of the city's *Nuit Blanche* all-night public arts festival, some encountered a dilapidated and muddy burgundy van, a set of deer antlers affixed to its hood, its roof covered in an embroidered buckskin rug with a couple of old armchairs secured on top, driving slowly through the streets, blaring Indigenous pow-wow[3] music (drumming and singing) from a large sound system. Eventually, the van pulled up on the curb at the headquarters to the Royal Bank of Canada (RBC), one of the world's largest financial institutions whose imposing two-tower edifice is literally made of gold infused into its glistening sheet-glass cladding. A crowd gathers, most of them non-Indigenous, to watch 'Gone Indian', a performance by Rebecca Belmore, perhaps Canada's best known and most celebrated Indigenous performance artist (Nagam, 2011). The title is a sly pun: the Indian is gone from these lands, eliminated to make room for the bustling financial district and larger city; but 'going Indian' was also a phrase from that same Canadian history to describe European settlers who developed what were perceived to be unhealthy attachments to the place and its people, being adopted into Indigenous communities (a crime – desertion – that, in Canada's early colonial days, was punishable by slow and painful death) or otherwise abandoning what the British called 'civility' for 'savage' ways (see Van Kirk, 1983).

Belmore's performance was layered and complex, blending Anishinaabe, Cree and settler symbolism. Near the outset, Belmore, barefoot and wearing feather-adorned army-green overalls and a black toque, placed several red cloth bags full of Canadian pennies at the periphery of the performance space and later cut them open with a knife, spilling the coins onto the sidewalk before tying the torn red fabrics to her ankle. Meanwhile, celebrated Cree actor and dancer Michael Greyeyes, dressed in full dance regalia, performed a series of choreographed modern dance routines, first to an Indigenous hip-hop track, next to a recording of pow-wow drumming and singing. While Greyeyes' movements referenced pow-wow dancing, they were original contemporary compositions, often exhibiting jerky, halting motions as if his body were at times possessed and/or constrained by unseen, unfriendly forces. The whole performance was quietly overseen and occasionally photographed by a silent Indigenous man conspicuously wearing dress trousers, a white collared shirt, a black tie, a black fringed buckskin jacket, and sunglasses (despite it being night-time). As the performance unfolded, Belmore, on her knees, used what appeared to be a heavy traditional stone mortar and pestle to attempt to grind the pennies as one might to corn or medicines to produce an edible or healing substance. The performance ended with Greyeyes drifting, as if in slow motion, through the space and Belmore giving up on her task. The pennies remained scatted on the ground and the company drove away in the van.

This piece was intentionally ambiguous in part because, to my mind, it attempted to haunt the colonial imagination precisely at the fraught intersection where, drawing on the work of Sherene Razack (2002), space meets place in a colonial settler state: in this case, the site where Indigenous land has been turned into a financial zone of speculation. This choice of location is by no means coincidental. As I have elaborated elsewhere, the theft of lands from Indigenous people, and the elimination of Indigenous presence on those lands, was always a financialised affair. All three key dimensions of the so-called FIRE sector (finance, insurance and real estate) were essentially born in the crucible of European imperialism and (settler-)colonialism: both stock markets and the joint-stock, limited liability corporation had their origins in Amsterdam and London in the financing of colonial ventures, settler-colonies and the slave trade (Haiven, 2017). Authors including Ian Baucom (2005), Anita Rupprecht (2016) and Zenia Kish and Justin Leroy (2015) have demonstrated that the origins of modern insurance laws and practices cannot be separated from the transformation of enslaved African human beings into speculative property. And Brenna Bhandar (2018), Aileen Moreton-Robinson (2015), Rachel O'Reilly (2018), and Cheryl Harris (1993) have all argued that the notion that land could become 'real estate; to be speculated upon and exchanged had its roots in the colonial transformation of territory into private property.

In Belmore's few public comments about 'Gone Indian' she has stressed that, in transporting a pow-wow into the financial district, she is attempting to create a spectacle not so much of remembrance of the past but a haunting image for the attendees, the vast majority of whom are urban settlers (see Haiven, 2012b). Before this space was a financialised place, the headquarters of Canada's largest bank, it was something, or somewhere, else. But the ceremony Belmore choreographed does not afford the viewer the satisfaction of the anthropological gaze so germane to settler colonies where, as Patrick Wolfe (2006) notes, the state attempts to continue its genocidal elimination of Indigenous presence on the land precisely by adopting, accommodating and appropriating its chosen versions of Indigenous 'culture'. 'We', the audience, arrive expecting to be entertained; we leave haunted by ghosts that were always already hidden in plain sight (see Gordon, 2008).

The choice of the RBC headquarters is quite specific. As Canada's largest bank not only does it inherit the legacies of financialised settler-colonialism, which for instance financed the fur trade on which the nation was built and the expansion of the railway which led to the mass displacement of multiple Indigenous peoples (see Haiven, 2017). RBC is also a key participant in the continued colonisation of the land today: the bulk of the savings and investments it manages are routed through firms on Canada's TSX stock exchange (in a building nearby to RCB) where, by some estimates, 60 per cent of global mining industry venture financing is generated (see Deneault and Sacher, 2012; Gordon and Webber, 2016). Indeed, Canada has repeatedly named the extractive industry, both at home and abroad, as one of its key strategic economic interests ('Mining Capital: How Canada Has Transformed Its Resource Endowment into a Global Competitive Advantage', 2013). This in spite of the fact that numerous international non-governmental organisations (including Human Rights Watch, Amnesty International and the United Nations) have condemned Canadian and Canadian-funded mining corporations for environmental and human rights abuses both within Canada and around the world, especially as they have affected (and, indeed, targeted) Indigenous people and Indigenous lands (Gordon and Webber, 2016; Veltmeyer and Petras, 2014).

Meanwhile, in Canada, settler-colonialism itself has taken on a financialised dimension. Since the 19th century, the Canadian government has imposed on Indigenous communities a form of poisoned 'self-governance' mandated through the Indian Act (first passed in 1876), a set of laws for the governance of Indigenous life that, at one time, included restrictions on Indigenous people's right to leave reservations without a pass authorised by a (white) 'Indian agent', their right to hunt and fish, their right to practice Indigenous spirituality and ceremonies, their right to organise politically, their right to hire lawyers, their right to use modern farming implements and their right to speak their languages (see Manuel and Derrickson, 2015). This Act also permitted the abduction of Indigenous children from their families to be placed in church-run residential schools, where they were severely punished for any behaviours deemed 'savage' (for example, speaking their language) and where they were subject to the horrific predations and abuses of the clergy and staff, all of which is a matter of public record and discussion thanks to a landmark legal case by survivors that resulted in a national Truth and Reconciliation Commission that was ongoing during Belmore's performance and which released its final landmark report in 2015 ('Honouring the Truth, Reconciling the Future: Final Report', 2015).

Today, the administration of settler-colonialism in Canada stresses Indigenous self-governance, but the top-down colonial framework still persists: as Shiri Pasternak (2015, 2016) has demonstrated, the Canadian government exerts profound and corrosive disciplinary pressure on Indigenous governments through financialised means. In the first place, the Canadian government holds the purse strings for funds that support nearly all services on Indigenous reservations and uses a series of laborious and disciplinary accounting and reporting mechanisms to constrain and delimit Indigenous communities' spending. Meanwhile, it holds out the threat of auditing and forced third-party management to dissuade those governments from taking actions that might jeopardise the colonial settler state's interests, notably blocking or intervening in attempts to locate extractive industries (for example, mines) or infrastructure (for example, pipelines) on Indigenous lands. Meanwhile, the same neoliberal governments have sought to fix the 'Indian problem' through financialised means. Responsibility for the endemic poverty and horrendous health and social indicators that characterise life on reservations is transferred from the Federal government's inaction and caustic paternalism towards the failure of markets in those spaces (see Altamirano-Jiménez, 2013; Sommerville, 2018). Numerous successive Canadian governments have sought to dissolve Indigenous collective title to lands and transform them into individual fee-simple holdings, the hope being that the introduction of private property will inspire entrepreneurialism, allow Indigenous people on reservations to borrow against their holdings, relocate to take advantage of labour markets elsewhere and, ultimately, lead them to become proper capitalist subjects (see Coulthard, 2014). Needless to say, this agenda has been strenuously rejected by many Indigenous nations who insist that their communal, non-commodified relationship to a land-base is at the heart of their existence as a people. For this reason, Wolfe (2006) and others including Glen Coulthard (2014) and Audra Simpson (2014) have noted that such market-oriented privatisation schemes are part of a long genocidal tradition of seeking to 'eliminate' Indigenous people.

All these dimensions factor into Belmore's performance. Settler-colonialism has advanced by leveraging financialised mechanisms to transform land into property by eliminating Indigenous presence. Her temporary reclaiming of the bank's space aims, in part, to reveal the imaginary and imaginative powers at work by transforming a financialised space back into an Indigenous place. It is not insignificant that Belmore here opts to work with pennies as well, an almost worthless unit of Canadian currency that the nation ceased to mint in 2012. Her attempts to crush or pulverise this ubiquitous fetish object, stands in, perhaps, for Indigenous attempts to grapple with the poisonous financialised spirituality or belief-system of settler-colonialism, which in the end is reducible only to the pathological logic of capital itself: accumulation at all costs.

If so, two or perhaps three unpayable debts are at work in this piece. In the first place, Belmore's failure to crush the coins, and Greyeye's ambivalent, fractured dance, may be read as resonant with the way in which financialised settler-colonialism, past and present, has sought to subsume or subscribe Indigenous people in a system that perpetually thwarts their thriving. As Paula Chakravartty and Denise Ferreira da Silva (2012) illustrate, the contemporary global financial order is one that is not only built on legacies of racism and colonialism, but one that, because of that, creates racialised financial subjects doomed to a kind of perpetual failure that is nonetheless profitable for others. In their reading, this financialised system places non-white people in a state of perpetual, unpayable debt, a debt incurred as a subject who was never intended to thrive or succeed within a white-supremacist economic system, even (especially) if that system now (self-servingly) declares itself a colour-blind capitalist meritocracy. Belmore and Greyeyes attempt to innovate Indigenous practices within a field of coins, in the shadow of the bank, surrounded by settler onlookers; their inability to succeed or thrive then becomes evidence of an unspoken and unspeakable debt that settler-colonialism imposes on Indigenous peoples and communities. As with the case of settler-colonial schemes to 'civilise' Indigenous people through the financialisation of their lands, the gift is poisoned (see Haiven, 2017).

Yet, at the same time, this performance might also be said to seek to awaken the audience's sensibility to the unpayable debts owed by settler-colonialism itself. With 13.5 million clients in a nation of 36 million, it is highly probable that the plurality of spectators at Belmore's performance were invested in RBC; in any case in this regard all of Canada's five hegemonic banks are equivalent: settler-colonial capitalist citizenship requires one be invested, one way or another, in both the symbolic and the real perpetuation of the financialised seizure and destruction of Indigenous lands via one's savings, investments, pensions and other financial activity (see Deneault and Sacher, 2012). Further, the enjoyment of the built environment and of the rights of citizenship anywhere in Canada, and certainly in its financial capital

Toronto, depends on a long history and legacy of financialised seizure of land and elimination of Indigenous presence (Bhandar, 2018). Hence both the space of the bank building and the material of the coins might be intended to awaken an awareness in the audience that they, too, are the product and the reproducers of a financialised form of settler-colonialism, and that this system implies an almost sublimely huge moral and also economic debt.

For instance, the reparation settlement for the survivors of the residential schools alone (the largest for a class action suit in Canadian history, with upwards of 34,000 claimants) amounted to over $3bn CAD (Galloway, 2016); were it to be seriously entertained (it is not), the monetary compensation and restitution for historical harms, attempted genocide and the systematic theft of Indigenous land would quite probably amount to a sum sufficient to bankrupt this G8 Nation.

Elsewhere, I have mused on the political utility of settlers in Canada embracing this imminent bankruptcy as a methodology by which to imagine a world beyond both financialisation and settler-colonialism, which I think is urgently necessary (Haiven, 2017). For now, I simply want to conclude by stressing that at stake in Belmore's summoning of the spectres of unpayable debts is the question of in what currency, or through what terms, such debts might be repaid. As Coulthard (2014) has noted, in the name of 'reconciliation' the Canadian government has made billions of dollars of new funding available in a kind of histrionic and hypocritical generosity: the money is, after all, derived ultimately from land and resources stolen from Indigenous people in the first place (Manuel and Derrickson, 2015). Indeed, even in spite of this 'generosity', multiple levels of Canadian state administration have been found guilty in court of systematically underfunding Indigenous communities and people (especially children) relative to non-Indigenous Canadians (see Cossette, 2017). By the same token, the settler-colonial state has strongly encouraged (and at times blackmailed) Indigenous governments to accept profit-sharing agreements with extractive corporations for the (ab)use of their lands, even though the environmental and social impacts are ultimately destructive to those communities (Pasternak, 2017). For these reasons, an increasing number of Indigenous nations and communities are resisting or rejecting monetary compensation or offers and, instead insisting on their sovereign rights to control access and use of their territories, a sovereignty (which should not be mistaken for a replica of the Westphalian European model) they are willing to defend through civil disobedience, blockades and, even, armed resistance (Coulthard, 2014; Barker, 2015; Barker, 2017).

If this trend continues the settler-colonial state of Canada will soon find itself unable to pay its debts for colonialism with its own minted currency: the currency itself is a key part of the system that exacts the violence that continues to incur the debt. If that is the case, amortising that debt will need to take place by other means, primarily through the cessation of the economic and social violence. But this is arguably ontologically impossible within the current order: the state and the form of financialised, settler-colonial capitalism with which it is entangled cannot endure a terminal challenge to the twinned logics (legal, political and economic) of private property and territorial state sovereignty that such a cessation would implicitly demand. Repayment of the debt would quite literally both imply and require a revolution.

Conclusion

If the above artworks have taught us anything, it is that systems and structures of financialised power fabricate and enforce unpayable debts on those people and communities whom they subordinate precisely in order to cover over the unpayable debts they themselves owe to the subordinated. As David Graeber (2011) argues, under financialisation, the unpayable debt of the subjugated is made to appear in quantitative, monetised terms precisely to help mask its origins in social violence and to individualise and pathologise the debtor to prevent them from creating bonds of solidarity within and beyond their communities, with those likewise encumbered. Meanwhile, the debt owed by the systems and structures of financialised power are rendered qualitative and moral at best, irrelevant at worst, in any case unactionable.

But, like an unquiet ghost, the deeper debt haunts: these profound unpaid, indeed *ontological* debts express themselves as contradictions and cataracts in the socio-economic and political fabric. Often, able to neither admit nor assuage the debt, those indebted systems take revenge in the form of punitive moralism or wanton cruelty: the hypocritical fetishisation of the figure of the debt-free child; the passion play that blames Greek debt (and German wealth) on allegedly national cultural characteristics, but nonetheless abandons a whole population to penury; the poisoned benevolence of Canadian settler-colonialism. Because ultimately these relationships are based on the exploitation and oppression germane to the contradictions of capitalist accumulation in a financialised world, they breed resentment and are riven with crises which, as they deepen, require that the dominant systems unleash ever more structural and systemic violence.

One might assess these and other artworks on the basis of how well they can reveal these underlying dynamics. But, more importantly, one might assess them to the extent they make visible, even for a moment, the potentials for solidarity, refusal and rebellion within and between those who are both abject debtor and secret creditor to an unchosen, destructive system. The latter is the crucial work of the radical imagination within, against and beyond financialisation.

Notes

1. https://www.socialdifference.columbia.edu/projects-/unpayable-debt-capital-violence-and-the-new-global-economy
2. Bredekamp made this point during a presentation as part of the 'Uncertain States' exhibition at the Akademie der Künste in Berlin in 2017, though I have not been able to locate it in print.
3. Pow-wows are an important part of indigenous North American cultural life and have specific regalia and music associated with them. Belmore herself uses this terminology.

References

Aalbers, M. B. (2012) (ed.) *Subprime Cities: The Political Economy of Mortgage Markets*. New York: Wiley.

'After 16 Refugees Drown, Greeks Rally Against EU-Turkey Swap Deal' (2018) *National Herald* (blog). 18 March 2018. https://www.thenationalherald.com/194160/after-16-refugees-drown-greeks-rally-against-eu-turkey-swap-deal/

Aitken, R. (2007) *Performing Capital: Toward a Cultural Economy of Popular and Global Finance*. New York: Palgrave Macmillan.

Aitken, R. (2015) 'Everyday Debt Relationalities: Situating Peer-to-Peer Lending and the Rolling Jubilee', *Cultural Studies* 29 (5-6): 845-68.

Altamirano-Jiménez, I. (2013) *Indigenous Encounters with Neoliberalism: Place, Women, and the Environment in Canada and Mexico*. Vancouver: UBC Press.

Barber, B. R. (2007) *Consumed: How Markets Corrupt Children, Infantilize Adults, and Swallow Citizens Whole*. New York: W. W. Norton.

Barker, A. J. (2015) '"A Direct Act of Resurgence, a Direct Act of Sovereignty": Reflections on Idle No More, Indigenous Activism, and Canadian Settler Colonialism', *Globalizations* 12 (1): 43-65.

Barker, J. (ed.) (2017) *Critically Sovereign: Indigenous Gender, Sexuality, and Feminist Studies*. Durham: Duke University Press.

Baucom, I. (2005) *Specters of the Atlantic: Finance Capital, Slavery, and Philosophy of History*. Durham, NC: Duke University Press.

Bauman, Z. (1999) *In Search of Politics*. Stanford, CA: Stanford University Press. http://www.loc.gov/catdir/description/cam0210/99071005.html

Beckles, H. (2013) *Britain's Black Debt: Reparations for Caribbean Slavery and Native Genocide*. Kingston, Jamaica: University Of West Indies Press.

Beech, D. (2016) *Art and Value: Art's Economic Exceptionalism in Classical, Neoclassical and Marxist Economics*. Chicago, Illinois: Haymarket Books.

Bello, W. (2013) *Capitalism's Last Stand?: Deglobalization in the Age of Austerity*. London: Zed.

Benjamin, W. (2006) *Berlin Childhood Around 1900* (trans. H. Eiland). Cambridge, MA: Belknap.

Berardi, F. (2009) *The Soul at Work: From Alienation to Autonomy* (trans. G. Mecchia and F. Cadel). Los Angeles, CA: Semiotext(e).

Bergfeld, M. (2016) 'Germany: In the Eye of the Storm',in *Europe in Revolt*, C. Príncipe and B. Sunkara (eds), 115-27. Chicago, Illinois: Haymarket Books.

Bergfeld, M. (2017) 'Germany's Willkommenskultur: Trade Unions, Refugees and Labour Market Integration', *Global Labour Journal* 8 (1).

Bhandar, B. (2018) *Colonial Lives of Property: Law, Land and Racial Regimes of Ownership*. Durham NC and London: Duke University Press.

Bhattacharya, T. (ed.) (2017) *Social Reproduction Theory: Remapping Class, Recentering Oppression*. London: Pluto Press.

Bourdieu, P. (1990) *Reproduction in Education, Society and Culture* (trans. J.-C. Passeron, 2nd ed.) London and Thousand Oaks, CA: Sage.

Bourdieu, P. (1993) in *The Field of Cultural Production: Essays on Art and Literature*. R. Johnson (ed.). New York: Columbia University Press.

Bürger, P. (1984) *Theory of the Avant-Garde*. Minneapolis, MN: University of Minnestoa Press.

Cantillon, B., Chzhen, Y., Handa, S. and Nolan, B. (2017) (eds) *Children of Austerity: Impact of the Great Recession on Child Poverty in Rich Countries*. Oxford, United Kingdom: United Nations Children's Fund and Oxford University Press.

Castoriadis, C. (1997a) 'Radical Imagination and the Social Instituting Imaginary' in *The Castoriadis Reader*, D. A. Curtis (ed.), 319-37. Cambridge and New York: Blackwell.

Castoriadis, C. (1997b) 'The Logic of Magmas and the Question of Autonomy', in *The Castoriadis Reader*, D. A. Curtis (ed.), 290-318. Cambridge and New York: Blackwell.

Cederström, C., and Fleming, P. (2012) *Dead Man Working*. Winchester, UK: Zero Books.

Chakravartty, P. and Ferreira da Silva, D. (2012) 'Accumulation, Dispossession, and Debt: The Racial Logic of Global Capitalism — An Introduction', *American Quarterly* 64 (3): 361-85.

Coates, T.-N. (2014) 'The Case for Reparations', *The Atlantic*, 2014. https://www.theatlantic.com/magazine/archive/2014/06/the-case-for-reparations/361631/

Cossette, M.-A. (2017) 'Fix First Nations Child Welfare System Now, Says Cindy Blackstock', CBC. 2 December 2017. http://www.cbc.ca/news/politics/blackstock-philpott-children-welfare-1.4420658

Coulthard, G. (2014) *Red Skin, White Masks: Rejecting the Colonial Politics of Recognition*. Minneapolis and London: University of Minnesota Press.

Crawford, B. (2017) 'It's the German Economy, Stupid! Economic Inequality, Not Immigration, Explains Far Right Rise in Germany', The Berkeley Blog. 27 September 2017. Available at: http://blogs.berkeley.edu/2017/09/27/its-the-german-economy-stupid-economic-inequality-not-immigration-explains-the-rise-of-the-far-right-in-germany/

Dalakoglou, D. (2013) '"From the Bottom of the Aegean Sea" to Golden Dawn: Security, Xenophobia, and the Politics of Hate in Greece', *Studies in Ethnicity and Nationalism* 13 (3): 514-22.

Davis, A. (2018) 'Defining Speculative Value in the Age of Financialized Capitalism', *The Sociological Review* 66 (1): 3-19.

De Verteuil, G. (2018) 'Immigration and Gentrification' in *Handbook of Gentrification Studies*, L. Lees and M. Phillips (eds), 428-43.

Deneault, A. and Sacher, W. (2012) *Imperial Canada Inc.* (trans. F. A. Reed and R. Philpot). Vancouver: Talon.

Derrida, J. (1994) *Specters of Marx: The State of the Debt, the Work of Mourning, and the New International*. New York: Routledge.

Deville, J. (2015) *Lived Economies of Default: Consumer Credit, Debt Collection and the Capture of Affect*. London and New York: Routledge.

Dienst, R. (2011) *The Bonds of Debt: Borrowing Against the Common Good*. London and New York: Verso.

'Documenta 14 Artists Pen Second Open Letter Defending Exhibition' (2017) *Art Forum*, 1 December 2017. https://www.artforum.com/news/documenta-14-artists-pen-second-open-letter-defending-exhibition-72702

Dymski, G. A. (2009) 'Racial Exclusion and the Political Economy of the Subprime Crisis', *Research on Money and Finance Discussion Paper*, March, 1-32.

Edelman, L. (2004) *No Future: Queer Theory and the Death Drive*. Durham NC and London: Duke University Press.

Elliott, L. (2015) 'What Was Good for Germany in 1953 Is Good for Greece in 2015', *The Guardian*, 6 July 2015. Available at: http://www.theguardian.com/business/2015/jul/06/germany-1953-greece-2015-economic-marshall-plan-debt-relief

Elliott, L. (2017) 'Child Poverty in Britain Set to Soar to New Record, Says Thinktank', *The Guardian*, 1 November 2017. Available at: https://www.theguardian.com/society/2017/nov/02/child-poverty-britain-set-to-soar-to-new-record-ifs

Engels, F. (1884) *The Origin of the Family, Private Property and the State*. https://www.marxists.org/archive/marx/works/1884/origin-family/

Feagin, J. R. (2014) *Racist America: Roots, Current Realities, and Future Reparations*. London and New York: Routledge.

Federici, S. (2012) *Revolution at Point Zero: Housework, Reproduction, and Feminist Struggle*. Brooklyn, NY and Oakland, CA: Common Notions (PM Press).

Federici, S. (2013) 'Commoning Against Debt', *Tidal: Occupy Theory, Occupy Strategy* 4: 20.

Fetter, B. (2017) 'Documenta 14: What Can We Still Learn from Art?', *PORTO ARTE: Revista de Artes Visuais* 22 (37): 289.

Fisher, M. (2014) *Ghosts of My Life: Writings on Depression, Hauntology and Lost Futures*. Winchester, UK: Zero Books.

Fisher, J. and Drobnick, J. (2012) 'Nightsense', *Public* 23: 35-63.

Flassbeck, H. and Lapavitsas, C. (2015) *Against the Troika: Crisis and Austerity in the Eurozone*. London and New York: Verso.

Francis, M. A. (2018) 'Documenta 14 , Kassel 10 June–17 September 2017', *Journal of Visual Art Practice* 17 (1): 126-8.

Fraser, A. (2012) 'There's No Place Like Home / L'1% C'est Moi', *Continent* 2 (3): 186-201.

Galloway, G. (2016) 'First Nations Leaders Want to Rethink Residential Schools Agreement', *The Globe and Mail*, 9 May 2016. Available at: https://www.theglobeandmail.com/news/politics/first-nations-leaders-want-to-rethink-residential-schools-agreement/article29948063/

George, S. (1990) *A Fate Worse than Debt* (2nd ed.). New York: Grove.

Gilman-Opalsky, R. (2016) *Specters of Revolt: On the Intellect of Insurrection and Philosophy from Below*. London: Repeater Books.

Giroux, H. A. (2001) *Theory and Resistance in Education: Towards a Pedogogy of the Opposition. Vol. II.* Westport, CT: Bergin and Garvey.

Giroux, H. A., and Searls Giroux, S. (2004) *Take Back Higher Education: Race , Youth, and the Crisis of Democracy in the Post-Civil Rights Era*. New York: Palgrave Macmillan.

Gordon, A. F. (2008) *Ghostly Matters: Haunting and the Sociological Imagination*. New edition. Minneapolis and London: University of Minnesota Press.

Gordon, T. and Webber, J. R. (2016) *Blood of Extraction: Canadian Imperialism in Latin America*.

Graeber, D. (2007) *Possibilities: Essays on Hierarchy, Rebellion and Desire*. Edinburgh, Oakland and West Virgina: AK Press.

Graeber, D. (2011) *Debt: The First 5000 Years*. New York: Melville House.

Groys, B. (2011) 'Art and Money', *E-Flux* 24 (April). Available at: http://www.e-flux.com/journal/art-and-money-2/

Haiven, M. (2011) 'Finance as Capital's Imagination?: Reimagining Value and Culture in an Age of Fictitious Capital and Crisis', *Social Text* 108: 93-124.

Haiven, M. (2012a) 'Can Pikachu Save Fannie Mae? Value, Finance and Imagination in the New Pokeconomy', *Cultural Studies* 26 (4): 516-41.

Haiven, M. (2012b) 'Halifax Nocturne versus (?) The Spectacle of Neoliberal Civics', *PUBLIC: Art, Culture, Ideas* 45 (July): 79-93.

Haiven, M. (2013) 'Finance Depends on Resistance, Finance Is Resistance, and, Anyway, Resistance Is Futile', *Mediations* 26 (1-2): 85-106.

Haiven, M. (2014) *Cultures of Financialization: Fictitious Capital in Popular Culture and Everyday Life*. London and New York: Palgrave Macmillan.

Haiven, M. (2017) 'The Uses of Financial Literacy: Financialization, the Radical Imagination, and the Unpayable Debts of Settler-Colonialism', *Cultural Politics* 13 (3): 348-69.

Haiven, M. (2018) *Art after Money, Money after Art: Creative Strategies Against Financialization*. London: Pluto.

Haiven, M. and Khasnabish, A. (2014) *The Radical Imagination: Social Movement Research in the Age of Austerity*. London and New York: Zed Books.

Harris, C. I. (1993) 'Whiteness as Property', *Harvard Law Review* 106 (8): 1707-91.

'Honouring the Truth, Reconciling the Future: Final Report' (2015) Ottawa: The Truth and Reconciliation Commission of Canada. Available at: http://www.trc.ca/websites/trcinstitution/File/2015/Honouring_the_Truth_Reconciling_for_the_Future_July_23_2015.pdf

hooks, b. (1994) *Teaching to Transgress: Education as the Practice of Freedom*. London and New York: Routledge.

Hubbard, P. (2017) *The Battle for the High Street: Retail Gentrification, Class and Disgust*. London: Palgrave Macmillan.

Jones, Reece (2017) *Violent Borders: Refugees and the Right to Move*. London and New York: Verso.

Jones, Rupert (2017) 'One in Four UK Retirees Burdened by Unpaid Mortgage or Other Debts', *The Guardian*, 17 February 2017. Available at: https://www.theguardian.com/money/2017/feb/17/one-in-four-uk-retirees-burdened-by-unpaid-mortgage-or-other-debts

Joseph, M. (2014) *Debt to Society: Accounting for Life under Capitalism*. Minneapolis: University of Minnesota Press.

Karoly, L. A. (1998) (ed) *Investing in Our Children: What We Know and Don't Know about the Costs and Benefits of Early Childhood Interventions*. Santa Monica, CA: Rand.

Kish, Z. and Leroy, J. (2015) 'Bonded Life: Technologies of Racial Finance from Slave Insurance to Philanthrocapital', *Cultural Studies* 29 (5-6): 630-51.

Klein, N. (2015) *This Changes Everything: Capitalism vs. the Climate*. New York: Knopf.

Koronaiou, A., Lagos, E., Sakellariou, A., Kymionis, S. and Chiotaki-Poulou, I. (2015) 'Golden Dawn, Austerity and Young People: The Rise of Fascist Extremism Among Young People in Contemporary Greek Society', *The Sociological Review* 63 (2): 231-49.

La Berge, L. C. (2015) 'Wages against Artwork: The Social Practice of Decommodification', *South Atlantic Quarterly* 114 (3): 571-93.

La Berge, L. C. (2019) *Wages Against Artwork: Socially Engaged Art and the Decommodification of Labor*. Durham NC and London: Duke University Press.

La Berge, L. C., and Hannah, D. (2015) 'Debt Aesthetics: Medium Specificity and Social Practice in the Work of Cassie Thornton', *Postmodern Culture* 25 (2).

Langer, B. (2002) 'Commodified Enchantment: Children and Consumer Capitalism', *Thesis Eleven* 69 (1): 67-81.

Lapavitsas, C. (2012) (ed.) *Crisis in the Eurozone*. London and New York: Verso.

Larratt-Smith, P. (2010) 'Marta Minujín in New York (Interview)', *Arte Al Día*, 2010.

Lazzarato, M. (2012) *The Making of the Indebted Man*. Boston, MA: MIT Press.

Lazzarato, M. (2015) *Governing by Debt* (trans. J. D. Jordan). South Pasadena, CA: Semiotext(e).

Malik, S. (2008) 'Critique as Alibi: Moral Differentiation in the Art Market', *Journal of Visual Art Practice* 7 (3): 283-95.

Manuel, A. and Derrickson, R. M. (2015) *Unsettling Canada: A National Wake-up Call*. Toronto: Between the Lines.

Martin, R. (2002) *Financialization of Daily Life*. Philadelphia, PA: Temple University Press.

Martin, R. (2015) *Knowledge LTD: Towards a Social Logic of the Derivative*. Philadelphia: Temple University Press.

Marx, K. and Engels, F. (1848) *The Communist Manifesto* (trans. S. Moore). Available at: https://www.marxists.org/archive/marx/works/1848/communist-manifesto/

'Mining Capital: How Canada Has Transformed Its Resource Endowment into a Global Competitive Advantage' (2013) Canadian Chamber of Commerce. Available at: http://www.chamber.ca/media/blog/130130_Mining_Capital.pdf

Moreton-Robinson, A. (2015) *The White Possessive: Property, Power, and Indigenous Sovereignty*. Indigenous Americas. Minneapolis: University of Minnesota Press.

Murray, D. (2018) *The Strange Death of Europe: Immigration, Identity, Islam* (updated ed.). London and New York: Bloomsbury.

Müser, K. (2017) 'Right-Wing AfD Politician Calls pro-Refugee Artwork "disfiguring"' DW. 17 August 2017. Available at: http://www.dw.com/en/right-wing-afd-politician-calls-pro-refugee-artwork-disfiguring/a-40137498

Mylonas, Y. (2018) 'Race and Class in German Media Representations of the "Greek Crisis"' in *The Media and Austerity: Comparative Perspectives*. London and New York: Routledge.

Nagam, J. (2011) '(Re)Mapping the Colonized Body: The Creative Interventions of Rebecca Belmore in the Cityscape', *American Indian Culture and Research Journal* 35 (4): 147-66.

Ndikumana, L. and Boyce, J. K. (2011) *Africa's Odious Debts: How Foreign Loans and Capital Flight Bled a Continent*. London: Zed.

Neuendorf, H. (2017) 'Germany's Far-Right Populist AfD Party Sues Documenta Over Financial Irregularities', *Artnet News*. 24 October 2017. Available at: https://news.artnet.com/art-world/afd-documenta-lawsuit-1126277

O'Reilly, R. (2018) 'Dematerializations of the Land/Water Object', *E-Flux* 90. Available at: http://www.e-flux.com/journal/90/191918/dematerializations-of-the-land-water-object/

Papadopoulos, G. (2018) 'Documenta 14 and the Question of Colonialism: Defending an Impossible Position between Athens and Kassel', *TBA (under Review)*.

'"Parthenon of Books" Constructed from 100,000 Banned Books Rises at Nazi Book Burning Site in Germany', (2017) *ArchDaily*. 10 July 2017. Available at: http://www.archdaily.com/875525/parthenon-of-books-constructed-from-100000-banned-books-rises-at-nazi-book-burning-site-in-germany

Pasternak, S. (2015) 'How Capitalism Will Save Colonialism: The Privatization of Reserve Lands in Canada: How Capitalism Will Save Colonialism', *Antipode* 47 (1): 179-96

Pasternak, S. (2016) 'The Fiscal Body of Sovereignty: To "Make Live" in Indian Country', *Settler Colonial Studies* 6 (4): 317-38.

Pasternak, S. (2017) *Grounded Authority: The Algonquins of Barriere Lake against the State*. Minneapolis: University of Minnesota Press.

Pettifor, A. (2017) *The Production of Money: How to Break the Power of Bankers*. London and New York: Verso.

'Preliminary Report' (2015) Athens: Truth Committee on Public Debt. Available at: http://cadtm.org/IMG/pdf/Report.pdf

Razack, S. (2002) (ed.) *Race, Space, and the Law: Unmapping a White Settler Society*. Toronto: Between the Lines.

Roos, J. (2019) *Why Not Default?: The Political Economy of Sovereign Debt*. Princeton NJ and London: Princeton University Press.

Rosler, M. (2013) *Culture Class*. Berlin: Sternberg Press.

Ross, A. (2014) *Creditocracy*. New York: OR Books.

Rupprecht, A. (2016) '"Inherent Vice": Marine Insurance, Slave Ship Rebellion and the Law', *Race & Class* 57 (3): 31-44.

Salzberger, R. P. and Turck, M. C. (2004) (eds) *Reparations for Slavery: A Reader*. Lanham, Md.: Rowman and Littlefield.

Schwartz, Y. (2017) 'Frauke Petry, the New Face of Germany's Anti-Immigrant Right, Talks to Tablet', *Tablet Magazine*. 7 February 2017. Available at: http://www.tabletmag.com/jewish-news-and-politics/224027/frauke-petry-tablet-interview

Servon, L. (2017) 'The Issue at the Heart of America's Great Unbanking', *Penn Wharton Public Policy Initiative* 44. Available at: https://repository.upenn.edu/pennwhartonppi/44

Sholette, G. and Ressler, O. (2013) (eds) *It's the Political Economy, Stupid: The Global Financial Crisis in Art and Theory*. London and New York: Pluto.

Shukaitis, S. (2015) 'Art Strikes and the Metropolitan Factory' in *Joy Forever: The Political Economy of Social Creativity*, M. Kozłowski, A. Kurant, J. Sowa, K. Szadkowski and J, Szreder (eds), 227-36. London: Mayfly.

Shukaitis, S. (2016) *The Composition of Movements to Come: Aesthetics and Cultural Labor after the Avant-Garde*. London, New York: Rowman and Littlefield.

Simpson, A. (2014) *Mohawk Interruptus: Political Life across the Borders of Settler States*. Durham: Duke University Press.

Soederberg, S. (2014) *Debtfare States and the Poverty Industry: Money, Discipline and the Surplus Population*. London and New York: Routledge.

Sommerville, M. (2018) 'Naturalising Finance, Financialising Natives: Indigeneity, Race, and "Responsible" Agricultural Investment in Canada', *Antipode*. Online version before inclusion in an issue.

Stakemeier, K. and Vishmidt, M. (2016) *Reproducing Autonomy: Work, Money, Crisis and Contemporary Art*. London: Mute.

Stanford, J. (2008) *Economics for Everyone: A Short Guide to the Economics of Capitalism*. Halifax and Winnipeg: Fernwood.

Taibbi, M. (2010) *Griftopia: Bubble Machines, Vampire Squids, and the Long Con That Is Breaking America*. New York: Spiegel and Grau.

Toussaint, E. (2015) *Bankocracy*. Belgium: Resistance Books, IIRE, CADTM. Available at: http://www.cadtm.org/IMG/pdf/Bankocracy_web.pdf

Urribarri, F. (2002) 'Castoriadis: The Radical Imagination and the Post-Lacanian Unconscious', *Thesis Eleven* 71 (1): 40-51.

Van Kirk, S. (1983) *Many Tender Ties: Women in Fur-Trade Society, 1670-1870*. Norman: University of Oklahoma Press.

Varoufakis, Y. (2016) *And the Weak Suffer What They Must?: Europe's Crisis and America's Economic Future*. New York: Nation.

Varoufakis, Y. (2018) *Adults in the Room*. Farrar, Straus and Giroux.

Velthuis, O. (2007) 'The Architecture of the Art Market', In *Talking Prices: Symbolic Meanings of Prices on the Market for Contemporary Art*, 21-52. Princeton NJ and London: Princeton University Press.

Veltmeyer, H. and Petras, J. F. (2014) *The New Extractivism: A Post-Neoliberal Development Model or Imperialism of the Twenty-First Century?* London: Zed Books.

Verlichak, V. (2010) 'Marta Minujín', *Art Nexus. 2010*. Available at: http://artnexus.com/Notice_View.aspx?DocumentID=21029

Vishmidt, M. (2013) '"Mimesis of the Hardened and Alienated": Social Practice as Business Model', *E-Flux* (blog). March 2013. Available at: http://www.e-flux.com/journal/%E2%80%9Cmimesis-of-the-hardened-and-alienated%E2%80%9D-social-practice-as-business-model/

Vishmidt, M. (2015) 'Notes on Speculation as a Mode of Production in Art and Capital', in *Joy Forever: The Political Economy of Social Creativity*, M. Kozłowski, A. Kurant, J. Sowa, K. Szadkowski and J. Szreder (eds) 47-64. London: Mayfly.

Wietecha, M. (2016) 'The Case for Investing in Child Health as a Matter of Our Nation's Security, Economy and Well-Being', Children's Hospital Association. 28 October 2016. Available at: https://www.childrenshospitals.org/research-and-data/pediatric-data-and-trends/2016/the-case-for-investment-in-child-health-as-a-matter-of-our-nations-security-economy-and-well-being

Wintour, P. (2016) 'Germany's Refugee Response Not Guilt-Driven, Says Wolfgang Schäuble', *The Guardian*. 4 March 2016. Available at: http://www.theguardian.com/world/2016/mar/04/germanys-refugee-response-not-guilt-driven-says-wolfgang-schauble

Wolfe, P. (2006) 'Settler Colonialism and the Elimination of the Native', *Journal of Genocide Research* 8 (4): 387-409.

Wolfe, P. (2016) *Traces of History: Elementary Structures of Race*. London; New York: Verso.

Wolff, J. (1984) *The Social Production of Art*. New York: New York UP.

Woznicki, K. (2018) *Fugitive Belonging*. Berlin: Diamond Paper.

Wyly, E. K. (2010) 'The Subprime State of Race', in *The Blackwell Companion to the Economics of Housing*, S. J. Smith and B. A. Searle (eds), 381-413. Oxford, UK: Wiley-Blackwell.

Zelizer, V. A. (1994) *Pricing the Priceless Child: The Changing Social Value of Children*. Princeton, N.J: Princeton University Press.

Zipes, J. (2002) *Breaking the Magic Spell: Radical Theories of Folk and Fairy Tales*. (Rev. and expanded ed.) Lexington: University Press of Kentucky.

9

Ecologies of indebtedness

Mark Featherstone

Imagining catastrophe

In the late 1990s the French philosopher, Jean Baudrillard, wrote a short essay, 'In the Shadow of the Millennium' (1998), concerned with the historical significance of the approaching year 2000. Given what has happened since what was called Y2K, it is hard to properly convey the low level panic that accompanied the impending arrival of the new millennium, but Baudrillard captured this through reference to the Beaubourg Clock, housed at the Pompidou Centre in Paris. In his piece, he explains that the Beaubourg Clock, which counted down the time to Y2K by the millisecond, is a symbol of impending catastrophe and millennial panic. Although Baudrillard does not provide details of the catastrophic imaginary that accompanied the approach of Y2K (probably because the arrival of the future produced endless narratives about the ending of this, that and the other), the panic centred around the belief that the world's computer systems would be unable to handle the turn from 1999 to 2000 and so might shut down completely. On the basis of this idea, the fantasy was that the world would be thrown into chaos. Nuclear launch systems would break down leading to the start of a potentially apocalyptic automated World War III. Even worse, the world's banking system, which had already made the leap into cyberspace, would collapse and ATMs would run dry. In short, Y2K would consume our lives in a scenario that would resemble the horrors of Arnold Schwarzenegger's 1984 film *The Terminator*, when the machines turn on humans, or Danny Boyle's post-millennial *28 Days Later*, when humans start to eat each other in a destroyed world.

Of course, the master of cool postmodern irony, Baudrillard, saw that the panic about year 2000 was really a traumatic projection of an event that had already happened and that had been endlessly replayed by Hollywood cinema and other narratives about 'the end'. In Baudrillard's (1998) view Y2K was really about the end of history, which had been announced by Francis Fukuyama (1989, 1992) a decade before we imagined the computers turning off, and that the countdown to Armageddon was simply an attempt to work through the end of modernity that had already happened. In this respect, Baudrillard's view of Y2K more closely resembled the story of Keanu Reeves' 1999 film, *The Matrix*, where the nightmare has already happened in some distant repressed past that allows life to carry on as though nothing had ever happened. If Y2K represented the delayed threat of *the return of the repressed*, when everything would actually break down and history would really collapse, Baudrillard explains that the catastrophists behind the Beaubourg Clock decided to err on the side of caution. He tells his reader that the clock suddenly disappeared, that it was locked away in a safe somewhere, so that nobody could see the approaching collapse of history.

In the same period, Baudrillard wrote another very short paper (similarly no more than a footnote to his wider corpus of work) entitled 'Global Debt and the Parallel Universe' (1996a), where the disappeared Beaubourg Clock comes back on a Times Square billboard. However, the trip from Paris to New York has not been uneventful, because the new clock is no longer concerned with the *countdown* to the millennium and the catastrophe of Y2K, but rather the infinite increase in or *count up* of the US national debt; as Baudrillard explains, this rises by hundreds of thousands of dollars each second. In taking up the comparison between these two clocks, Baudrillard tells us that, while the French timepiece represented a delimited catastrophe which will happen when 0 arrives, there is a sense in which the US debt counter represents a more contemporary, endless catastrophe, comparable to the nightmare Walter Benjamin (2003) imagines in his work on the philosophy of history, because it is infinite and piles numbers upon numbers into the infinite future. Again, Baudrillard, the postmodern catastrophist par excellence, is not down about the infinity of debt. He explains that because there is no end to US or, for that matter, global debt, there is no point worrying about it. We can never pay these debts back. In this respect, these numbers are weightless, transcendental, and – in a world which gave up God in the 19th century when Nietzsche proclaimed that the Father was no more – meaningless. Indeed, he imagines that the North Americans have only turned their debt into a spectacle because they know there is no real burden. In this respect, the US's infinite debt is, ironically, a sign of the power, and the full spectrum dominance of what Baudrillard (1996a) terms the 'American Empire' (Hardt and Negri, 2000), because nobody is about to try call this money in.

According to this view, the debt clock is a sign of US superiority, and its only real function is to allow North Americans to imagine some kind of catastrophe, which (much like a Hollywood film) becomes necessary because it can never happen in real life. In Baudrillard's view, the superiority of the Americans over the French is, therefore, concerned with their understanding that the catastrophe has already happened, somewhere in the dim and distant past when history gave way to the endless procession of signs, and that there is no point hiding the timepiece of catastrophe. On the contrary, what we really need to do is hang onto the imagination of catastrophe in order to convince ourselves that there is some kind of history, some kind of society, some kind of significance to collapse in the first place. This is exactly what Baudrillard (1996a) imagines the New York debt clock captures in its representation of what he calls the 'exorbital' dimension of debt. It imagines these numbers matter, even though it communicates the exact opposite in its transformation of these surreal numbers into a spectacle of exorbitance and power beyond responsibility.

Confronting reality

This is where we were in the late 1990s. We know what has happened to the 'American Empire' in the period since Baudrillard, the prophet of postmodern endings, declared the banal catastrophe of Y2K and infinite indebtedness (1996a). In 2001, the Empire came face to face with *catastrophe in reality* in New York, home of the debt counter, when the great symbol of global capitalist power, the World Trade Centre, was brought down. On the back of Bin Laden's attack on the home of US economic power, President George W. Bush plunged the Empire into the 'war on terror' and a \$3trillion conflict in Iraq in order to demonstrate American power and the truth of a vision that could have been inherited from Baudrillard himself – *Empire no longer lives in reality, but rather makes and sets the terms of what is real.* Although this seems wildly utopian today, we must not forget that this was the world of Bush, Blair and the neoliberal elites until very recently.

Where Baudrillard thought that the postmodern procession of signs and symbols was a catastrophe, but one we should not worry about too much since it had abolished the very ground of significance that would make it worth worrying in the first place, the Bush/Blair group (which would later include Sarkozy, Berlusconi and others) were utopian fantasists of the highest order who thought that the postmodern was an invitation to remake reality on their own terms. If the war on terror and the attempt to turn Iraq into a US outpost in the Middle

East was part of this conceit, the global financial system was a similar exercise in utopian hubris. As Ole Bjerg has shown in his book *Making Money* (2014) the fantasy of global financialisation resides in the idea that it is possible to make money out of money without reference to real production. In this respect money is absolutely virtual.

Given this situation it is shocking that, over the course of recent history, Marxists and critical thinkers who have suggested that the world might need to change to take into account various limits have been branded utopian fools by people who better understand the harsh reality of politics and economics (Gray, 2009; Featherstone 2017). This is especially the case today when the leaders of what is now a bankrupt Empire want to trade on a high-tech version of the North American frontier myth where one can pan for gold and suddenly strike it rich. Of course, the links between stock market profiteering and gambling, the city of Las Vegas (coincidentally one of Baudrillard's favourite haunts), and American mythology are clearly made by writers such as Mark Taylor (2004) and Urs Staheli (2013). What Staheli, in particular, shows is how Wall Street managed to rationalise risk-taking in order to create the fantasy of reasonable and more or less scientific speculation on the future. In the utopian world of financialisation, this allowed the fantasy of the US, where for example everybody would own their own plot of land, to become a reality through a housing market based on what we would come to call NINJA loans (No Income, No Job) and processes of securitisation capable of distributing and dissolving risk through innovations (now infamous financial instruments, including CDOs or Collateralised Debt Obligations), where risky loans were packaged with secure investments in order to offset risk.

The hubris of George W. Bush's housing market reforms, which opened up the market to people with no income, was thus based both on the idea that everybody should be able to become part of the property-owning democracy and on the fantasy of financialisation, where banks are able to leverage well beyond their actual assets in order to make loans on money they do not have. As Ole Bjerg (2014) has shown, the financial magic of this process, which is perfectly symmetrical with Baudrillard's (1996a) theory of the inflationary nature of hyper-reality, is that banks make money from nothing because they receive interest repayments on money they never had in the first place. On the one hand, the banks thus made money out of nothing, but on the other – and from the point of view of those who bought into the neoliberal fantasy of the right to home ownership (which we can coincidentally trace back to the philosophy of John Locke who imagined that working the land and owning private property is what makes us human) – these institutions also created vast quantities of debt that had very real impacts. Of course, in one respect, Baudrillard (1996a) was perfectly correct in his assessment of the meaninglessness of debt: since there was nothing behind the debt issued by the banks, one could say it did not exist.

Certainly, this is how lenders behaved in the postmodern Empire of finance. It was easy to make and lend money because it did not really exist and, in instances where home owners were forced to default, systems of securitisation would mean that lenders could not lose. In fact, from this point of view, there was only upside (and ever more growth), since the lender would pick up the bricks and mortar left behind by the now homeless owner who had understandably bought into the fantasy of the neoliberal universe where credit appeared safe and secure because boom and bust was thought to be a relic of some distant past before banks worked out how to conjure money out of thin air. As a result, however, the upside of the industrial production of fictitious capital was less apparent for the debtor for whom debt was very real, since they needed to make repayments with money made in the real economy. It is precisely this dimension of indebtedness that Baudrillard (1998) misses in his account of global debt, and it is this dimension that eventually led to the global economic crash of 2008 and subsequent collapse of growth. Where Baudrillard dismisses the consequence of exorbitant debt on the basis that it can never be repaid, and banks took a similar view on the basis that they would never have to account for debts they had sold on to investors, debtors were ultimately responsible for servicing debts made by irresponsible lenders. In their world, debt took on enormous weight.

In the case of those taking on NINJA loans or over-leveraging their own salaries based on an idea of a constantly rising market, the problem was that the neoliberal fantasy of home ownership was not based in the reality of the real economy. The result was the subprime crisis – which infected the entire global economy by virtue of, first, the way processes of securitisation paradoxically distributed risk to dilute exposure, and second, the way financialisation drove investment in order to ensure the maintenance of cash flow in the real economy – and the credit crunch that destroyed growth, particularly in nations where finance had become the motor of the economy. It is, therefore, an unhappy coincidence that a year after Baudrillard's death in 2007, the global financial system, which was in many ways representative of the virtual, integral order he imagined in works such as *The Perfect Crime* (1996b) and *The Intelligence of Evil or Lucidity Pact* (2005), collapsed and what he had written about in terms of the 'exorbital' (orbital and excluded), sci-fi debt became a very real burden upon the masses who had been seduced by the fantasy of neoliberal ideology where we can have anything we desire because it is possible to make money from nothing and grow the economy on nothingness. The death of the prophet of postmodernism, and his concept of the virtual economy that floated somewhere above the world without consequence, was therefore somehow repeated in the demise of the global financial system whose corpse we continue to pick over today, in what Ulrich Beck (Beck and Beck-Gernsheim, 2002) might have called zombie capitalism or zombie globalisation. In the contemporary period (which makes Baudrillard's vision of the hyper-real economy seem like it was written in some fantastical period of history long ago), we live under conditions where 'exorbital' debt hangs over people like a dead weight.

The paradox of the apparent materiality of this dense dead weight of debt is, of course, that it is invisible, simultaneously everywhere and nowhere, and for this reason impossible to confront head on. This is why we pick over the bones of the postmodern economy, which staggers on under the pretence that the 2008 financial crash never took place, in a ghoulish parody of Baudrillard's vision that we might talk about in terms of 'post-mortemism'. What is post-mortemism? In basic terms, Baudrillard's zombie form represents the realisation of the corruption of Empire in the rise and fall of the so-called 'Islamic State' (IS), in the suicidal violence in the ruins of Syria and Iraq, and in the collapse of the global financial system through the seemingly endless depression that hangs over society where default and bankruptcy is an ever-present threat. Of course, there is no real growth, no development, and no modernity under these conditions. If the postmodern was concerned with what Baudrillard writes about in terms of the projection of the modern into signs and symbols and the rearticulation of the idea of progress in the inflationary potential of the virtual, the 'post-mortem' is about what happens when we have to manage the paradoxical dead weight of the abstract and the pollution of the virtual. Why post-mortem? The answer is because we are working through Baudrillard's sci-fi past now, looking for workable responses to the toxins of postmodern abstraction, and trying to begin again on the other side of the end of history.

The cancellation of the future

But how is it possible to think the new outside the dialectic which conditioned our thinking about the future from Plato on through Hegel to Marx, until it was eventually abolished in the postmodern? In many respects, debt is a reflection of the paralysis of the present which makes it impossible to move, to change and to imagine the future. In the case of the Greeks, who invented the idea of freedom in response to their tragic struggles with the gods (who were in many respects the ultimate creditors), this paralysis involves a fatal effort to somehow hold society together under pressure of German demands for repayment. Unlike their ancient ancestors who understood the nature of tragedy, the contemporary Greeks were seduced by the fantasy of neoliberalism and sought to build a shiny new world of money around the 2004 Athens Olympics, only to find themselves caught in a debt trap.

The Greeks now find themselves punished by the gods of neoliberalism, trying to hold up the sky, like the ancient Titan, Atlas. Their choice is a stark one – either default and let the sky fall in or manfully (my use of this gendered term here is deliberate to signify the phallic nature of the struggle to survive the neoliberal state of nature) endure under an impossible burden for ever more. In this respect, the Greek lot is perfectly representative of the fate of their tragic mythological heroes by virtue not only of its fatality, but also of its mythic dimensions that appeal to issues of individual psychology, social and political philosophy, and finally environmental concerns around the limits of nature. In each case, the moral of the Greek tragedy is that the cost of hubris is inescapable debt and an eternity of punishment. It is the very mythic generality of this story, which enables a connection between ancients and postmoderns or 'post-mortems', that means that indebtedness is simultaneously highly rational, in that it can be calculated in numbers, but also entirely affective, in respect of the way it transforms into an atmosphere and therefore becomes 'ultra-rational', where ultra means 'more than' or 'beyond'. In this way, we might say that the metaphor of the Greeks supporting the sky is absolutely real, because in a sense their struggle concerns the effort to prevent the experience of indebtedness clouding the space-time of their world or crushing their existence. Contrary to Baudrillard's (1996a) theory of 'exorbital' debt (orbital, excluded, exorbitant), this vision of debt is closer to Ulrich Beck's (1992) conceptualisation of 'radiation' that spreads out to invade every space and a more or less infinite span of time. If Beck's space-time is radioactive, and full of the pollution of high modernity, the contemporary Greek world is infected with indebtedness, since there is nowhere that is not exposed to the effects of the burden of the exorbitance of the postmodern, financial system, and no imaginable future that will not have to count the costs of the hubris of Empire where money was a creationist fiction.

In the language of Felix Guattari (2014), we could say that debt has polluted the three ecologies of mind, social, and environment, in respect of the ways it plunges the debtor into depression and despair, captures society in a state of post-mortem immobility, and transforms nature into a thing to be plundered in the name of making ever more money in order to escape from the abyss of indebtedness brought about by the orgy of virtualisation. In each case what the debtor loses to debt is the possibility of the future, which is exactly what the Italian thinker Franco Berardi (2015) means when he talks about the time of indebtedness: the future is precisely what disappears into depression, immobility, and the destruction of the world in a desperate attempt to increase productivity. This is the bind of the post-mortem period of history, which captures the way that *depression* reinforces itself in manic attempts to escape that only create more despair, *social immobility* tends to reproduce itself in a desperate lack of imagination brought about by the abandonment of thought for practical action, and *industrial efforts* designed to increase production and value simply destroy the future by working people into the ground and consuming the planet that underwrites the existence of life itself. Moreover, the three ecologies that indebtedness pollutes are interrelated and tend to interact in the emergence of a self-sustaining machine for the creation of degradation, despair and depression. In this machine, depression over the state of debt and the cancellation of the future results in a lack of imagination and mobile thought that reinforces existing behaviours where escape is sought through the same old modern and post-modern commitment to expansion and growth.

In the context of post-mortemism this is no kind of solution to the problem of indebtedness because efforts to increase industrial production in a state of low growth punishes exhausted people and plunders the world. By contrast, the postmodern response, where expansion is premised on virtuality, knowledge, and information, simply threatens to pile up more debt: what this approach neglects is that the basis of value resides in the interaction of human producer and the natural world. In both approaches debt increases, in the form of either ecological debts that will have to be repaid in the future or more numbers on the virtual debt meter which will simply vanish over the horizon of our economic and environmental (in)solvency. This ultimately reflects the fact that there is nowhere else to grow into.

Why is there nowhere to grow into? The answer is that planetary space-time is exhausted and the only way to keep moving forward is to keep borrowing ever more with the promise of repayment sometime in the distant future. This is, essentially, the bind of contemporary post-mortemism, which means that it is not only hard to see a way out of the generalised state of debt, but also difficult to imagine how processes of globalisation produced by modern and then postmodern innovation will continue to develop. The economic problem here is that a slowdown in the circulation of financial exchange, and a reduction in the availability of easy credit to drive modernisation, produces pressure on real wages, makes work harder to come by, and produces an atmosphere of fear and suspicion of others who, in the neoliberal world at least, are always competitors for scarce resources. Under these conditions, it may be that the ever-present danger of financial bankruptcy translates into a wider process of symbolic disinvestment, default and withdrawal, which is exactly what Bernard Stiegler suggests in his three-volume study, *Disbelief and Discredit* (2011, 2012, 2014b). Here, the failure of finance is no longer isolated to the economic sphere, but rather spreads to infect the wider symbolic, and eventually social, system that starts to break down under the weight of the abstract violence produced by a state of unmanageable indebtedness.

Moreover, this state, characterised by the cancellation of the future in indebtedness and disinvestment, produces a crisis in individual subjectivity, which Stiegler (2012) captures through the idea of the new 'disindividual' and Gerald Raunig (2016) writes about in terms of the 'dividual', defined by a recognition of the failure to be able to act in the world in meaningful ways by virtue of a debt burden that colonises the entirety of space-time. In their recent work on an alternative politics of debt, Davies, Montgomerie and Wallin (2015) call this depressive situation 'financial melancholia' and explain how the feelings of loss – of possibility, of the future – lodge themselves deep inside the indebted subject and eat away at their sense of self. Given the neoliberal demand to act, to take risks, to perform, this post-mortem incubation of loss, and ultimately death, becomes inescapable: there is no safe space where the depressed dividual can try to convert their melancholia into mourning, simply because the neoliberal system punishes weakness, depression and despair as these conditions symbolise failure and, most importantly, uncompetitiveness. Under these conditions, financial melancholia starts to shade into feelings of exhaustion, an inability to survive the brutal economic landscape of indebtedness and heightened competitiveness, and deep existential despair about life, other people, and the possibility of change. In this respect the contemporary state of debt resembles Marx's (1990) vision of history and death which weighs on the minds of the living like a nightmare and produces a situation that recalls Sartre's famous play, *No Exit* (1989). Akin to Sartre's characters, caught up in the hell of sociability, there is no way out of the nightmare of indebtedness for the contemporary neoliberal subject, who is always indebted to somebody else.

The new debt reality and its ecological critique

The contemporary Italian thinker Maurizio Lazzarato (2012) suggests that it is this condition of imprisonment that makes the contemporary debt society a control society. In this vision, first explained by Deleuze (1997) in his expansion of Foucault's theory of discipline, the individual, or *divided dividual*, is captured in networks of power that make it impossible to move. What reference to Stiegler's (2014a) work adds to this insight is a theory about the way this state of capture itself becomes difficult to articulate, because of a state of symbolic misery that transforms the state of indebtedness into a kind of post-political, post-human fact comparable to the factual fossils concerning the origins of the universe and so on, which Quentin Meillassoux (2009) writes of in his work on finitude. This state of symbolic misery (explained by Christian Marazzi's (2008, 2011) work on the relationship between finance and language) involves the reduction of language to, first, a kind of technical, operative, programmatic machine that rejects expression in the name of precision, and, second, the translation of this mechanised, communicative, form into numbers and facts that reduce the world to a series of quantitative measures. In this situation there is no room for expression, or political debate, because the world is made up of facts, most of which are concerned with the communication of debt responsibility and performance linked to the need to produce profit in order to service this responsibility. We might call this stark, objective, world, which paradoxically takes on a kind of cold, hard, materiality even though it is made in abstract numbers and calculations, *the new debt reality*. Given this situation it is not wholly surprising that the new depressive global debt reality has started to produce a culture of escapism that stretches from Donald Trump's fantasy of building walls to prevent migrants making their way into the US, through the British debate about the relative merits of escape from the EU, to the late Steven Hawking's theory of exoplanets that might allow humanity to start again somewhere else.

While Trump, who rose to the office of President off the back of the decline of the US since Baudrillard (2005) wrote about the integral power of Empire, imagines escape through a politics of withdrawal and disinvestment in the world, and the British supporters of Brexit fantasise about a similar break with the structures of Europe that cost too much and undermine state sovereignty, Hawking and Russian billionaire Yuri Milner conceive of a planetary exodus on the back of spacecraft the size of microchips (Radford, 2016). Although the scales of these visions of escape differ, it would seem to me that they are broadly comparable in their sense of the bankruptcy of the contemporary global social, political, and economic system. On the one hand, we should withdraw from the global scene, which has enmeshed us in inescapable indebtedness, in the name of a return to a state before absolute interconnectivity (Trump, Brexit), or on the other hand, we should look to take flight from the world into the cosmos on the basis that our home planet is no longer big enough to sustain our way of life (Hawking). However, I would suggest that the problem with both of these perspectives is that they fail to address the real problem with the contemporary global system, which is less connectivity or the *smallness* of the world, but rather the way in which we have come to inhabit the planet, which is precisely what is disclosed by the contemporary debt reality. In the final pages of this chapter, then, I want to consider the possibility of a middle way, somewhere between Trump's call for withdrawal and Hawking's vision of cosmic escape, centred on the reconciliation of humanity with the scale of world. In this respect, I suggest an ecological critique of the contemporary global debt society, based upon a recognition of the etymology of the term 'eco' which, as Guattari explains in his *Three Ecologies* (2014), can be tracked back to the Greek word '*oikos*' which means economy, nature, and essentially home.

Against the state of indebtedness, my critique is concerned with developing an outline for a sustainable home, on the grounds that our current global reality has become a kind of monstrous, alien, abstract 'unhome', and thinking through a response somewhere between withdrawal and escape which recognises both the reality of interconnectivity and the finitude of our earth-bound status, but is no less utopian than either Trump or Hawking for this realism.

I want to start with a critique of Baudrillard based in the translation of the postmodern into what I have sought to call 'the post-mortem'. Where Baudrillard (1996a) claims that 'exorbital debt' renders indebtedness irrelevant, because it can never be repaid, my view is that what the magnitude of global debt actually discloses is its irreducibility. This means both that debt will continue to increase and that it is inescapable. Although debt can never be repaid, this does not mean that the contemporary debt reality suspends the need to struggle to make repayments. This is precisely the problem of the current situation, where debtors labour like tragic heroes to try to manage an unmanageable burden. Like the mythic figure of Sisyphus, their task is an impossible one. Given the irreducibility of debt, I would suggest that what needs to happen is an underlining of the Foucauldian/Barthesian view that the individual is no more. Although this was a key insight of the postmodern, and forms the basis of contemporary theories of the post-human, this realisation has not penetrated neoliberal ideology, which continues to communicate the idea that people are somehow free of external constraint and can pick and choose how they relate to others, institutions, and their wider environment.

This notion of the sovereign individual is, of course, a key conceit standing behind capitalist thought more generally, but I think it is one that should be rejected, simply because what the irreducible state of indebtedness reveals is that the much vaunted neoliberal person who expresses their essential freedom through the market is in actual fact a divided 'dividual', to use Raunig's (2016) term, founded in deeply depressing debt relations. From this point of view the neoliberal individual, *homo debitum*, is a kind of fatal, tragic figure and the only response to the reduction of freedom implicit in the rise of the dividual is depression and melancholia. However, this is the case only from *inside* the perspective of neoliberal thought, where the individual *is* freedom and should, consequently, live life in the black. Given this position, of course, the dividual is always, and can only ever be, a figure defined by lack. In this regard, the only way to resist the horror of dividualism would seem to be to take the Nietzschean (1990) stand against debt, and the general experience of indebtedness, and reject all forms of dependence and judgement in the name of a kind of hyper-individualism. However, the alternative is to step outside the neoliberal framework and recognise that the Nietzschean position made sense in the modern and perhaps even the postmodern world, but does not make sense under conditions of post-mortemism, because there is nowhere else to escape to unless one takes Hawking's view that humans should look to achieve escape velocity. Should one reject this neo-Platonic (2002) theory of the need to abandon terrestrial life for the heavens, and reach the conclusion that the Nietzschean superman was always a tragic figure whose identity was based in struggle, the solution to the problem of indebtedness might be the translation of the dividual into a kind of ecological model of identity and, centrally, subjectivity. Here the 'self' exceeds itself in the 'other', the other becomes the locus of the 'social', the social is rooted in the finitude of the biosphere, and the biosphere in turn projects itself into the existence of self, other, and more generally life itself (that is to say, the biosphere enables, contains, and sustains life).

In this way the dividual – who lacks under conditions of neoliberal indebtedness, falls into depression, and can see no way out of their predicament – becomes a figure of excess in relation to (1) the other and (2) the wider world. Under these conditions the political economy of austerity, which threatens to cast a shadow over the future of the low-growth society, is recast in ecological terms. There is no doubt that austerity must be part of the response to the post-mortem society, simply because endless growth is no longer possible in the context of the ruins of modernity, which reflect the ageing of the capitalist world, which weighs heavy upon the eco-system, turning it into a space of lack. Centrally, however, the negativity of the austere is a construction premised upon the point of view of the neoliberal individual which demands that they exist in isolation from the other and the world. The alternative is to recast austerity in terms of (1) the irreducibility of indebtedness, (2) the figure of the individual who exceeds themselves in the limit of otherness, and (3) the idea of the gift economy explored by first, Marcel Mauss (see for example Mauss, 2001) and later, Georges Bataille (1991). Here the dividual expends what they no longer need in the other, who is similarly prodigal in their vision of the world, founded upon a conceptualisation of nature that extends itself in existence. In this vision of excess, which Bataille (1991) rooted in a cosmic imaginary of solar radiation, the austerity of the individual disappears into the excess of the dividual who recognises that existence itself is never indivisible, but rather based in infinite difference and complex interaction.

But the invention of this sustainable, post-growth, red-green, society would require a massive cultural shift away from the inheritances of modernity, postmodernity, industrial, and post-industrial capitalism, to a stance where we would recognise and realise dividualism and expend what we no longer need in others who would equally live ecologically sustainable lives. The problem with this vision is, of course, that the concept of need is entirely relative, and no longer really means anything in the postmodern debt society, where needs are infinite and shade into desires which are endlessly manufactured by media and projected into the future. What is need? There is no sense of the significance of need in the wake of the exorbitance of modernity and postmodernity, where technology buried nature under the structures of civilisation. What is required today is, therefore, a new conceptualisation of the idea of need, which could be based in a return to the ancient notion of 'measure' or moderation, grounded in an understanding of the limits of environmental sustainability.

The space for this revision is present in the contemporary problematic of infinite need and endless desire brought about by the new debt reality. That is to say that these distortions are already unsustainable, and contribute to the infinite extension of indebtedness. In this respect, the break or emergence of critical space essential for the rethinking of the meaning of human necessity has already happened. This is perhaps what economic austerity measures have produced, though the left has not yet fully recognised this potential, because it remains concerned with the more limited issue of the uneven application of austerity. It is, of course, essential that this inequality is addressed and that the new austerity of the dividual that exceeds itself in the other and world is evenly distributed. At the moment, what we see across Europe is an attempt to impose austerity at the bottom in order to leave those at the top free to make massive profits in the flawed assumption that some of this money will flow down, create growth, and restart the neoliberal system based on financialisation and consumerism. Unfortunately, this appears to be a wholly inadequate strategy, primarily because the monstrous debt burden precludes a return to the postmodern economic norm.

In the new historical period I have sought to call post-mortemism, where symbolic misery leads to the collapse of the politics of the near future, I would suggest that there can be no return to modern or postmodern economy. In my view, the kind of ecological contract set out above rooted in the excessive nature of the dividual is necessary because it is inevitable that the neoliberal machine will have to give way to a new sustainable form based in gifting in order to secure human survival. In his book on the gift economy, *Given Time*, Derrida (1994) opposes Mauss' theory (2001) of the necessary gift because of its totalitarianism. From Derrida's point of view, there is ironically no freedom in the gift as Mauss (2001) conceives it, because one is always obliged to up the ante on the other's present. Of course, this was the point of Mauss' theory. The idea was always that the gift knits society together, creates obligation and responsibility, and produces relationships that endure through time. It is precisely this obligatory or necessary relationality, or we might say responsibility, that Derrida wants to escape in the name of freedom from what he considers the totalitarianism of the gift. When one takes into account the context of Derrida's critique – that he considers the gift to be representative of the time of indebtedness found in actual socialist systems – it is possible to understand his suspicion of Mauss' sleight of hand (the gift that is not really a gift, but rather an obligation). However, the problem with this critique is that actual socialist societies, such as the Soviet Union or Maoist China, were never really based in the kind of economics we find in Mauss (2001) or Sahlins (1974): they maintained a class division, in the shape of separation of party and people, regardless of what they might have claimed to the contrary, and also completely neglected the critique of the exploitation of nature found in the early Marx (1988).

This is why I think the contemporary equation of capitalism and freedom, and the use of this economic-political complex to critique socialist politics and economics, ultimately falls flat. That is to say that what the liberal, democratic, capitalist critique of actual socialist systems (which were always perversions of true Marxist thought where the (in)dividual is rooted in social and natural structures through the concept of the 'species-being'), eventually produced was the neoliberal individual who seemed completely ignorant of their necessary relationship to others and the world. The eventual result of this conceit was financialisation, which was based in a rejection of limits of material production, and – in the post-mortem phase we currently occupy – the state of global indebtedness, that represents the return of the repressed sphere of materiality that has become a research object of the new post-humanism. In light of the problem of post-mortemism, the real issue with the Derridean (1994) critique of the totalitarian time of the gift is, therefore, that big ideological debate is no longer about a political choice between the authoritarian state that limits freedom in the name of corrupt redistribution and liberal capitalism that embraces freedom and lets people become who they are, because the former politics have left the scene and the latter system has fallen into bankruptcy and has itself become a kind of global authoritarianism obsessed with the maintenance of abstract financial regulation in the name of defence of the social, political, and economic status quo.

In the face of this machine, which favours abstraction over materiality, the political debate between actual socialist systems and liberal democratic capitalism has become a philosophical struggle between a desperate post-modernism, concerned to manage indebtedness in order to continue to create excessive value on the back of the exploitation of the natural world, and a recognition that there is no way back through the post-mortem to either modernity or postmodernity because global indebtedness symbolises the need for radical change, a kind of utopian break, and the creation of some new way of living. In this respect, there is a sense in which the truly radical response to global indebtedness would involve the emergence of a new kind of totalitarianism, shorn of its relationship to Nazism and Stalinism. The emergence of this new social, economic, and cultural form, which we might name 'totalitarianism' on the basis of its emphasis on totality, would rely upon a novel natural-social contract. Recalling Heidegger's (2010) notion of the ontological basis of sociability, 'being-with' (*Mitsein*), Merleau-Ponty's (1969) theory of the irreducible connection between self and world, 'being-in-world', and Arne Naess' (2008) deep ecological vision of a world, where everything is interconnected in the formation of a kind of global mesh, the radicalism of this new form would reside in its emphasis on sustainability, vulnerability, and limitation in the context of an understanding of ecological metabolism. Against contemporary neoliberal post-politics, which asserts the objectivity of economic regulation, my view is, therefore, that this ecological totalitarianism would be equally post-political in its focus on the necessity of escape from the horror of the global debt society into a new sustainable social, political, economic, and centrally cultural, form able to sustain a future for generations to come. In the new eco-totalitarianism there could be no individual hubris or insistence that it is somehow possible to live in the black. This is precisely what leads to the horror of indebtedness. Neoliberalism wants to imagine and preserve the fantasy that repayment in full is possible with the result that the sovereign individual becomes a miserable dividual characterised by lack.

Surely the scale of global indebtedness, which Baudrillard (1996a) wrote about in the late 1990s, means that this vision is no longer possible. On the contrary the new totalitarianism would show that debt is irreducible and the truth of the world is red, where *redness* signifies infinite indebtedness and a collective or communistic appreciation of this inescapable fact. This perspective is, centrally, exactly what David Graeber (2011) writes about in his massive history of debt, when he points out that indebtedness is written into everyday life through a kind of 'immanent communism' that means that we are always in debt to those who came before, those who support us in the present, and those who enable our futures. The flip side of this debt is that we have an infinite responsibility to others who came before, live in our world, and will follow us in the future, which recalls Emmanuel Levinas' (1969, 1999) work on ethics and otherness. Where Graeber stops, however, is in his lack of recognition of the way in which our indebtedness and responsibility extend to the natural world that underwrites our existence. It is this that ultimately grounds the essential *ontological truth of indebtedness* that cannot be reduced to some kind of financial burden that it is possible to escape. Finally, it is only when we make this cultural shift, recognise the ontological necessity of indebtedness, and cast off the limited economic understanding of debt that leads to the pretence that payment in full is possible, that we will paradoxically cancel the reality of global indebtedness in its complete realisation. At this point we will escape the misery of post-mortemism, start to live in recognition of the way the self exceeds itself in other and world, and cancel the global debt burden in a new ecology of irreducible indebtedness. Ironically, the secret to debt relief resides in the realisation of the universality of indebtedness.

References

Bataille, G. (1991) *The Accursed Share: Volume I: Consumption.* New York: Zone Books.

Baudrillard, J. (1996a) 'Global Debt and Parallel Universe', *Liberation.* 16 October 1996.

Baudrillard, J. (1996b) *The Perfect Crime.* London: Verso.

Baudrillard, J. (1998) 'In the Shadow of the Millennium (Or the Suspense of the Year 2000)' in *Ctheory.* Available online at: http://www.ctheory.net/articles.aspx?id=104

Baudrillard, J. (2005) *The Intelligence of Evil or the Lucidity Pact.* Oxford: Berg.

Beck, U. (1992) *Risk Society: Towards a New Modernity.* London: Sage.

Beck, U. and Beck-Gernsheim, E. (2002) *Individualization: Institutionalized Individualism and its Social and Political Consequences.* London: Sage.

Benjamin, W. (2003) 'On the Concept of History' in *Walter Benjamin: Selected Writings: Volume IV: 1938-1940.* Cambridge, Mass: Harvard University Press. 389-401.

Berardi, F. (2015) *And: Phenomenology of the End.* New York: Semiotext(e).

Bjerg, O. (2014) *Making Money: The Philosophy of Crisis Capitalism.* London: Verso.

Davies, W., Montgomerie, J., and Wallin, S. (2015) *Financial Melancholia: Mental Health and Indebtedness.* London: PERC.

Deleuze, G. (1997) 'Postscript on Control Societies' in *Negotiations: 1972-1990.* New York: Columbia University Press. 177-183.

Derrida, J. (1994) *Given Time: Volume I: Counterfeit Money.* Chicago: University of Chicago Press.

Featherstone, M. (2017) *Planet Utopia: Utopia, Dystopia, and Globalisation.* London: Routledge.

Fukuyama, F. (1989) 'The End of History?' *The National Interest* (16): 3-18.

Fukuyama, F. (1992) *The End of History and the Last Man.* New York: Free Press.

Graeber, D. (2014) *Debt : The First 5000 Years.* New York: Melville House.

Gray, J. (2009) *False Dawn: The Delusions of Global Capitalism*. London: Granta.
Guattari, F. (2014) *The Three Ecologies*. London: Bloomsbury.
Hardt, M. and Negri, A. (2000) *Empire*. Cambridge, Mass: Harvard University Press.
Heidegger, M. (2010) *Being and Time*. Albany, New York: SUNY Press.
Lazzarato, M. (2012) *The Making of the Indebted Man: Essay on the Neoliberal Condition*. New York: Semiotext(e).
Levinas, E. (1969) *Totality and Infinity: An Essay on Exteriority*. Pittsburgh, PA: Duquesne University Press.
Levinas, E. (1999) *Otherwise Than Being, or, Beyond Essence*. Pittsburgh, Penn.: Duquesne University Press.
Marazzi, C. (2008) *Capital and Language: From the New Economy to the War Economy*. New York: Semiotext(e).
Marazzi, C. (2011) *Capital and Affects: The Politics of the Language Economy*. New York: Semiotext(e).
Marx, K. (1988) 'Estranged Labour' in *The Economic and Philosophic Manuscripts of 1844 and The Communist Manifesto*. New York: Prometheus Books. 69-85.
Marx, K. (1990) *The Eighteenth Brumaire of Louis Bonaparte*. London: Lawrence and Wishart.
Mauss, M. (2001) *The Gift: Forms and Functions of Exchange in Archaic Societies*. London: Routledge.
Meillassoux, Q. (2009) *After Finitude: An Essay on the Necessity of Contingency*. London: Continuum.
Merleau-Ponty, M. (1969) *The Visible and the Invisible*. Evanston, Ill: Northwestern University Press.
Naess, A. (2008) *Ecology, Community, and Lifestyle*. Cambridge: Cambridge University Press.
Nietzsche, F. (1990) *On the Genealogy of Morals and Ecce Homo*. New York: Vintage.
Plato (2002) *Five Dialogues: Euthyphro, Apology, Crito, Meno, Phaedo*. London: Hackett.
Radford, T. (2016) 'Stephen Hawking and Yuri Milner Launch $100m Star Voyage', *The Guardian*, 12th April.
Raunig, G. (2016) *Dividuum: Machinic Capitalism and Molecular Revolution*. New York: Semiotext(e).
Sahlins, M. (1974) *Stone Age Economics*. London: Routledge.
Sartre, J.-P. (1989) *No Exit: And Three Other Plays*. London: Vintage.
Staheli, U. (2013) *Spectacular Speculation: Thrills, the Economy, and Popular Discourse*. Stanford: Stanford University Press.

Stiegler, B. (2011) *The Decadence of Industrial Democracies: Disbelief and Discredit: Volume I.* Cambridge: Polity.

Stiegler, B. (2012) *Uncontrollable Societies of Disaffected Individuals: Disbelief and Discredit: Volume II.* Cambridge: Polity.

Stiegler, B. (2014a) *Symbolic Misery: Volume I: The Hyperindustrial Epoch.* Cambridge: Polity.

Stiegler, B. (2014b) *The Lost Spirit of Capitalism: Disbelief and Discredit: Volume III*: Cambridge: Polity.

Taylor, M. C. (2004) *Confidence Games: Money and Markets in a World without Redemption.* Chicago: University of Chicago Press.

Index

A

Adkins, Lisa 19, 22, 107, 132–3, 134
advertising
  online trackers 155–6, 158–9
  of short-term loans on TV 185
  targeted at children 203–4
advice sector, UK 120–3
  budgeting using the CFS 126–8
  challenges of 'deficit debtors' 138–9
algorithmic analytics *see* digital subprime
'American Empire', Baudrillard 232, 233–6
anti-foundationalism 30–1
antisemitism 62, 66
Art after Money, Money after Art (Haiven) 197
artworks depicting unpayable debts 195–221
'austere creditors' 122, 138
austerity *see* economic austerity

B

balanced budgets, household 123
Ban, C., Eurozone bond markets33 33
banking sector
  creation of money from debt 54–5, 56, 60, 66, 191, 234–5
  quantitative easing (QE) 31–2
  regulation of credit 184–8
  shadow banking 34
  versus non-financial sector 63–4
  see also central banks; interest rates
Barahona de Brito, Alexandra, social memory 78
Barr, C., intergenerational inequality 96
Bataille, Georges 17, 23, 243
Baudrillard, Jean
  approach of millennium 231–3
  'exorbital' debt 23, 233, 235–6, 241
  meaninglessness of debt 234–5
Bauman, Zygmunt 5, 94, 109, 204
Beck, Ulrich 236, 237
Belmore, Rebecca, performance artist 214–16, 217–18
Benjamin, Walter 203, 232
Bentham, Jeremy, 'Defence of Usury' 181–3, 189
Berardi, Franco, the time of indebtedness 238
Berlant, L., 'cruel optimism' 11, 131, 136, 140, 146
big data analytics 147, 149, 150–1
  overcoming opacities of 153–5
biopower/biopolitics, Foucault 13, 176, 189
Bjerg, Ole, debt drive 19–20, 49–67, 234
Bonds of Debt, The (Dienst) 11
Bowsher, Joshua, Truth Committee on Greek Public Debt 20–1, 69–88
browser profiling 157
budgeting 120–1
  advice on 126–8
  'deficit budget sheet' 123
  within intimate relationships 128–32
Burton, D., usury
  interest rate limit, 1571 Act 179
  prohibition of in the Bible 178

C

capital (assets) and inequality 40
capitalism 2, 8
  artwork depicting payday loans for children 202–4
  collapse of, Streeck 8–10, 176
  and the debt crisis 175–6
  and drive for economic growth 50–3
  social inequalities created by 190
  and unpayable debts 200
Cartwright, Laura 21
Castoriadis, Cornelius 196
catastrophe, imagining 231–3
central banks 29, 31–2, 54, 191
  Bank of England 175, 180
  ECB 33, 45, 69, 75, 209
Chakravartty, Paula 218
children
  employment by artists 205
  facing future of unpayable debt 205–6
  living in poverty 205
  payday loan shop for 202–3
  under capitalism 203–4
Christmas Carol, A (Dickens) 3–4
class
  based on an economy of assets 44
  creditors versus debtors 72, 83, 124
  rentier 36–40
  shift from job to wealth-related 40–1
collateral (securities) markets 33
colonialism, Canada 215–20
Common Financial Statement (CFS) 120, 126–8
Communist Manifesto, The (Marx and Engels) 3, 4, 203

competition versus cooperation 58–9
conspiracy theories 66
Consumer Credit Act (1974, amended 2006) 186
consumer debt 121, 175
'good' versus 'bad' debts 91, 109, 111
see also household debt
consumer spending as an escape from debt 135–6
consumerism 10–11
Coulthard, Glen 217, 219
credit cards
regulation on interest rates 184, 186–8
subprime 148
UK debt 92–3
young adults' use of 101–2
credit-worthiness assessments 145, 147–9
basing on user's social ties 160–2
'cruel optimism', Berlant 11, 131, 132, 136, 140, 146
Cullen, Darren, 'Pocket Money Loans' 23, 195, 203, 204–5, 206
Curran, D., financial risk-class 37–8

D

Davies, William, 'financial melancholia' 239
Davis, Mark 21
Dawney, Leila 21
'death drive', Žižek 66–7
Debt of the Living, The (Stimilli) 16–17
Debt or Democracy (Mellor) 191
debt economy, Lazzarato 72, 73–4, 87
Debt: The First 5,000 Years (Graeber) 177
debt as power 11, 13, 72, 124, 189, 191, 197
'deferral' of life objectives, young people 91–112
'deficit debtor' 128, 138–9
living in 'deficit time' 138–9
Deleuze, Gilles, control society 12, 13, 22, 240
DeMuth, Christopher, usury laws 184
Depository Institutions Deregulation and Monetary Control Act (1980), US 187
depression experienced by debtors 238, 239, 242
deregulation of credit markets 184, 186, 187, 190
Derrida, Jacques 2, 3, 17, 244
desire versus drive within capitalism 50–3, 64–5
Deville, Joe 12–13, 22
Di Muzio, T., debt as power 11
Dickens, Charles 3–4
Dienst, Richard, *The Bonds of Debt* 11
digital subprime 146–7
companies practising 148–9
detecting fleeting visibilities of 153–5
opacity of techniques 150–1
research challenges 149–52
techniques 147–8
tracking the trackers 155–60
Disbelief and Discredit (Stiegler) 239
disciplinary structuring of indebted life 120, 124, 132, 138–9, 140
the 'dividual' 239, 242–3, 244
Documenta 14 Festival (2017) 206–13
Dodd-Frank Act (2010), US 188, 189
drive of contemporary capitalism 49–50
as 'death drive' 66–7
into debt 57–67
versus desire 50–3, 64

E

ecological critique of global debt society 241–7
economic austerity 7, 243, 244
enforced on Greece 69, 76–7, 81, 208–9
technical (financial) analysis 31–5
economic growth 1, 31–2
consumer demand driving 53, 64
macroeconomics of 49–50
parable of the 11th round 57–62, 64–5
tied to debt 29, 55–7
Eisenstein, Charles, competition and economic growth 59
Engels, Friedrich 3, 9, 19, 203
'entrepreneurs of the self', Foucault 71, 73
Equal Credit Opportunity Act (1974), US 159
European Central Bank (ECB) 29, 33, 45, 69, 75, 209

F

Facebook, harvesting of data from 160–1
fantasy
of desire (to consume) and drive 52
of utopian world of financialisation 233–6
Ferreira da Silva, Denise 218
fiat money, created by central banks 53, 54
financial apartheid, trend towards 64
Financial Choice Act (2017), US 188
Financial Conduct Authority (FCA), UK 175, 186–7
financial crisis (2007-8) 28–31, 71–2
and austerity 34–5, 38
and the financial risk-class, Curran 37–9

link to deregulation of credit markets 186, 187–8
post-crisis monetary policy, Gane's analysis 31–2
similarities to current rise in consumer debt (2017) 121, 175
sociological analyses of the post-crisis present 32–3
financial education policy initiatives 94–5
'financial melancholia' 239
financial versus productive economy 62–4
financialised neoliberalism, resistance to 71, 85
'flawed consumers', Bauman 94
Foucault, Michel 12, 13, 73
free market in credit provision vs. regulation 176–7, 180–1, 183–4, 187–8
freedom 242, 244, 245
Freud, Sigmund, and the uncanny 13–14
Fukuyama, Francis, end of history 2, 231–2

G

Gabor, D., Eurozone bond markets 33
gambling compulsion 52
Gane, Nicholas 22
analysis of QE 31–2, 34
critique of usury 175–92
Germany, Minujín's artwork on Greek debt repayment 206–13
Ghostery, browser tool 155, 156
gift economy 4, 243, 244
Given Time (Derrida) 244
gold standard 53–4
'Gone Indian', Indigenous performance art 214–20
'good' versus 'bad' debts 91, 109, 111
Gordon, Avery, hauntology of power 202
Graeber, David, history of debt 177, 178–9, 197, 220, 246
greed, inexplicable to economic thought 65
Greek debt crisis, Greece 20–1, 69–71
arguments of TCPD against social debt 82–3
counter-memory of Greece's innocence 83–6
memory-making of truth commissions 77–81
performative art 206–13
Greyeyes, Michael, actor and dancer 214–15, 218
growth *see* economic growth
Guattari, Felix, *Three Ecologies* 238, 241
guilt for Greek debt, analysis of TCPD 71–4, 79–81

H

Haiven, Max, financialisation 4, 5, 22–3
Harvey, David 6
Hawking, Steven, vision of cosmic escape 240–1, 242
Heidegger, M., 'being-with' 246
'Help to Buy ISA', UK 104
hierarchy of debt, Lazzarato 72
home ownership 103–4, 234–5
Horsley, Mark 10–11
household debt 1–2, 35–40
advice sector perspective 121–3
as securitised debt 41–3
housing
operation as an asset 43
unaffordable for young adults 103–4
see also mortgages
How Will Capitalism End? (Streeck) 9
HTTP profiling 157
human rights law 78–9, 80, 83
human rights movement 77–8
human rights victimhood 85–6

I

identity of online users, tracking of by credit-scoring companies 147–8, 151–2, 156–8
illiquid loans, transformation to liquidity 41–2
'imaginary', debt as 195–8
income deductions 122, 123, 185–6
Indian Act (1876), Canada 216
Indigenous people in Canada, past and present injustices 214–19
inequality 31–2, 93–4
and austerity 34, 244
based on asset/wealth distribution 40, 41, 42
intergenerational 95–6
Ingham, Geoffrey 15–16, 17, 18, 178
innocence of Greek citizens 81, 83–6
Intelligence of Evil or Lucidity Pact, The (Baudrillard) 235–6
interest rates
charging of, moral issues 190–1
credit cards 184, 187
payday lenders 149
rise of and household debt 121
student loans 101
usury laws 178–83
International Monetary Fund (IMF) 29, 69, 80, 84, 87, 209
investment, lack of 7–9
irreducibility of debt 241–2
'Islamic State' 211–12

J

Jews, conspiracy of 66
job insecurity 91, 92, 94, 96, 99, 109
Johnson, Peter 182
Joseph, Miranda 17–18, 36, 85, 139–40, 197

K

Kassel, Germany 207, 208, 212
Kirwan, Sam 21
Konings, Martijn 120, 133–4, 137, 139, 140, 189–90
Kreditech 149, 160–1

L

La Berge, Leigh Claire, decommodifcation of labour 204
Lapavitsas, C., modern-day *rentiers* 36–7
Lazzarato, Maurizio 11, 72–4
  debt repayment 124–5, 138
  indebtedness of young people 96
  mnemotechnics of debt, Greece 74, 77, 81
legislation
  usury 179–80
Lenddo, credit scoring using social networks 160
leveraging, Minskian household 43
Levinas, Emmanuel, ethics and otherness 246
Levy, David, perceptions of risk-taking 181
Lietaer, Berhard, parable of the eleventh round 57–9
'the lipstick effect' 135
Liquidated (Ho) 5
liquidity 5, 7
  mistaken by sociologists for illiquidity 42, 44
  securitisation 41–2
  transformation of debt into 44, 45
Lived Economies of Default (Deville) 12
  see also mortgages; payday lending

M

macroeconomics 49–50, 74–5
Making of the Indebted Man, The (Lazzarato) 11
Making Money (Bjerg) 234
Malik, S., young people's debt 96
Marazzi, Christian 71, 240
marriage trends 108
Martin, Randy 6, 201–2
Marx, Karl 17, 18, 203, 239, 245
Maurer, Bill, money-credit link 145, 146
Mauss, Marcel, gift economy 17, 23, 244–5
McClanahan, Annie, uncanny homes 13–14
McFall, Liz 153
McLaughlin, Jillian 151
media discourse on Greek debt crisis 76–7
Meillassoux, Quentin, finitude/symbolic misery 240
Mellor, Mary 93, 191
memory project, TCPD, Greece 70–1
  'Greek Debt Truth Commission' 79–81
  guilt and responsibility 71–4
  human rights 77–9
  innocence counter-memory 77–9
  media discourses 76–7
  mnemotechnics of debt 74–7
Merkel, Angela, German Chancellor
  lookalike in art work Decoumenta 14 Festival 206–7
  open-door policy towards Syrian refugees 210–11
Merleau-Ponty, M, 'being-in-world' 246
Merrill, Douglas 148, 151, 155
Merton, Robert, anomie in the US 9
Mill, John Stuart, on usury 183–5, 188, 189
Miller, Zinaida 78
'Minskian households' 27, 43–4
Minsky, Hyman 43, 175–6
Minujín, Marta
  'Parthenon of Books', Kassel 207–8, 212
  'Payment of Greek Debt to Germany with Olives and Art', Athens 212–13
Mirowski, Philip 177
'mnemotechnics' of debt, Greece's truth committee 70–87
mobile banking 134–5
money creation from debt 55–62, 66, 191, 234–5
Montgomerie, Johnna
  'financial melancholia' 239
  UK household debt 125
  US credit card industry 187
Moore, Suzanne, social attitudes about poor people 94
moral aspects of finance and debt 3–4, 94–5
mortgages
  securitised 43
  subprime loans 199, 234, 235
  young adults 103–4
Mylonas, Yiannis, media discourses of Greek crisis 76

N

Nature of Money, The (Ingham, 2004) 15–16

Nazi Holocaust, Germany's moral debts 211
negative outlook of young adults 106–10
neoliberalism 189–90
Never Let a Serious Crisis Go To Waste (Mirowski) 177
Nietzsche, F. 72, 232, 242
NINJA (No Income, No Job or Assets) loans 199, 234, 235
No Exit (Sartre) 239–40
normalisation of borrowing 92–3

O

Occupy Wall Street Movement 64
'odious debt' 80, 83–4
On the Genealogy of Morals (Nietzsche) 72
operating system fingerprinting 157
overdrafts, young people 101–2, 109

P

parable of the eleventh round 57–62
  and economic growth 64–5
  and financial versus productive economy 62–4
payday lending 185–6
  Pocket Money Loans art project 202–3
  regulation 186–7, 189
  see also digital subprime
pension participation, young adults 104–6
Perfect Crime, The (Baudrillard) 235–6
perpetual debt, drive towards 57–61
Pettifor, Ann, new politics of money 10, 15, 186, 191–2
Piketty, T., emergence of wealth or patrimonial society 40
'Pocket Money Loans' artwork, Cullen 202–6
Polanyi, K. 11
post-mortemism 236, 238–9, 245
  austerity as response to 243
  translation of postmodern into 241–2
postmodern(ism), Baudrillard 231–2, 233
Postone, M., financial crisis and its aftermath 30–1
precarious jobs, young people 91, 92, 99–100
Production of Money, The (Pettifor) 191
profiling of online behaviour patterns 156–60

Q

Quantcast tracker 158–9
quantitative easing (QE), Gane's analysis of 31–2

R

radical imagination 196
Raunig, Gerald, lack of the 'dividual' 239, 242
reality
  'American Empire' confronting 233–6
  new debt reality 240–2
refinancing 43
refugee crisis, Germany's handling of 210–11
regulation of credit markets 184–8
  failure of 189–90
  to provide cheaper credit, Pettifor 15, 16
  usury laws 179–80
relationship budgeting 128–32
religious history of usury 178–9
religious thinking about finance 15
rentiers (modern risk-class) 36–9
repayment of debt 124–5
  insolvency as the only solution 138–9
  speculative practices suspending 133–4
  and temptations to overspend as an escape 134–7
  within intimate and familial relationships 128–32
  Wonga's sliders 154
responsibility for Greek debt, TCPD analysis 71–4
risk-class 19, 37–9
Robbins, R., debt as power 11
Royal Bank of Canada HQ, artwork performed in front of 214–19

S

Sartre, Jean-Paul 12, 13, 17, 239–40
Sayer, Andrew, attack on usury 191
Schuld (guilt, shame and debt) 211
Scott, John, class in Britain 39–40
securitised debt of households 41–3, 133, 134, 199
Selmic, Radman, analysis of Greek crisis 74–5
shared budgeting 128–32
short-term credit market *see* payday lending
Simpson, Audra 217
Smith, Adam 180–1, 183–4
social debt, TCPD arguments against 82–3
social inequality *see* inequality
social media data, harnessing of 149, 160–2
social sciences, move away from economics 29–31
socialist societies 244–5
sovereign bonds, downgrading of 29, 33
sovereign debt, Greece 70–83
Spectres of Marx (Derrida) 2
speculation, financial 6, 36–7, 137, 234

'speculative time' 21, 132–4, 139
Spokeo, people search engine 151–2
Spooner, Joseph, 'austere creditors' 122
Staheli, Urs, risk-taking in Wall Street 234
Standing, Guy, 'precariatised mind' 106, 124
the state, marketisation of 189–90
Stavrakakis, Yannis 72
Stiegler, Bernard, *Disbelief and Discredit* 8, 16, 239
Stimilli, Elettra, *The Debt of the Living* 16–17
Streeck, Wolfgang, collapse of capitalism 8, 9–10, 176
student debt 96–7, 100–2
Syrian refugees, Germany's open-door policy 210–11
Syriza government, Greece 69–70, 87, 209

T

TCP fingerprinting 157
Temin, P., usury laws 184
temporal dynamics of debt, young people 98, 100
temporal frameworks of debt repayment 119–20, 124–5, 132–3
ThreatMetrix, tracker tool 156, 157
Three Ecologies (Guattari) 241
totalitarianism 244, 245–6
Troika 69, 208–9
Trump, Donald 14, 188, 189
Truth Commission on Public Debt (TCPD), Greece 20, 70–88
Turner, Catherine, human rights 78–9

U

uncanny/unhomely (abandoned) homes, McClanahan 13–14
uncertainty about the future, young adults 106–10
university tuition fees 92, 96, 98
unpayable debts 195, 198–202
- art, role and importance of 197–8
- between past, present and future generations 202–6
- Greece's debt to Germany 206–13
- imagination, debt as structure of 195–7
- owed to Indigenous people in Canada 218–20

unsecured credit 92–3
- young adults and students 96–7, 101–2

usury
- contemporary debate 176–7
- history of 178–84
- original meaning of 176
- post-crisis return of 188–9
- regulation of credit 184–8

utopias and dystopias 2, 11–12, 16, 23

V

value of debt 139, 140
van der Velden, Lonneke 153
victimhood 85–6
Von Uexkull, J., ecosystem theory 13
Voth, H.-J., usury laws 184

W

wage stagnation 40, 43, 71, 93, 100, 101, 105, 199
Walker, Rosie 21
Wallin, Sara, 'financial melancholia' 239
Wealth of Nations, The (Smith) 180
wealth, unequal distribution of 40
welfare as social debt 74
wergeld (worth payment) 17, 18
Why We Can't Afford the Rich (Sayer) 190
Wilson, Thomas, *A Discourse Upon Usury* 179
Wolfe, Patrick 215–16
Wonga, payday lender 149, 153–4, 158, 160

Y

Y2K, millennial panic 231–2
young people and debt 91–110
Yu, Persis 151, 152
Yuran, Noam, greed and the pursuit of money 65

Z

Zelizer, Viviana, shared budgeting 129
ZestFinance, US 148–9, 155
Zinman, J., credit card interest 187
Žižek, Slavoj
- on antisemitism 66
- debt as a 'death drive' 66–7
- from desire to drive 50–3
- real vs. symbolic 53–4
- 'symbolic castration' 60

Zweckrationalität (legalism) 8